American Government: The Facts Reorganized

GENERAL LEARNING PRESS • 250 James Street, Morristown, New Jersey 07960

Library of Congress Catalog Card Number   74-79052

ISBN 0-382-18039-9

Preface

In the initial planning stages of this project, we knew that we were going to write a new and useful kind of American government book. Our confidence stemmed not from any certainty that we were better able to analyze government than our professional colleagues, but from the fact that we were participating in an entirely new instructional system for an American government course. This system, devised by General Learning Press, features a concise "core" textbook with a series of specially prepared "associated units" whose treatment expands upon various areas of the general subject matter. This unique system seemed ideal for such courses as American government, American history, or the American political experience, which involve so many different topics and such a variety of approaches.

As the project progressed, the parameters of this system contributed to the final product, even beyond expectation. The system allows the instructor flexibility, permitting emphasis to be placed on those areas and problems considered most important. The design of the system allows the core book authors to concentrate upon the task of finding a meaningful, consistent theme—without having to abandon the equally important objective of presenting the standard materials relating to American government.

The General Format

In the core text an attempt has been made to provide a unifying theme around which a system of associated units may be clustered. Within the context of the main theme, we have endeavored to accommodate and present the basic facts and materials of American government. Wherever possible, these basic materials are noncontroversial and reliably described.

Simultaneously, we have tried to produce an important, relevant analysis of American government—and our analysis does not attempt to remain noncontroversial. On the contrary, we intend that our analysis stimulate thought, provoke discussion, and channel divergent thoughts and opinions into head-on collisions. Arguments that go past one another are pointless and destructive, but arguments that actually engage a different point of view can be productive.

Most American government textbooks attempt a unifying theme, and most of them fail in one way or another. Either the text gives due treatment to all of the major viewpoints and substantive areas, in which case the "unifying theme" disappears in the mass of materials, or the text preserves a theme or "approach" at the cost of excluding materials and opinions that are important.

It is difficult to solve this problem within the conventional format, but the new, instructional system affords greater flexibility. The associated units accompanying the core book perform four main functions: First, several of the units cover important areas in more depth and detail than a core book is able. For example, the courts are discussed within the framework of our analysis, but due attention is not given to several important, conventionally treated themes of constitutional development. Nevertheless, these themes are alluded to and developed more fully in an associated unit within the system.

Second, several of the units represent important points of view that are different from our own. Too often, American government textbooks try to accommodate varying points of view with the insipid formula, "Some political scientists say X, while others say Y." To us, this tactic seems to suggest implicitly that "It's just a matter of opinion," or worse, that differing opinions are not matters to be taken seriously. We do have a point of view, but we should never wish to exclude from consideration other points of view. The associated units permit other approaches and opinions to speak for themselves.

Third, there are a very few occasions where our analysis in the core book indicates a completely unusual presentation of facts and materials; in such cases, as the material on political participation, the associated units may be the sole bearers of conventional wisdom.

Finally, the associated units and the core text represent the living community of interests that is in the heart of an academic discipline. Nothing could make the reality of intellectual community more salient for students than this joint undertaking, diverse in orientation and particular interests, yet focused by broad, shared intentions.

The Transformation Paradigm

A preliminary word regarding the organization of the core text may prove helpful. As its title suggests, this book aims primarily to reorganize the facts of American government. We have tried very diligently not to omit facts ordinarily included; and we have tried not to reinterpret or change those facts to suit our own purposes and arguments. We have, however, reorganized the facts to allow several approaches heretofore thought to be incompatible. This variety in approach should allow the reader to place facts in a broader, more fundamental framework.

As a kind of shorthand, we have called this broader framework the *transformation paradigm*. A *paradigm* is a pattern, and the pattern of American government is discontinuous—that is, American government has undergone a *transformation* of its basic form, or pattern. We believe that the recognition of this transformation is essential for an adequate understanding of the American experience.

This paradigm has something in common with radical and revolutionary analyses. The latter very often involve *reinterpretations of history*—Marxists reinterpret history in materialistic terms; radical feminists call for a "herstory"; black nationalists demand a black history. It is impossible to urge a radical departure from conventioned interpretations of the *present* without, at least implicitly, insisting upon a reinterpretation of the *past.* For whether one finds it interesting or not, everyone supposes that a real past preceded the real present; a new interpretation of the present implies a new interpretation of the past.

We said that our paradigm shares something with radical analyses, and, for the most part, we do not actually reinterpret the past, but refocus attention upon what it is, and what is not, the history of America. Some American government texts pay considerable attention to American history, while others treat it very lightly. In general, the assumption goes unchallenged that the history of the founding of the American republic is the history of our present-day institutions. We find that this interesting, largely valid history of America bears only indirectly upon our present-day form of government—an opinion, to which most political scientists probably would assent. What we have done is to separate the facts and the history of what we call the *American Republic* from the facts of what we call the *American Nation-State.* We have tried to pinpoint the time and the occasion of the transformation of America from one form of government (discussed and analyzed in Part I) to another form of government (discussed and analyzed in Part II).

Brief introductions are included at the beginnings of Parts II and III. Part I serves as an introductory section, its primary purpose being the explication of key concepts and terms used throughout the text. This section will become more meaningful after part or all of the main text has been read.

❋ ❋ ❋ ❋

Elliot Zashin of the University of Texas was our collaborator during an earlier phase of work on our project to produce an American government textbook. Although he did not join us to write this version, he did offer advice and encouragement throughout the project.

Karen Anne Bell read and criticized every stage of the manuscript. She very helpfully recovered the main ideas in Chapters 2 and 7 when writing problems had almost obscured them.

Carol Z. Rothkopf of General Learning Press edited our manuscript and blended much-appreciated support and well-taken criticisms.

We would also like to thank Alessandra Lippucci of the University of Texas for reading several early chapter drafts; Marta Jacobs for finding a crucial book in San Francisco and H. Malcolm Macdonald, Government Department at the University of Texas, for the use of his personal library.

Finally, we thank our students, especially those who pursue knowledge and understanding as well as grades and degrees.

R. A. B.

March 1974 *Walnut Creek, California*

D. V. E.

Austin, Texas

Contents

x

Part I
American Government: An Overview

Chapter 1
The Experience of Politics

It would be nice if, instead of talking about what we are going to say, we could simply say it. But the language of political science is dotted with technical terms, a specialized vocabulary—and to complicate matters, the specialized vocabulary is somewhat inconsistently employed. (To be blunt about it, some political scientists use a language that other political scientists cannot understand and vice versa.) We have tried to confine ourselves to ordinary English in this book, and to self-revealing methods of analysis. Nevertheless, we, too, have our peculiar definitions and particular emphases. This introductory chapter is designed to clarify those definitions for what follows.

Power, Authority, and Politics

There is a tremendous amount of literature in political science on the subjects of power and authority, some of which tries to distinguish between the two concepts, some to equate the terms—but always, definitions and discussions of politics get around to references to power, authority, or both. David Easton defines politics as "the authoritative allocation of values"[1] for a society; Harold Lasswell defines politics as "Who gets what, when, how."[2] The former definition

1. David Easton, *The Political System* (Knopf, 1953).
2. Harold Lasswell, *Politics: Who Gets What, When, How.* (McGraw-Hill, 1936).

2

stresses the tendency of politics to transform power into authority. The latter definition, by contrast, stresses the tendency of politics to transform authority into power. Seen in one light, or again in certain of its manifestations, politics is that human activity or process by which power (superior strength, knowledge, resources, or the like) is channelled and contained within institutions of authority (implying legitimacy or "rightness"). But, in a different manifestation, politics is the process that subordinates considerations of legitimacy to those of power—"who gets what."

This is a book about the American political experience, about our own experiences of politics. Consequently we must pursue this problem of the ambivalent nature of politics a bit further because most people (so it seems to us) recoil from the ambivalent or paradoxical. And this (possibly healthy) tendency of the mind to avoid such experiences may also lead us away from just that category of experiences that is the paradoxical, ambivalent center of the experience of politics itself. For in politics we find at once the producer and destroyer of human order. Amidst the disintegration of Greek civilization, Aristotle found in politics "the queen of the sciences"; today in the United States, we find everywhere an aversion to politics, wrecker of the rule of law and destroyer of integrity in government. "There is no political science," said Richard Nixon in October 1973.

Politics is where power and authority are. We always find politics, then, where we find governments, for governments typically lay claim to the legitimate exercise of force or coercion in a society. But societies will usually produce and respect institutions of authority besides the government—the Church and religious authority in the Middle Ages; universities and scientific authority in contemporary times—which inevitably also are politicized. Indeed, if the authority of the extra-governmental institution of authority is very great (like that of the Church in the Middle Ages, or the schools today), then politics will draw the institutions together, creating an often unstable admixture of competing claims to authority and ambiguous exercises of power. Such a situation, apparently, exists today. The government is deeply involved in our schools at every level, from heavy funding of research and tuition loans at the university level to (often controversial) attempts to influence or control integration policies and educational policies in primary and secondary education (which, by the way, is itself institutionalized by state and local governments). Conversely, experts (by virtue of their educational certification) exert extensive influence and authority throughout the governmental structures, as we shall show presently.

In order to provide a language for describing and analyzing the political experience in America, we have devised a special definition of politics, which is discussed in the next section. And to provide a unified focus upon the governmental institutions of America (which, we shall argue, have been drastically modified in the present century), we have adopted a specialized use of the term, political representation.

The term *political representation* occurs in common parlance about politics, but it has a special meaning in our analysis. We are all familiar with the ordinary meaning of "political representation." A country is generally said to have representative institutions when its legislative officers hold office by virtue of popular elections that are held frequently and are open to competition. The executive, too, is elected, either by direct popular vote or by electors who are themselves elected by the people. In this sense, the United States is representative, as are the United Kingdom, France, and many other countries. But to understand politics more fundamentally, we must clarify the sense in which *any* viable political society is representative, whether it holds elections or not.

In the ordinary sense of the term, there can be extensive disagreement about whether a government is truly representative of its people. For example, Marxists in general will contend that the government of the United States is not truly representative of its people since (among other things) the political parties that participate in the electoral process represent special interests—"the ruling class" in Marxist terms —and not exclusively the workers. A typical response made in behalf of the United States system will hold that the party monopoly provided by the Soviet constitution makes choice impossible, which in turn makes true representation impossible. But this is a disagreement about which government better represents "the people."

There is no question that both governments represent their respective political societies. The Soviet Union operates a great military machine, which can and does make war against other political societies, and the same is true for the

United States. The Soviet Union can and does enter into military and economic agreements with other countries, as does the United States. And so did tsarist Russia in the nineteenth century, when there were no elections there at all. In other words, the ability of a government to represent its political society effectively has little if anything to do with whether its institutions are "representative" in the ordinary sense of the term. As the political theorist Eric Voegelin puts it, "Political societies . . . must have an internal structure that will enable some of its members—the ruler, the government, the prince, the magistrate, etc. . . to find habitual obedience for their acts of command; and these acts must serve the existential necessities of a society, such as the defense of the realm and administration of justice . . . ."[3]

When we talk about political representation here, we are interested in the conditions that make it possible for some members of a political society to act for the society as a whole—to exercise ruling power. The internal organization that makes political representation possible is neither always present, nor can it be produced suddenly. Such organization develops over time, and this process is called the *articulation* of political society. As a result of this process of political articulation "we find human beings, the rulers, who can act for the society, men whose acts are not imputed to their own persons but to the society as a whole."[4]

In our analysis of the United States, we make a distinction designed to simplify our discussion. We say that a government *represents* a political society, and we distinguish between "external" and "internal" representation.

External representation indicates the political society seen from without. We might know very little about the internal organization of a country—the People's Republic of China, for a good example—and yet find that country effectively and undeniably represented as an existing, viable political society. Its representatives can threaten us with physical destruction, prohibit our entry into its territory, enter into contracts and agreements with our country and others, and so forth. These are all manifestations of a state's external representation.

---

3. Eric Voegelin, *The New Science of Politics* (University of Chicago Press, 1952), pp. 36-37.
4. Ibid., p. 37.

Internal representation is the political society experienced from within. The articulated institutions of a society—president, king, parliament—and the consequent relations among its members, constitute the common framework within which reality is perceived by individuals in the society. To a member of a political society, its externality is one important component of the society (that is, the fact that the state is seen from the outside as a society capable of waging war, negotiating treaties, and so on, is for most citizens an important and meaningful feature of the state), but internal arrangements are also of great importance, as we shall see in Part II.

The articulation of the American Republic, and then the American Nation-State, naturally involved many political disputes. In order to maintain a unified discussion of American politics occurring in two such different forms of political representation, we shall need a definition of politics that is both broad and focused, and it is to that task that we now turn.

Politics in America

People act in the world in accordance with their image of reality—their set of beliefs about the kind of world they live in. People have different experiences: they have different biographies (different lives) and different perspectives (different positions from which they view the world). Thus two people often act differently in the same situation, or think differently about the same thing. We all know this is true, and so we are not surprised when people differ. Because everyone is different, whenever two people come into contact, or interact, there will be some degree of difference or conflict in their reality images, and hence there are likely to be differences or conflicts between them.

All interaction among people thus involves differing reality images. When the subject of the difference is the question of who is to decide which reality image is correct or will prevail, we call it a *political* interaction. In a political interaction, the dispute shifts from the truth or falsity of the reality images held by the two disputants to the question of which of the disputants should determine, or should be allowed to determine, which reality image will be accepted as correct. What is really happening in a case like this is that the dispute is over claims to *authority.*

Of course, this is a complex world we live in, and no one can be expert in every aspect of it, or even understand all ot it. All of us must rely on other people as experts on various aspects of the world. Students rely on teachers, children rely on parents, invalids rely on doctors, presidents rely on advisors. In each of these cases, one party serves as an authority—a person whose position, experience, knowledge, or personality is believed to qualify him as an expert whose advice, interpretation, or understanding can and should be relied upon by others as correct, or at least as more likely to be correct than the views of someone without his qualities.

In cases where everyone recognizes the same authority on a matter, there is no politics. At certain times in history, for example, the pope was recognized by all Christians as *the* authority on Christianity. But at other times the pope's authority was challenged, and this was a clear instance of politics in the Church.

It may seem strange to think of politics in the Church, at least if one generally believes that politics are confined to the civil government. But we have already noted that politics occur where authority and power occur—when the Church had great authority, politics finally could not be avoided. And neither, of course, can politics be avoided in the powerful government of the United States, despite the rather amusing demands (often made by politicians) that politics be "kept out of" this or that event, such as the selection of a vice-presidential successor to Spiro Agnew.

What is important to realize here is that in such instances—and also, for example, in the case of the professor who claims to be an authority for the student, or in the case of the book that claims to be an authority for the reader (as, obviously, this one does)—the same things may happen. The authority may be accepted, in which case there is no politics, only dictation or education. Or the authority may not be accepted—it may be combatted by another religious leader, another presidential candidate, another professor, another book; or it may even be resisted by the religious subject, the rebellious citizen or voter, the student, or the reader. No matter what the case, when a claim to authority is resisted, we have the beginning of an instance of politics.

As we conceive it here, *politics is dispute over claims*

to authority concerning the nature of reality. Thus it involves two key factors: a disputed claim to authority, and the interpretation of reality. (Presently, we shall consider also the factor of *level* of dispute.)

In the 1972 presidential election, for example, Richard Nixon and George McGovern each sought and received—though not without political contest—the authority to run for president representing the Republican and the Democratic parties. They then each sought the authority to run the country for the next four years. It is certainly true that they had different reality images—different beliefs about what kind of world we live in and how it should be changed. So do most people. But what made the presidential election truly political was the fact that each of them was competing for a position of authority—the presidency—that only one of them could be granted. Even if Nixon and McGovern had shared the same reality image (the same foreign policy for Vietnam and the same policies for coping with poverty, for example), their contest would still have been a political battle. But, in cases where the candidates are in harmony on policy, the battle is waged more clearly in terms of personal qualities of the candidates—for example, who seems more trustworthy, more knowledgeable, and more decisive—in short, who seems a better candidate for being our chief governmental authority for the following four years.

We live in a political society in which authority is extensively specialized. That is, claims to expertise are typically made within specialized ranges of knowledge. Any major university, for example, contains several different schools (such as Arts and Sciences and Business), and within those schools will be scores of departments (such as Political Science and Marketing). Within those scores of departments will be dozens of subfields, or areas of specialization (such as American Politics and International Relations). All told, hundreds and hundreds of specializations will be institutionalized in a university; combinations of these permit many thousands of specialities, each with different levels of achievement possible. Of course, universities are not the only source of specialization in the society, but they illustrate the extent to which knowledge in our society has become differentiated. This differentiation has two sorts of political consequences. First, conflict over authority is *limited* because of the limited kinds of claims it is possible for most authorities to make. They are authorities, but only within specialized areas. Moreover, they all have a stake in the general validity of the society's knowledge, because their own expertise is a "part" of the whole system. But second, the same highly differentiated system makes for an unlimited variety of (limited) conflicts over authority. Because knowledge is so specialized, it is rather difficult, to say the least, to settle political disputes "once and for all." New claims to authority in specialized areas constantly present themselves, partly because they are constantly being newly created, challenging the previous arrangements. We need only think of issues like drugs, the environment, sex and morality, crime control—the list goes on—to realize that many of the disputes centering around these issues are the result of new knowledge, new specializations, conflicts among experts over who *really* knows the answers.

These are disputes over claims to authority concerning the nature of reality, but they are, by and large, disputes *within* the same overall structure of authority. Put another way, they are disputes associated with specializations—subdivisions—of a common framework, or structure. Even at a general level, when a McGovern runs against a Nixon, we have a broad, policy-level dispute over authority *within the same structure*. Disputes at this level—within the structure—whether specific or general, might be called conventional politics. That is, they are disputes about reality, but they implicitly acknowledge another level of authority that is not disputed. Indeed, it is the common acceptance of this structure of authority that makes disputes within it possible at all.

There is another level of dispute that inspires a nameless dread or a fierce exhilaration in people. This, the level of disputes over ultimate authority concerning reality—disputes over the structure within which reality is "disputed about"—are the stuff of genuine revolutions and epochal changes in man's history. The founding of the American republic involved politics at the level of structure. But the transformation of America also involved basic structural changes, and disputes over ultimate authority concerning the nature of reality have reemerged in the twentieth century. These great, ideological disputes about the nature of reality are extremely difficult to grasp and to cope with. For one thing, although we are all surrounded by world-threatening forces, such as the possibility of nuclear war, we live in a society so specialized that no individual seems capable of responding to the situation. One response, we believe, would be to take the possibilities of a course like this one more seriously. Here, at the beginning of this book, we will try to indicate why an introductory American government course is politically important. At the end of the book, after our analysis of American politics has been presented, we discuss the topic again —hopefully in even more persuasive terms.

Standing Knowledge on its Head

For many years now, the introductory course in American government has been held in low esteem. The introductory American government course, like so many introductory courses in other fields as well, has suffered at least in part because of the bureaucratization of education. As political scientists have become more specialized, the consensus as to what should be the content and "approach" of an American government course has weakened; and students, oriented more and more to a hierarchical model of knowledge, have come increasingly to find the course a prerequisite for the more serious, upper-level courses.

The process of differentiation of knowledge in American colleges and universities began around the turn of this century, as universities began to departmentalize along disciplinary lines (following the model of the great German universities). But it was the transformation of America, and especially the tremendous expansion of the educational system during the later stages of the transformation, that stimulated and conditioned a virtually unchecked process of differentiation. The conversion of the leading political scientists to behavioralism—the study of politics as an empirical science—in the 1920s laid the basis for extensive organizational specialization. By the 1950s, when the highly visible "behavioral revolution" in political science occurred, the possibilities for professional specialization were almost unlimited.[5] Conversely, the possibility of becoming a professional *generalist* was almost nil. In the first place, the would-be generalist could scarcely find a generalist under whom to study; in-

5. For an account of the development of the discipline of political science in America, with special attention to the "behavioral revolution" of the 1920s and 1950s, see Arthur Jensen, "History and Political Science." In S. M. Lipset, ed., *Politics and the Social Sciences* (Oxford University Press, 1969).

stead, he would have to study under a very large (and growing) number of specialists, and try to integrate all of that knowledge himself. In the second place, even if he could accomplish such a gigantic task, there would probably be no position available for one so trained, at least not in one of the large, expanding universities. For the academic "market" itself expanded by differentiating: in general, each new addition to an expanding political science department *brought a new course with him or her.* Of course, this movement from generalization to differentiation was not unique to political science. Most departments and disciplines, especially if they were at all scientifically oriented, underwent similarly rapid expansion through differentiation. As the size of departments doubled and redoubled, the number of different courses and specializations did not remain static; rather, the number of subfields and specializations grew very rapidly. By the 1960s, a new word—"multiversity"—had been coined to name the huge bureaucracies that contained all of these specialists in all of these disciplines (some old, many new, and most claiming scientific status). And, so prodigious has been the output of the multiversities that the proud claim could be made that of all the scientists who have ever existed, from the beginning of science itself, over ninety percent are alive and working today.

In the meantime, the introductory American government course has been, as it were, emptied of reliable content. Like the general practitioner in medicine, the political science generalist became a rare phenomenon, and not a particularly respected figure at that. Afflicted by the "trained incompetence" of narrow specialization, political scientists conducted or, often, presided over desultory sessions with this or that text that tried to be all things to all people. Lacking consensus at that level, what else could be done?

Of course, there were exceptions. Some individuals have resisted the trend toward specialization. A few new colleges have instituted interdisciplinary, nonbureaucratic curricula explicitly in reaction to the problems we are discussing. And in any case, the mood and expectations of the introductory course today are decidedly different on many university campuses. For the salad days of expansion are past, and we return, perforce, to the problematic task of teaching what is known, and what must be discovered, about American government. In a way, we are the beneficiaries of a great cultural achievement, for the bureaucratic expansion of education has produced a norm of "school for school's sake"—we must take certain courses of study in order to get into college where, in turn, we must satisfy certain prerequisites in order to get into our major which, in turn, is prerequisite to admission to postgraduate education. But, ironically, this cultural achievement is realized in a way that quite eludes the individual: seen from the "outside," the university is the institutionalization of a prodigious amount of knowledge; but the farther "into" the university one gets, the farther away from all that knowledge he finds himself. First the individual picks (more or less arbitrarily) a school or college; then a department ("major") within the college; then a specialization within the department. By the time a person reaches the graduate level in the multiversity, he is quite *separated* from the knowledge institutionalized by the university. Is there any way to reverse this process?

Actually, the process is reversing itself. The dynamic we have described above is one *conditioned by expansion;* indeed, it *is* expansion. But there is no unlimited, ever-growing supply of humans to keep pace with the system's geometric growth rate, and now the system must consolidate. This, therefore, is the time that new, typical patterns for the introductory course will be set, and how those patterns develop portends much for the future of American politics. The text we have written, with its complementary series of associated units, provides a core analysis along with a flexible format. And it presumes that *this* is the important, demanding, exciting level of intellectual study. It is at this level, in this and related courses, that major political-intellectual problems must be identified and solved; it is to some of the major ones that this book addresses itself.

Suggested Further Reading

The development of contemporary approaches to the study of political science are covered in the following works.

For a discussion of the methods for studying political science, see:

Roderick Bell. "Approaches to the Study of American Government." General Learning Press, 1974.

The following volumes are collections of readings on the behavioral (scientific) approaches to the study of politics:

James C. Charlesworth. *Contemporary Political Analysis.* Free Press, 1967.

Heinz Eulau. *Political Behavior in America: New Directions.* Random House, 1966.

For a collection of essays representing various social science approaches to the study of politics, consult:
Seymour Martin Lipset, ed. *Politics and the Social Sciences.* Oxford University Press, 1969.

An already classic account of the development of the study of political science will be found in the following volume:
Albert Somit and Joseph Tannenhaus. *The Development of American Political Science.* Allyn and Bacon, 1967.

For an interesting, brief account of the development of political science studies, see:
Stephen L. Wasby. *Political Science: The Discipline and its Dimensions.* Scribner's, 1970. Chapters 7 and 8.

A collection of essays on approaches to the study of political science will be found in:
Roland Young. *Approaches to the Study of Politics.* Northwestern University Press, 1958.

For more recent reactions to behavioralism, see:
George Graham and George Carey. *The Post-Behavioral Revolution.* McKay, 1972.
Michael Haas and Henry S. Kariel. *Approaches to the Study of Political Science.* Chandler, 1970.

Interesting analyses of authority, which we have argued is of the essence of politics, include the following:
Hannah Arendt. "What Is Authority?" *Between Past and Future.* Meridian, 1961.
David Easton. *The Political System.* Knopf, 1953.
Harold Lasswell. *Politics: Who Gets What, When, How.* McGraw-Hill, 1936.
Robert Nisbet, "Authority," *The Sociological Tradition.* Basic Books, 1966.

Among studies of the contemporary uses of authority and changes in its use that the reader will find helpful are the following:
Richard Peters. "The Changing Face of Authority," *Authority, Responsibility, and Education.* Atherton, 1966.
John Schaar, "Legitimacy in the Modern State," *Power and Community.* Edited by P. Green and S. Levinson. Vintage, 1971.

The most helpful study of representation, as we use the concept:
Eric Voegelin. *The New Science of Politics.* University of Chicago Press, 1952.

An interesting survey of the development of the concept of representation in political philosophy is found in:

Hannah Pitkin. *The Concept of Representation.* University of California Press, 1972.

Finally, a number of important essays and articles on the concept of political power and the ways to study and measure it have been collected in the following volume:

Roderick Bell, David V. Edwards, and R. Harrison Wagner. *Political Power: A Reader in Theory and Research.* Free Press, 1969.

Part II
The American Republic

Introduction

When we study the government of the United States, we are studying the exercise of ruling power. When we study politics, we are studying disputes about who should exercise such power, how far such power should extend, and to what ends it should be employed. In the language we are employing, these are fundamentally disputes over claims to authority concerning the nature of reality—who possesses such authority, and how it is to be employed.

When we study the government and politics of the United States, a focus upon the nature and problems of democracy is unavoidable. The history of the United States, from its inception in the eighteenth century to the present day, has been marked by controversies over the nature and place of democracy in our government.

In *The Federalist Papers* (a series of brief essays written in support of the Constitution by James Madison, Alexander Hamilton, and John Jay), Madison made a distinction between a republic, "by which I mean a government in which the scheme of representation takes place" and a "pure democracy." According to Madison, "The two great points of difference between a democracy and a republic are: first, the delegation of the government in the latter to a small number of citizens elected by the rest; secondly, the greater number of citizens and greater sphere of country over which the latter may be extended."[1]

---

1. Federalist No. 10, the discussion of the role of factions and interests in government. Clinton Rossiter, ed., *The Federalist Papers* (Mentor, 1961), pp. 81–82.

But if pure democracy was not favored by the dominant faction of the Founding Fathers, a representative form of government that we would term democratic clearly was. However, there were extensive and fundamental disputes over the form it should take among those establishing a government for the United States, as we shall rediscover shortly. And this debate was soon extended into dispute over the extent and kind of authority any government can claim over its citizens.

Thus, in order to clarify the problem of democratic government in America, we have divided our discussion of the government and politics of America into two main parts, "The American Republic" and "The American Nation-State." The republic was a form of democratic political representation that was articulated under the assumption of *limited government*—that there was a limit to the authority that *any* government, no matter what its form, could claim. The nation-state, on the other hand, is a form of democratic political representation that was articulated under the assumption of *unlimited* governmental power.

In the United States today, there is no generally accepted limit to governmental power, although this disquiets some. In Part III we shall detail the means by which such unlimited power is exercised, and in the conclusion we shall look into the deeper problems and challenges associated with the exercise of unlimited power now and in the years to come. But here, in Part II, we are concerned with the democratic exercise of limited ruling power. Even though the days of the republic are behind us, it is important to understand its institutions and its problems, for several reasons.

First, the major institutions of government under which we still operate, although in drastically modified fashion, were articulated in the years of the American republic. This can be a source of great confusion if we do not recognize how these institutions operated in the republic—under different assumptions about the nature and extent of governmental ruling power—and how they have been modified in the nation-state.

Second, we need a basis for comparison in order to ponder and discuss the problem of the lack of limitation upon governmental power. Most of us were born in a world dominated by nation-states that were in a continuing state of crisis; a return to limited government might be one alternative to this situation. But before we could recommend it, we must know what a democratic, limited government would be like. Thus we need to examine what our limited, republican government was like before we can determine whether or not we could or should return to something like it.

Finally, there is a third reason, which is not purely utilitarian. The American republic was a unique political society—huge, rich, and exciting. Unfortunately, in a concise study of the American political experience we cannot reconstruct fully the historical American republic. However, our brief examination should reveal its significance.

Part II contains three chapters, corresponding to the stages in the articulation of the institutions of the American republic. These institutions did not, as is sometimes incorrectly supposed, spring fullblown from the Constitution of 1787. Nor were many of these institutions planned by the framers of the Constitution. Chapter 2 shows the tensions between the internal and external demands on the form of political representation that plagued the incipient political society. Caught between the strong revolutionary demand for freedom from ruling power, which came from within the society, and the demand for adequate force to back up contracts and treaties, which came from outside, from other political societies, a coalition of political leaders forged a constitution that was designed to cope with these necessities. Chapter 3 then traces the articulation of the institutions that tended to democratize the republic, securing to the people themselves the benefits and great burdens of self-government. Finally, Chapter 4 describes the fully articulated American republic—how the people exercised their power, how their power was limited, and what the consequences were for the individual.

Chapter 2
The Radical Break

The American republic was unique at its inception because it diverged from the current general assumption that kingship was indispensable. For centuries European political societies had been represented by kings. In England, the power of the monarch had been sharply contested, and the nation was torn by civil war between 1640 and 1660. The Restoration (1660–1688), however, had reestablished the monarchy. And it was, of course, the power of the English king, George III, against which the American colonies rebelled.

The rebellion was successful, but it produced quite a problem, too. During the Revolutionary War, the colonies had joined together under a provisional government in their common cause against England. Now they were faced with the problem of establishing ruling power among themselves, even though their main basis for common political society was their *opposition* to ruling power.

The Declaration of Independence, as we have already noted, was a political act *par excellence,* because it openly challenged the authority of the king of England over his colonists and asserted as an alternative authority "The Thirteen United States of America, In Congress." The basis for this claim to authority was explicitly stated at the outset of the document as "the laws of Nature and of Nature's God." The revolutionary war that followed the Declaration was a continuation—by military means—of this political conflict.

It is easy for us, some two hundred years later, to see

this as the major political conflict in America at that time. We generally assert that "the colonies rebelled," as though a consensus about the proper locus and nature of authority existed. But, in fact, another major political conflict raged. It was the dispute between the "loyalists" and the "revolutionaries" over whether the world should be seen from the view of, and interpreted for the colonists by, King George, or whether it should be seen from the view of, and interpreted for others by, the signers of the Declaration and their supporters. In fact, no consensus was to be found. One of the great historians of the American republic, Andrew McLaughlin, describes the revolution as a civil war, "where [George] Washington, not [the British General] Howe, was in the enemy's country."[1] As much as a third of the colonial population—many of them men of substance and position in prerevolutionary days—were loyal to the crown of England, and regarded the revolutionaries as the enemy. During the war many of these loyalists ("Tories") were killed and after the war, tens of thousands of them were expelled.[2] In effect, then, this dispute was settled by force. The Tories were killed or banished. But the cost to the new political society of such a solution was great; not only did the country lose valuable human resources, but support was thereby lent to an attitude among the people that threatened the viability of any ruling power at all, and helps account for the conspicuous absence of efficient ruling power under the Articles of Confederation.

That attitude was well expressed in Thomas Paine's *Common Sense*, which McLaughlin has characterized as "the most popular book of that generation":

> In its pages one could read that government is a necessary evil, and that palaces of kings are built on the ruins of the bowers of paradise. If men believed this, they naturally believed that a return to nature would be a return to happiness; and if . . . government . . . was necessary, it should be looked on with suspicion . . . . Such philosophy was of wide influence in that generation and the next.[3]

The ruling power of government was, as such, unpopular among many, and this revolutionary philosophy expressed

1. Andrew McLaughlin, *The Confederation and the Constitution, 1783-1789.* (Collier Books, 1962), p. 37. This study was originally published in 1905.
2. Ibid., pp. 37–38.
3. Ibid., p. 39.

itself—or was at least indirectly acknowledged—in the Articles of Confederation, which kept national government under severe restraint.

The first instrument of national government for the thirteen ex-colonies, the Articles, made a radical break from European political organization by leaving the whole function of the king untended. Each state sent a delegation (which had one vote) to a congress, which had—"on paper"—just those powers necessary to establish the United States as a politicial society among other political societies in the world, and to regulate a few internal matters of common concern. As the text of the Articles (see p. 25) reveals, this meant primarily the power to make war and peace, and to manage diplomatic matters. In addition, it had the power to perform certain "housekeeping" duties of general interest, such as establishing post offices and regulating coinage.

But there was no executive office at all, and the judicial power was quite limited. Even the provision for the appointment of a member of Congress to preside over its sessions was limited to no more than one year in any term of three years, "in fear of kingly authority."[4] It required the assenting votes of nine of the thirteen states in order to take important action, and even then there were no means by which the states could be made to comply. To obtain money for raising an army; for instance Congress (*with* the consent of nine states) had to requisition, or request, the money from the states. If a state did not come up with the money, that was the end of it. Moreover, the provisions of the Articles could not be altered save by unanimous consent of the thirteen states.

This situation may sound a little like the United Nations —a "league of friendship" relying extensively on voluntary compliance by its constituent members. But it was not the same because the several states were not sovereign states able to make their own way in the world. That is, the states had the means necessary for *internal* representation—they had simply modified their colonial governments a bit—but they lacked the means for *external* representation. The Articles of Confederation, plainly, were to provide that means for all of the states, but without the disagreeable aspects of internal ruling power.

This structure set the stage for further political disputes

4. Ibid., p. 46.

both within the government—over questions of internal representation—and between the government and other governments—over questions of external representation. The philosophical justification for rejection of the king—that governments derive their just powers from the consent of the governed—raised the question of whether or not individuals owed obedience to a government that was unable to provide physical security, economic justice, and the other proclaimed responsibilities of government.

An interesting instance of how this restraint upon internal ruling power destroyed the new government's ability to represent itself externally to other political societies arose in Rhode Island. At a time when the value of the continental currency—the paper money issued by the Second Continental Congress to pay debts—was falling rapidly, economic justice for the debtor class (farmers and common people) was hard to come by. During the war, foreign loans and occupying armies brought in large amounts of coin to the country, but after the war this "hard money" flowed out as war profiteers and speculators spent their gains freely (for example, buying luxury imports). Paper money issued without the adequate backing of specie (coin or bullion) soon resulted in a situation in which debtors were required to pay back loans with hard money, because creditors would not accept the nearly worthless paper money being issued. In most states, owing to property restrictions on voting and conservative rules of apportionment in the legislatures, the backers of hard-money policies were able to defeat the advocates of paper money, who wished to relieve the plight of the debtors with greater issues of legal tender paper. But in Rhode Island, the radicals won power and issued paper money. Terrible civil strife ensued there when creditors refused to accept the worthless paper money. Then laws were passed in Rhode Island that allowed a debtor to give notice publicly of his attempt to pay with legal tender, and then be free of debt if the creditor refused to accept payment or avoided the debtor. (The laws, because the public notices began with the words "Know ye," were called the "Know ye laws.") In Massachusetts, where the paper-money party had been defeated in voting, the desperate farmers resorted to armed insurrection in Shays' Rebellion of 1786.[5]

---

5. A fuller description of these events can be found in Homer Cary Hockett, *Political and Social Growth of the American People, 1492–1865* (Macmillan, 1941, 3rd ed.), pp. 249–255. See also John Fiske, *The Critical Period of American History, 1783–1789* (Houghton Mifflin, 1916), pp. 163–184.

Against this background, Congress, under the Articles, attempted to honor its considerable war debts. Not only did it need money to operate at all, but Congress at least had to pay the interest, and hopefully some of the principle, on its debt to foreign nations. If it failed to do so, the United States could not be counted as a credible power, or indeed as a real political society at all, by the nations with which commercial and diplomatic intercourse was essential. The insufficiency of the provision in the Articles that allowed Congress to raise money only by requisitions on the hard-pressed states was realized at once, and an amendment was submitted to the states that would have allowed Congress to collect a duty of five percent (in hard money) on all imports for payment of principle and interest on the debt. Rhode Island alone refused to assent. This, of course, defeated this important proposal. Congress subsequently had to borrow from Holland (one of the few nations that would now lend to the United States), and requisition the states. But still the debt mounted and revenues decreased. Even though trade flourished and many private interests prospered in those days of vigorous trade, many debtors suffered and the national government went deeper into debt.

These disputes are particularly interesting for our inquiry because they reveal disputes about the nature of reality (is paper money good? should it be recognized as such?) and various claims to the authority to resolve the disputes by both hard-money and paper-money advocates on divergent grounds. The hard-money advocates attributed financial authority to goods and gold, while the soft-money advocates pointed to the acts of Congress and relied on "the rights of man" to justify escaping past debt by printing and distributing paper money. The politics of these monetary disputes were virulent and ominous in their implications for internal representation in the new kingless American republic.

But, troublesome as the problem of internal order was in some states, it was not this problem that led the Federalists—the coalition of political leaders that forged the Constitution of 1787—to try to replace the Articles. The discontent of debtors notwithstanding, the state governments were in most places sound, with conservative, one might even say aristocratic, elements well in control. Liberal and, as we shall see presently, even brilliant land policies encouraged thriving settlements and the amelioration of much domestic discontent. But there were grave difficulties in external representation. The agents of the new government were quite able, but they were agents of an inadequate political representative, Congress, under the Articles of Confederation. In England, John Adams faced ministers who refused to make an agreement on commerce, intimating that they doubted whether the Articles gave Congress the power to make a treaty the states would be bound to observe. Other nations, which had treated the Americans well during the war in order to embarrass the British, now were slow to deal with the, to them, rather dubious new government with no king. In France, Thomas Jefferson reported that "we are the lowest and most obscure of the whole diplomatic tribe."[6] The situation was similar elsewhere. The various states even began to deal with foreign markets on their own, and tariff wars, in which states established varying policies protecting their own particular commercial interests, ensued.

The Americans had rejected the king as their representative, and the legitimacy of kingly and aristocratic authority as well (see Article VI, p.26). But they were left without a form of political representation that would be recognized by other political societies.

We have seen how disputes about authority concerning the nature of reality had crippled the representative of the new political society, Congress under the Articles. Not only was the authority of the king rejected, but the jealous care with which the states protected themselves from a central ruling power destroyed the ability of Congress to represent the nation externally. Nevertheless, much was learned and much was discovered about political possibilities under the Articles. First, the Articles revealed with particular clarity what powers were necessary for adequate external representation, and what powers could be left to the people, to the local authorities or to the states. After several years of trying to represent the nation without the power to do so, the Congress had revealed to the Federalists just what powers were essential for effective political representation. Second, a new means of expansion, competitive with, but radically different from and superior to the colonial system employed by the European powers, had been devised. A discussion of this new means of expansion will be found in the next chapter, as it figures decisively in the articulation of political society under the Constitution of 1787; but, as we

6. Quoted in ibid., p. 247.

shall see, it was a system hit upon during the struggle for representation under the Articles.

THE ARTICLES OF CONFEDERATION—1781
Condensed[7]

"Articles of Confederation and perpetual Union between the States of [the thirteen original colonies].

ARTICLE I

The Stile of this confederacy shall be "The United States of America."

ARTICLE II

Each State retains its sovereignty, freedom, and independence, and every Power, Jurisdiction and right, which is not . . . expressly delegated to the United States, in Congress assembled.

ARTICLE III

The said States hereby severally enter into a firm league of friendship . . . for their common defence . . . and their mutual and general welfare, binding themselves to assist each other against all force . . . or attacks made upon them . . . .

ARTICLE IV

. . . the free inhabitants of each of these States . . . shall be entitled to all privileges and immunities of free citizens in the several States . . . .

If any Person guilty of, or charged with, treason or felony . . . shall flee from Justice, and be found in any of the United States, he shall, upon demand of the Governor or executive power, of the state from which he fled, be delivered up . . . to the state having jurisdiction . . . .

Full faith and credit shall be given in each of these States to the . . . acts . . . of every other State.

ARTICLE V

For the more convenient management of the general interests . . . delegates shall be annually appointed, in such manner as the legislatures of each State shall direct, to meet in Congress . . . .

---

7. *Journals of the Continental Congress*, vol. XIX, pp. 214ff. Reprinted in Forrest McDonald and Ellen Shapiro McDonald, eds., *Confederation and Constitution, 1781–1789* (University of South Carolina Press, 1968), pp. 21–29.

No State shall be represented in Congress by less than two, nor by more than seven Members; and no person shall be . . . a delegate for more than three years in any term of six years; nor shall any . . . delegate . . . (receive) any salary, fees or emolument of any kind.

. . . each State shall have one vote.

Freedom of speech and debate in Congress shall not be impeached or questioned in any Court, or place out of Congress . . . .

ARTICLE VI

No State, without the Consent of . . . Congress assembled, shall send any embassy to, or receive any embassy from, or enter into any . . . agreement . . . with any king, prince, or state; nor shall any person holding any office . . . under the United States, of any of them, accept of any present . . . office or title of any kind whatever from any king, prince or foreign state; nor shall the United States in Congress assembled, or any of them, grant any title of nobility.

No two or more States shall enter into any treaty . . . or alliance whatever between them, without the consent of the United States in Congress assembled, specifying accurately (the details) . . . .

No State shall lay any imposts or duties, which may interfere with any . . . treaties, entered into by the United States . . . .

No vessels of war shall be kept up in time of peace by any State, except . . . as shall be deemed necessary by the United States . . . ; nor shall any body of forces be kept up by any State . . . except . . . as . . .(by) Congress . . . shall be deemed requisite . . . for the defence of such State; but every State shall always keep up a well regulated militia . . . .

No State shall engage in any war without the consent of . . . Congress assembled, unless such state be actually invaded by enemies . . . .

ARTICLE VII

When land-forces are raised by any State for the common defence, all officers of or under the rank of colonel, shall be appointed by the legislature of each State respectively . . . .

ARTICLE VIII

All charges of war . . . and all other expences . . . incurred for the common defence or general welfare, and allowed by . . . Congress assembled, shall be defrayed out of a common treasury, which shall be supplied by the several States in proportion to the value of all land within each State . . . . The taxes for paying that proportion shall be laid and levied by the authority and direction of the legislatures of the several States within the time agreed upon by the United States in Congress assembled.

ARTICLE IX

The United States . . . shall have the sole and exclusive right and power of determining on peace and war . . . —of sending and receiving ambassadors—entering into treaties . . . —of establishing rules for deciding in all cases, what captures on land or water shall be legal . . . —of granting letters of marque and reprisal in times of peace—appointing courts for the trial of piracies . . . on the high seas and establishing courts for receiving and determining finally appeals in all cases of captures, provided that no member of Congress . . . be . . . a judge . . . .

The United States in Congress assembled shall also be the last resort on appeal in all disputes . . . between two or more States . . . . [There follows a close description of procedures to be used].

The United States . . . shall also have the sole and exclusive right and power of regulating . . . coin struck by their own authority, or by that of the respective States—fixing the standard of weights and measures . . . —regulating the trade and managing all affairs with the Indians . . . —establishing or regulating post-offices . . . —appointing all officers of the land forces . . . —appointing all the officers of the naval forces . . . — . . . and directing their operations.

The United States . . . shall have authority to appoint a committee, to sit in the recess of Congress, to be denominated "A Committee of the States," . . . —to appoint one of their number to preside, provided that no person be allowed to serve in the office of president more than one year in any term of three years; to ascertain the necessary sums of money to be raised . . . and to appropriate and apply the same . . . —to borrow money, or emit bills on the credit of the United States . . . —to build and equip a navy . . . .

The United States . . . shall never [exercise the foregoing powers] . . . unless nine States assent to the same . . . .

ARTICLE X

The committee of the States, or any nine of them, shall be authorized to execute, in the recess of Congress, such of the powers of Congress as . . . Congress . . . shall . . . vest them with . . . .

ARTICLE XI

Canada acceding to this confederation . . . shall be admitted into . . . this union: but no other colony shall be admitted into the same, unless such admission be agreed to by nine States.

ARTICLE XII

All bills of credit emitted, monies borrowed and debts contracted by, or under the authority of Congress, before the assembling of the United States, in pursuance of the present confederation, shall be . . . a charge against the United States, for payment and satisfaction whereof the said United States, and the public faith are hereby solemnly pledged.

ARTICLE XIII

Every State shall abide by the determinations of the United States in Congress . . . and the Articles of this confederation shall be inviolably observed by every State, and the union shall be perpetual; nor shall any alteration . . . be made in any of them; unless such alteration be agreed to in a Congress . . . and be afterwards confirmed by the legislatures of every State.

And Whereas it hath pleased the Great Governor of the World to incline the hearts of the legislatures we respectively represent in Congress, to approve of, and to authorize us to ratify the said articles of confederation and perpetual union.. Know Ye that we . . . do . . . fully and entirely ratify and confirm . . . the said articles . . . .

In Witness whereof we have hereunto set our hands in Congress. Done at Philadelphia in the state of Pennsylvania the ninth day of July, in the Year of our Lord one Thousand seven Hundred and Seventy-eight, and in the third year of the independence of America.

Kingless Representation: The Constitution of 1787

The government or representative of a political society, as we have said, is seen from the inside *and* from the outside. It is clear from the nature of the Articles of Confederation that they were established primarily for purposes of external representation. Indeed, the Articles were a more formalized continuation of the provisional government that had been formed to prosecute the war against England. However, it is also quite clear that the problem of internal representation—the problem of ruling power for the representative—held sway, and remembrance of the tyranny felt under kingship thus prevented the establishment of effective external representation.

Given the provision requiring unanimous consent among the states in order to amend the Articles, the movement to "render the constitution of the federal government adequate to the exigencies of the Union," as the resolution calling for a constitutional convention put it, came not from the Congress, but from a conference of men eager to form a more powerful federal government. The most influential interpretation of the composition and motives of this group of Founding Fathers has been that of Charles Beard. In his *Economic Interpretation of the Constitution,* he pointed to the clear indications that it was the propertied class and their motives for economic stability and personal gain that produced the Constitution of 1787.[8] Such men constituted the majorities of most of the state legislatures, for wage-earners were typically excluded from voting in the states by property requirements, while small farmers were relegated to minority status in the state legislatures by means of conservative apportionment schemes.[9] However, to say that the motives of the Founders of the Constitution were primarily economic does not deny that they were also public-spirited, and it is quite consistent with our contention that the Constitution of 1787 was primarily a means for establishing effective external representation.

In the eighteenth century, the nations of Europe vigorously pursued the policy known as "mercantilism." Basically, this policy assumed that the strength of a nation was gauged in terms of the amount of bullion (silver and gold) that the nation possessed. The competition for colonies, the complex trade and commerce agreements, and the wars of these nations were all of a piece with mercantilism. Consequently, a concern for external representation and a concern for favorable commercial agreements, hard-money policies, and so forth, could not be separated. In Europe, the aristocracy (royalty and nobility) and the bourgeoisie (merchants and traders) of a nation were allied: both elements wanted to bring as much bullion as possible into the nation.

In America, the new political society was trying to cast off its colonial status—which had served to provide a means by which the mother country could get more bullion in trade for products—and to get into the game as a sovereign nation.

---

8. Charles A. Beard, *An Economic Interpretation of the Constitution* (Macmillan, 1913). See also the major critique by Robert E. Brown, *Charles Beard and the Constitution* (Norton, 1956).
9. Hockett, *Political and Social Growth of the American People,* p. 283.

As for the economic interpretation, the Founders may be thought of as a bourgeoisie without a king with whom to be allied. Their task was to create a substitute for a king, an effective representative of the political society whose strength, like that of the kings of Europe, would protect the interests of the merchants and increase with their success.

When the Constitutional Convention assembled in Philadelphia in 1787, with all of the states (except Rhode Island) eventually represented, a sort of coup d'état, a seizure of power, was in the making. The fifty-five members of the secret meetings were largely agreed upon their main task, which was to establish a national government with coercive ruling power. Of course there was no thought of reverting to a monarchy; the selection of the leader of the revolutionary forces, George Washington, as presiding officer testified amply to that. But Alexander Hamilton had long contended that the Congress must have "complete sovereignty in all that relates to war, peace, trade, finance, and management of foreign affairs," while Washington had by 1786 come to think that the United States could not "exist long as a nation without having lodged somewhere a power which will pervade the whole Union in as energetic a manner as the authority of the State governments extends over the several States." And early in the debates, Gouverneur Morris pointed out that the national government must have "a complete and compulsive operation."[10]

On the basis of their experience with the Articles of Confederation, the delegates were generally agreed as to what coercive powers must be held by a national government; indeed, most of these powers were already enumerated in the Articles. The powers of taxation and commercial regulation clearly had to be added, and then "naturalization, bankruptcy, patents, copyrights, the punishment of counterfeiting, and the power of coercion . . . exhaust the list" of other powers the Convention could think of.[11] That these powers should be vested in a Congress was already presumed; and with the agreement that the government would have coercive powers, the establishment of a national judiciary to adjudicate its laws followed as a matter of course. Moreover, the establishment of an independent executive was agreeable to most, although the question of the method of selection served as a focus for

10. Ibid., p. 287.
11. Ibid., p. 285.

dispute. But the states needed effective external representation, and the enumeration of the president's powers that was eventually included in the Constitution indicates quite clearly that he was to substitute for a king in the mode of external representation. Internally, however, he was to be considerably dependent on Congress.

The debates and compromises of the Constitutional Convention should be understood in the context of the broad unity of purpose that motivated the delegates. To be sure, the Constitution touched off sharp disputes concerning the nature of reality, but the gravest of these disputes occured during and after the struggle over ratification. The Federalists were well organized, and basically knew what they sought; the disputes among themselves were mainly over how best to achieve their goals, and over which among them would most profit by the arrangements.

The critical question, then, once the powers of the national government were determined, was—who shall control the national government? Or, in our terms, who shall have authority to employ the powers of the government in interpreting and determining the nature of reality for the citizens of the United States? The major disputes arose first between the large states and the small states over representation in the national legislature, and then between the northern and southern delegates concerning slavery and differing sectional economic interests.

The focus of greatest debate concerned two competing images of ideal reality that dealt with the nature of national ruling power, "The Virginia Plan" and "The New Jersey Plan," as they came to be called. Out of these debates grew the collective decision to establish a *dual* government, state and national, with both governments operating directly on the people. The basic question concerned the locus of authority: in whom would it be vested and over whom would it be exercised. At first, both plans had envisioned a federal government using its coercive powers against recalcitrant *states;* but it was pointed out that this would be tantamount to civil war. Force would be used against *individuals* (if considerable numbers were involved), and the national laws would be enforced by the mechanisms of a complete judicial system. However, the Virginia Plan proposed a Congress of two houses, and separate executive and judicial branches, which was the traditional model derived from England. (Parliament consisted of an upper house, the House of Lords, and a lower house, the House of Commons; in colonial government, the king had appointed a governor.) Moreover, the Virginia Plan proposed that both houses be "in proportion to population or contribution to the common treasury" (population was the best indicator of wealth).[12]

Eventually, the New Jersey Plan accepted most of the elements of the Virginia Plan, but it held fast to the idea of a single-house Congress with equal representation from all the states. (Hence, the plans were also known as the "big state" and "small state" plans.) Madison and Hamilton continued to insist that sectional differences, not large state versus small state differences, were more likely sources of dispute, but the issue seemed locked on size and representation. Perhaps this was fortunate because the economic differences between the South and the North might well have proved impossible of resolution had the issue been drawn there. In any case, after much debate, after special meetings, and after almost adjourning over the issue, the Convention accepted the "great Compromise," which produced a lower house based on population, and an upper house representing the states equally.

An illustration of how sectional differences might have stymied or wrecked the convention (had sectionalism become the main focus) is provided by the question of slave representation. Population was used to determine representation in the lower house, and it was used also as a basis for direct taxation on the states. Direct taxation could only be laid in proportion to the population of the state. But southern delegates held that population was not a good index of state wealth in the South because, they contended, slaves were not the equals of white men as wealth producers. However, they wished to count slaves equally with whites for the purpose of representation (although, of course, the slaves could not vote). Not surprisingly, the North took the opposite view that slaves should be counted equally for taxation, since they were in the South nothing but wealth-producers; and for the same reason, they should not be counted at all for representation purposes. The compromise agreement was to count three-fifths of the slaves for both taxation and representation. This compromise had the further function of facilitating the justification for denying slaves the right to "life, liberty, and the pursuit of happiness" because they were not (yet) considered

---

12. Ibid., p. 289.

to be full men and, of course, it is "all men" who are "created equal" and thereby "endowed by their Creator" with these "inalienable rights."

Although the question of state representation caused the most bitter debates, the problem of the executive was perhaps the most difficult one facing the Convention. Despite resistance to any reappearance of a kingly figure, the idea of an independent single executive soon prevailed and, given the widespread recognition of the importance of external representation for the new republic, this is not surprising. Unless there were an office that could represent the United States without being hamstrung by Congress, the new government's agents would fare little better in foreign places than had the agents of the Confederation. Yet the executive had been the agent of the king in the colonies, and the favored practice after the revolution had been to elect an executive in the legislative branch, thus assuring his relative weakness. Very few of these propertied delegates would give serious consideration to popular elections (indeed, "democrat" was a term of opprobrium among them), and in any case a very scattered vote would likely occur in popular elections. The creation of the device known as an electoral college thus was greeted as one of the triumphs of the Convention.

Much of what appeared as the final draft of the Constitution was the work of a Committee on Details. It drew heavily upon the Articles of Confederation and upon practices that had long been established in English-speaking political society. The final great decision was to submit the Constitution to conventions of delegates in each state, with ratification to depend upon agreement by nine of the states. In effect, not only Congress under the Articles, but the state legislatures as well, were partially bypassed. One might say that the plan was for a majority of states to secede from the Confederacy, and to reform under the Constitution of 1787. However one thinks of it, it must be realized that the Constitution was the work of a definite minority of the people, conservative (relative to the common people), and resolved to establish national ruling power for the purpose of external representation.

The Constitution that the convention produced is a spare, well-written document of only seven articles, each of which contains sections to make its provisions explicit. While certain of its provisions have since been changed by amendments, and certain other provisions were temporary in their relevance or application, the greater part of the document described the major elements of the new government (with the notable omission of political parties, which had yet to emerge, as we shall see in the next chapter). How accurately its provisions and prescriptions describe the conduct of politics and government in the American nation-state today is another question, with which we shall grapple in Part III.

THE CONSTITUTION OF THE UNITED STATES—1787

We the People of the United States, in Order to form a more perfect Union, establish Justice, insure domestic Tranquillity, provide for the common defence, promote the general Welfare, and secure the Blessings of Liberty to ourselves and our Posterity, do ordain and establish this Constitution for the United States of America.

ARTICLE I

Section 1. All legislative Powers herein granted shall be vested in a Congress of the United States which shall consist of a Senate and House of Representatives.

Section 2. The House of Representatives shall be composed of Members chosen every second Year by the People of the several States, and the Electors in each State shall have the Qualifications requisite for Electors of the most numerous Branch of the State Legislature.

No Person shall be a Representative who shall not have attained to the age of twenty five Years, and been seven Years a Citizen of the United States, and who shall not, when elected, be an Inhabitant of that State in which he shall be chosen.

Representatives and direct Taxes shall be apportioned among the several States which may be included within this Union, according to their respective Numbers, which shall be determined by adding to the whole Number of free Persons, including those bound to Service for a Term of Years, and excluding Indians not taxed, three fifths of all other Persons. The actual Enumeration shall be made within three Years after the first Meeting of the Congress of the United States, and within every subsequent Term of ten Years, in such Manner as they shall by Law direct. The Number of Representatives shall not exceed one for every thirty Thousand, but each State shall have at Least one Representative; and until such enumeration shall be made, the State of New Hampshire shall be entitled to chuse three, Massachusetts eight, Rhode-Island and Providence Plantations one, Connecticut five, New-York six, New Jersey four, Pennsylvania eight, Delaware one,

Maryland six, Virginia ten, North Carolina five, South Carolina five, and Georgia three.

When vacancies happen in the Representation from any State, the Executive Authority thereof shall issue Writs of Election to fill such Vacancies.

The House of Representatives shall chuse their Speaker and other Officers; and shall have the sole Power of Impeachment.

Section 3. The Senate of the United States shall be composed of two Senators from each State, chosen by the Legislature thereof, for six Years; and each Senator shall have one Vote.

Immediately after they shall be assembled in Consequence of the first Election, they shall be divided as equally as may be into three Classes. The Seats of the Senators of the first Class shall be vacated at the Expiration of the second Year, of the second Class at the Expiration of the fourth Year, and of the third Class at the Expiration of the sixth Year, so that one third may be chosen every second Year; and if Vacancies happen by Resignation, or otherwise, during the Recess of the Legislature of any State, the Executive thereof may make temporary Appointments until the next Meeting of the Legislature, which shall then fill such Vacancies.

No Person shall be a Senator who shall not have attained to the Age of thirty Years, and been nine Years a Citizen of the United States, and who shall not, when elected, be an inhabitant of that State for which he shall be chosen.

The Vice President of the United States shall be President of the Senate, but shall have no Vote, unless they be equally divided.

The Senate shall chuse their other Officers, and also a President pro tempore, in the Absence of the Vice President, or when he shall exercise the Office of President of the United States.

The Senate shall have the sole Power to try all Impeachments. When sitting for that Purpose, they shall be on Oath or Affirmation. When the President of the United States is tried the Chief Justice shall preside: And no Person shall be convicted without the Concurrence of two thirds of the Members present.

Judgment in Cases of Impeachment shall not extend further than to removal from Office, and disqualification to hold and enjoy any Office of honor, Trust or Profit under the United States: but the Party convicted shall nevertheless be liable and subject to Indictment, Trial, Judgment and Punishment, according to Law.

Section 4. The Times, Places and Manner of holding Elections for Senators and Representatives, shall be prescribed in each State by the Legislature thereof; but the Congress may at any time by Law make or alter such Regulations, except as to the Places of chusing Senators.

The Congress shall assemble at least once in every Year, and such Meeting shall be on the first Monday in December, unless they shall by Law appoint Absence a different day.

Section 5. Each House shall be the Judge of the Elections, Returns and Qualifications of its own Members, and a Majority of each shall constitute a Quorum to do Business; but a smaller Number may adjourn from day to day, and may be authorized to compel the Attendance of absent Members, in such Manner, and under such Penalties as each House may provide.

Each House may determine the Rules of its Proceedings, punish its Members for disorderly Behaviour, and, with the Concurrence of two thirds, expel a Member.

Each House shall keep a Journal of its Proceedings, and from time to time publish the same, excepting such Parts as may in their Judgment require Secrecy; and the Yeas and Nays of the Members of either House on any question shall, at the Desire of one fifth of those Present, be entered on the Journal.

Neither House, during the Session of Congress, shall, without the Consent of the other, adjourn for more than three days, nor to any other Place than that in which the two Houses shall be sitting.

Section 6. The Senators and Representatives shall receive a Compensation for their Services, to be ascertained by Law, and paid out of the Treasury of the United States. They shall in all Cases, except Treason, Felony and Breach of the Peace, be privileged from Arrest during their Attendance at the Session of their respective Houses, and in going to and returning from the same; and for any Speech or Debate in either House, they shall not be questioned in any other Place.

No Senator or Representative shall, during the Time for which he was elected, be appointed to any civil Office under the Authority of the United States, which shall have been created, or the Emoluments whereof shall have been encreased during such time; and no Person holding any Office under the United States, shall be a Member of either House during his Continuance in Office.

Section 7. All Bills for raising Revenue shall originate in the House of Representatives; but the Senate may propose or concur with amendments as on other Bills.

Every Bill which shall have passed the House of Representatives and the Senate, shall, before it becomes a Law, be presented to the President of the United States; If he approve he shall sign it, but if not he shall return it, with his Objections to that House in which it shall have originated, who shall enter the Objections at large on their Journal, and proceed to reconsider it. If after such Reconsideration two thirds of that House shall agree to pass the Bill, it shall be sent, together with the Objections, to the other House, by which it shall likewise be reconsidered, and if approved by two thirds of that House, it shall become a Law. But in all such Cases the Votes of both Houses shall be determined by yeas and

Nays, and the Names of the Persons voting for and against the Bill shall be entered on the Journal of each House respectively. If any Bill shall not be returned by the President within ten Days (Sundays excepted) after it shall have been presented to him, the Same shall be a Law, in like Manner as if he had signed it, unless the Congress by their Adjournment prevents its Return, in which case it shall not be a Law.

Every Order, Resolution, or Vote to which the Concurrence of the Senate and House of Representatives may be necessary (except on a question of Adjournment) shall be presented to the President of the United States; and before the Same shall take Effect, shall be approved by him, or being disapproved by him, shall be repassed by two thirds of the Senate and House of Representatives, according to the Rules and Limitations prescribed in the Case of a Bill..

Section 8. The Congress shall have Power To lay and collect Taxes, Duties, Imposts and Excises, to pay the Debts and provide for the common Defence and general Welfare of the United States; but all Duties, Imposts and Excises shall be uniform throughout the United States;

To borrow Money on the credit of the United States;

To regulate Commerce with foreign Nations, and among the several States, and with the Indian Tribes;

To establish an uniform Rule of Naturalization, and uniform Laws on the subject of Bankruptcies throughout the United States;

To coin Money, regulate the Value thereof, and of foreign Coin, and fix the Standard of Weights and Measures;

To provide for the Punishment of counterfeiting the Securities and current Coin of the United States;

To establish Post Offices and post Roads;

To promote the Progress of Science and useful Arts, by securing for limited Times to Authors and Inventors the exclusive Right to their respective Writings and Discoveries;

To constitute Tribunals inferior to the supreme Court;

To define and punish Piracies and Felonies committed on the high Seas, and Offences against the Law of Nations;

To declare War, grant Letters of Marque and Reprisal, and make Rules concerning Captures on Land and Water;

To raise and support Armies, but no Appropriation of Money to that Use shall be for a longer Term than two Years;

To provide and maintain a Navy;

To make Rules for the Government and Regulation of the land and navel Forces;

To provide for calling forth the Militia to execute the Laws of the Union, suppress Insurrections and repel Invasions;

To provide for organizing, arming, and disciplining, the Militia, and for governing such Part of them as may be employed in the Service of the United States, reserving to the States respectively, the Appointment of the Officers, and the Authority of training the Militia according to the discipline prescribed by Congress;

To exercise exclusive Legislation in all Cases whatsoever, over such District (not exceeding ten Miles square) as may, by Cession of Particular States, and the Acceptance of Congress, become the Seat of the Government of the United States, and to exercise like Authority over all Places purchased by the Consent of the Legislature of the State in which the Same shall be, for the Erection of Forts, Magazines, Arsenals, dock-Yards, and other needful Buildings;—And

To make all Laws which shall be necessary and proper for carrying into Execution the foregoing Powers, and all other Powers vested by this Constitution in the Government of the United States, or in any Department or Officer thereof.

Section 9. The Migration or Importation of such Persons as any of the States now existing shall think proper to admit, shall not be prohibited by the Congress prior to the Year one thousand eight hundred and eight, but a Tax or duty may be imposed on such Importation, not exceeding ten dollars for each Person.

The Privilege of the Writ of Habeas Corpus shall not be suspended, unless when in Cases of Rebellion or Invasion the public Safety may require it.

No Bill of Attainder or ex post facto Law shall be passed.

No Capitation, or other direct, Tax shall be laid, unless in Proportion to the Census or Enumeration herein before directed to be taken.

No Tax or Duty shall be laid on Articles exported from any State.

No Preference shall be given by any Regulation of Commerce or Revenue to the Ports of one State over those of another; nor shall Vessels bound to, or from, one State, be obliged to enter, clear or pay Duties in another.

No Money shall be drawn from the Treasury, but in Consequence of Appropriations made by Law; and a regular Statement and Account of the Receipts and Expenditures of all public Money shall be published from time to time.

No Title of Nobility shall be granted by the United States; And no Person holding any Office of Profit or Trust under them, shall, without the Consent of the Congress, accept of any present Emolument, Office, or Title, of any kind whatever, from any King, Prince, or foreign State.

Section 10. No State shall enter into any Treaty, Alliance, or Confederation; grant Letters of Marque and Reprisal; coin Money; emit Bills of Credit; make any Thing but gold and silver Coin a Tender in Payment of Debts; pass any Bill of Attainder, ex post facto Law, or Law impairing the Obligation of Contracts, or grant any Title of Nobility.

No State shall, without the Consent of the Congress, lay any Imposts or Duties on Imports or Exports, except what may be absolutely necessary for executing its inspection Laws: and the net Produce of all Duties and Imposts, laid by any State on Imports or Exports, shall be for the Use of the Treasury of the United States; and all such Laws shall be subject to the Revision and Controul of the Congress.

No State shall, without the Consent of Congress, lay any Duty of Tonnage, keep Troops, or Ships of War in time of Peace, enter into any Agreement or Compact with another State, or with a foreign Power, or engage in War, unless actually invaded, or in such imminent Danger as will not admit of delay.

ARTICLE II

Section 1. The executive Power shall be vested in a President of the United States of America. He shall hold his Office during the Term of four Years, and, together with the Vice President, chosen for the same term, be elected, as follows

Each State shall appoint, in such Manner as the Legislature thereof may direct, a Number of Electors, equal to the whole Number of Senators and Representatives to which the State may be entitled in the Congress: but no Senator or Representative, or Person holding an Office of Trust or Profit under the United States, shall be appointed an Elector.

The Electors shall meet in their respective States, and vote by Ballot for two Persons, of whom one at least shall not be an Inhabitant of the same State with themselves. And they shall make a List of all the Persons voted for, and of the Number of Votes for each; which List they shall sign and certify, and transmit sealed to the Seat of the Government of the United States, directed to the President of the Senate. The President of the Senate shall, in the Presence of the Senate and House of Representatives, open all the Certificates, and the Votes shall then be counted. The Person having the greatest Number of Votes shall be the President, if such Number be a Majority of the whole Number of Electors appointed; and if there be more than one who have such Majority, and have an equal Number of Votes, then the House of Representatives shall immediately chuse by Ballot one of them for President: and if no Person have a Majority, then from the five highest on the List the said House shall in like Manner chuse the President. But in chusing the President, the Votes shall be taken by States, the Representation from each State having one Vote; A quorum for this Purpose shall consist of a Member or Members from two thirds of the States, and a Majority of all the States shall be necessary to a Choice. In every Case, after the Choice of the President, the Person having the greatest Number of Votes of the Electors shall be the Vice President. But if there should remain two or more who have equal Votes, the Senate shall chuse from them by Ballot the Vice President.

The Congress may determine the Time of chusing the Electors, and the Day on which they shall give their Votes; which Day shall be the same throughout the United States.

No Person except a natural born Citizen, or a Citizen of the United States, at the time of the Adoption of this Constitution, shall be eligible to the Office of President, neither shall any Person be eligible to that Office who shall not have attained to the Age of thirty five Years and been fourteen Years a Resident within the United States.

In Case of the Removal of the President from Office, or of his Death, Resignation, or inability to discharge the Powers and Duties of the said Office, the Same shall devolve on the Vice President, and the Congress may by Law provide for the Case of Removal, Death, Resignation or Inability, both of the President and Vice President, declaring what Officer shall then act as President, and such Officer shall act accordingly, until the Disability be removed, or a President shall be elected.

The President shall, at stated Times, receive for his Services a Compensation, which shall neither be encreased nor diminished during the Period for which he shall have been elected, and he shall not receive within that Period any other Emolument from the United States, or any of them.

Before he enter on the Execution of his Office, he shall take the following Oath or Affirmation:—"I do solemnly swear (or affirm) that I will faithfully execute the Office of President of the United States, and will to the best of my Ability, preserve, protect and defend the Constitution of the United States."

Section 2. The President shall be Commander in Chief of the Army and Navy of the United States, and of the Militia of the several States, when called into the actual Service of the United States; he may require the Opinion, in writing, of the principal Officer in each of the executive Departments, upon any Subject relating to the Duties of their respective Offices, and he shall have Power to grant Reprieves and Pardons for Offences against the United States, except in Cases of Impeachment.

He shall have Power, by and with the Advice and Consent of the Senate, to make Treaties, provided two thirds of the Senators present concur; and he shall nominate, and by and with the Advice and Consent of the Senate, shall appoint Ambassadors, other public Ministers and Consuls, Judges of the supreme Court, and all other Officers of the United States, whose Appointments are not herein otherwise provided for, and which shall be established by Law; but the Congress may by Law vest the Appointment of such inferior Officers, as they think proper, in the President alone, in the Courts of Law, or in the Heads of Departments.

The President shall have Power to fill up all Vacancies that may happen during the Recess of the Senate, by granting Commissions which shall expire at the End of their next Session.

Section 3. He shall from time to time give to the Congress Information of the State of the Union, and recommend to their Consideration such Measures as he shall judge necessary and expedient; he may, on extraordinary occasions, convene both Houses, or either of them, and in case of disagreement between them with respect to the time of adjournment, he may adjourn them to such time as he shall think proper; he shall receive ambassadors and other public ministers; he shall take care that the laws be faithfully executed, and shall commission all the officers of the United States.

Section 4. The President, Vice President, and all civil officers of the United States, shall be removed from office on impeachment for, and conviction of, treason, bribery, or other high crimes and misdemeanors.

ARTICLE III

Section 1. The judicial power of the United States shall be vested in one Supreme Court, and in such inferior courts as the Congress may from time to time ordain and establish. The judges, both of the supreme and inferior courts, shall hold their offices during good behavior, and shall, at stated times, receive for their services, a compensation, which shall not be diminished during their continuance in office.

Section 2. 1. The judicial power shall extend to all cases, in law and equity, arising under this Constitution, the laws of the United States, and treaties made, or which shall be made, under their authority;—to all cases affecting ambassadors, other public ministers and consuls;—to all cases of admiralty and maritime jurisdiction;—to controversies to which the United States shall be a party; —to controversies between two or more States;—between a State and a citizen of another state;—between citizens of different States—between citizens of the same State claiming lands under grants of different States, and between a State, or the citizens thereof, and foreign States, citizens or subjects.

2. In all cases affecting ambassadors, other public ministers and consuls, and those in which a State shall be party, the Supreme Court shall have original jurisdiction. In all the other cases before mentioned, the Supreme Court shall have appellate jurisdiction, both as to law and fact, with such exceptions, and under such regulations as the Congress shall make.

3. The trial of all crimes, except in cases of impeachment, shall be by jury; and such trial shall be held in the State where the said crimes shall have been committed; but when not committed within any State, the trial shall be at such place or places as the Congress may by law have directed.

Section 3. 1. Treason against the United States shall consist only in levying war against them, or in adhering to their enemies, giving them aid and comfort. No person shall be convicted of treason unless on the testimony of two witnesses to the same overt act, or on confession in open court.

2. The Congress shall have power to declare the punishment of treason, but no attainder of treason shall work corruption of blood, or forfeiture except during the life of the person attainted.

ARTICLE IV

Section 1. Full faith and credit shall be given in each State to the public acts, Records, and judicial Proceedings of every other State. And the Congress may by general Laws prescribe the Manner in which such Acts, Record and Proceedings shall be proved, and the Effect thereof.

Section 2. The Citizens of each State shall be entitled to all Privileges and Immunities of Citizens in the several States.

A Person charged in any State with Treason, Felony, or other Crime, who shall flee from Justice, and be found in another State, shall on Demand of the executive Authority of the State from which he fled, be delivered up, to be removed to the State having jurisdiction of the Crime.

No Person held to Service or Labour in one State, under the Laws thereof, escaping into another, shall, in Consequence of any Law or Regulation therein, be discharged from such Service or Labour, but shall be delivered up on Claim of the Party to whom such Service or Labour may be due.

Section 3. New States may be admitted by the Congress into this Union; but no new State shall be formed or erected within the Jurisdiction of any other State; nor any State be formed by the Junction of two or more States, or Parts of States, without the Consent of the Legislatures of the States concerned as well as of the Congress.

The Congress shall have Power to dispose of and make all needful Rules and Regulations respecting the Territory or other Property belonging to the United States; and nothing in this Constitution shall be so construed as to Prejudice any Claims of the United States, or of any particular State.

Section 4. The United States shall guarantee to every State in this Union a Republican Form of Government, and shall protect each of them against Invasion; and on Application of the Legislature, or of the Executive (when the Legislature cannot be convened) against domestic Violence.

ARTICLE V

The Congress, whenever two thirds of both Houses shall deem it necessary, shall propose amendments to this Constitution, or, on the Application of the Legislature of two thirds of the several States, shall call a Convention for proposing Amendments, which, in either Case, shall be valid to all Intents and Purposes, as Part of this Constitution, when ratified by the Legislatures of three fourths of the several States, or by Conventions in three fourths thereof, as the one or the other Mode of Ratification may be proposed by the Congress; Provided that no Amendment which may be made prior to the Year One thousand eight hundred and eight shall in any Manner affect the first and fourth Clauses in the Ninth Section of the first Article; and that no State, without its Consent, shall be deprived of its equal Suffrage in the Senate.

ARTICLE VI

All Debts contracted and Engagements entered into, before the Adoption of this Constitution, shall be as valid against the United States under this Constitution, as under the Confederation.

   This Constitution, and the Laws of the United States which shall be made in Pursuance thereof; and all Treaties made, or which shall be made, under the Authority of the United States, shall be the supreme Law of the Land; and the Judges in every State shall be bound thereby, any Thing in the Constitution or Laws of any State to the Contrary notwithstanding.

   The Senators and Representatives before mentioned, and the Members of the several State Legislatures, and all executive and judicial Officers, both of the United States and of the several States, shall be bound by Oath or Affirmation, to support this Constitution; but no religious Test shall ever be required as a Qualification to any Office or public Trust under the United States.

ARTICLE VII

The Ratification of the Conventions of nine States, shall be sufficient for the Establishment of this Constitution between the States so ratifying the Same.

   done in Convention by the Unanimous Consent of the States present the Seventeenth Day of September in the Year of our Lord one thousand seven hundred and Eighty seven and of the Independence of the United States of America the Twelfth in witness whereof We have hereunto subscribed our Names, . . .

Ratification of the Constitution

As we have seen, debate within the Constitutional Convention was less a dispute about the nature and necessity of national ruling power than a series of disputes about how to divide the relative advantages of such ruling power within the group. Ratification of the Constitution posed a different set of problems because it required that the hitherto secret works of the convention become public. However, the Federalists (as they gladly called themselves, to play down the issue of nationalism) still used that previous secrecy to advantage by getting a flying start on the Anti-federalists, disorganized and disadvantaged as the latter were by not even knowing what they were to oppose.

At an earlier stage in the articulation of the republic, during the Revolutionary War, the issue of kingless representation had assumed the proportions of civil war, with the issue settled in favor of the anti-royalists through coercion when thousands upon thousands of Tories were killed or banished. Now the issue reemerged, and the shoe was on the other foot, since the Federalists now needed to try to establish effective, national ruling power. But this time the hostility among the people toward central ruling power was not advantageous for the Federalists; instead, the people opposed them because they still disliked ruling power. Coercion, now, was out of the question as no effective coercive agency existed, and in addition, support—not opposition—was needed. If the supporters of the king had been dealt with by force, the opponents of nationalism were dealt with by exclusion.

The concern for adequate external representation and the concomitant requirement for national ruling power was a view of reality quite beyond the ken of small farmers and wage earners. The Federalists were the merchants, planters, lawyers, and financial speculators of the seaboard. They were men whose fortunes and identities were involved with the mercantile policies of the nations of that day, and the common people saw in the Federalists' machinations an attempt to extend their local political domination to a national basis. The common people saw this, that is, when they had a chance to see those machinations at all. The advantage—at least temporarily—in this dispute over the most desirable repository of governmental authority was with the Federalists. First, the wage-earners of the seaboard cities, being without property, were for the most part politically unenfranchised; since they could not vote, their opposition could never really express itself in the state ratifying conventions. Second, the Federalists "rushed" a few key states in order to forestall the opposition of the small farmers and settlers. Pennsylvania was the first large state to ratify (Delaware was the first state), and a motion was made in the state assembly for a ratifying convention even before Congress had received official notification of the Constitutional Convention's action. Only a month was allowed for election of delegates and six weeks before the convening of the meeting. Thus the Federalists at the Pennsylvania convention outnumbered the Anti-federalists two to one, and virtually all of them came from Philadelphia and the eastern counties. The Anti-federalists from the back counties never had a chance, in those days of hard travel and slow communications, to marshall their forces of resistance. Third, much of the opposition to the Federalists occurred in the (then) western areas. In Vermont, Kentucky, and Tennessee, where statehood had been anticipated but never became fact under the Articles, universal manhood suffrage had been the practice from the start (partly in order to attract settlers). These democratically minded people did not like the looks of the aristocratic, anti-democratic Federalists, but they did not have an opportunity to prevent ratification.

But, as time went by, the Anti-federalists became more organized. They could not in any case have been ignored entirely because the Constitution needed more support than just that of the small monied classes. Despite their readiness to resort to fast tactics and occasional intrigues, the Federalists had to do something to allay the fears of the Anti-federalists, and even win some of them over. They thus promised to support a number of amendments to the Constitution. The ten amendments that eventually passed are the well-known "Bill of Rights."

THE BILL OF RIGHTS

The First Ten Amendments to the Constitution,
Ratified in 1791

AMENDMENT I

Congress shall make no law respecting an establishment of religion, or prohibiting the free exercise thereof; or abridging the freedom of speech, or of the press; or the right of the people peaceably to assemble, and to petition the Government for a redress of grievances.

AMENDMENT II

A well regulated Militia, being necessary to the security of a free State, the right of the people to keep and bear Arms, shall not be infringed.

AMENDMENT III

No Soldier shall, in time of peace be quartered in any house, without the consent of the Owner, nor in time of war, but in a manner to be prescribed by law.

AMENDMENT IV

The right of the people to be secure in their persons, houses, papers, and effects, against unreasonable searches and seizures, shall not be violated, and no Warrants shall issue, but upon probable cause, supported by Oath or affirmation, and particularly describing the place to be searched, and the persons or things to be seized.

AMENDMENT V

No person shall be held to answer for a capital, or otherwise infamous crime, unless on a presentment or indictment of a Grand Jury, except in cases arising in the land or naval forces, or in the Militia, when in actual service in time of War or public danger; nor shall any person be subject for the same offence to be twice put in jeopardy of life or limb; nor shall be compelled on any criminal case to be a witness against himself, nor be deprived of life, liberty, or property, without due process of law; nor shall private property be taken for public use, without just compensation.

AMENDMENT VI

In all criminal prosecutions, the accused shall enjoy the right to a speedy and public trial, by an impartial jury of the State and district wherein the crime shall have been committed, which district shall have been previously ascertained by law, and to be informed of the nature and cause of the accusation; to be confronted with the witnesses against him; to have compulsory process for obtaining witnesses in his favor, and to have the Assistance of Counsel for his defence.

AMENDMENT VII

In Suits at common law, where the value in controversy shall exceed twenty dollars, the right of trial by jury shall be preserved and no fact tried by a jury, shall be otherwise re-examined in any Court of the United States, than according to the rules of the common law.

AMENDMENT VIII

Excessive bail shall not be required, nor excessive fines imposed, nor cruel and unusual punishments inflicted.

AMENDMENT IX

The enumeration in the Constitution, of certain rights, shall not be construed to deny or disparage others retained by the people.

AMENDMENT X

The powers not delegated to the United States by the Constitution, nor prohibited by it to the States, are reserved to the States respectively, or to the people.

The amendments that constituted this Bill of Rights reveal that what the Anti-federalists continued to fear was the arbitrary exercise of kingly authority by the national government. Their fears proved well-founded, as we shall see in the next chapter. In fact, the Bill of Rights had not even been ratified when the Federalists violated the Fourth Amendment with their Alien and Sedition Acts. Historians agree that the promise by the Federalists to support the Bill of Rights was a necessary compromise to garner enough votes in key states to win ratification. Once the minimal mark of nine states was passed, the others fell into line. All, that is, except for Rhode Island, that tiny bastion of radical democracy, which had refused all along to deal with the hated Federalists. It was not until 1790, when Congress under the new Constitution threatened Rhode Island with a suspension of commercial intercourse, that the state yielded and ratified.

Just as people today tire of political disputes—important as they may be, such as those over the war in Indochina or the Watergate affair—so did the early Americans grow weary of political disputes. Perhaps partly for this reason—and certainly because the popular revolutionary General Washington lent his prestige and support to the new government—the

Constitutional government of 1789 was accepted surprisingly well. In most states, the Anti-federalists did not even try to win seats in Congress and the Federalists swept to victory. A government representing national ruling power had been established. But the Constitution did not completely describe an articulated or well-developed political society. In particular, the relations among the members of the society that would have to obtain in order for effective ruling power to exist were by no means completely enumerated. Moreover, the question of whether the apparently incompatible demands upon the form of political representation—the external demand for effective national ruling power versus the internal demand for freedom from such power—could be resolved in political union remained unanswered. To be sure, the Federalists had by dint of planning and effective organization won the first round; but if the Anti-federalists could organize resistance at the popular level and among disgruntled and deposed state leaders, they might yet prevail. They set out to do just that.

The scene was set for yet another dispute over authority. We shall see in the next two chapters how virulent the conflict that emerged from two quite different reality images became. We also shall see the emergence of a more fundamental dispute over claims to authority—that led eventually to the Civil War, and lent especial poignance to a remark attributed years later to Benjamin Franklin by James McHenry, a Maryland delegate to the Constitutional Convention: "A lady asked Dr. Franklin Well Doctor what have we got a republic or a monarchy—a republic replied the Doctor if you can keep it" [sic].[13]

Suggested Further Reading

Insightful application of our approach to political analysis of the American Republic will benefit considerably from a good sense of the history of the period. While none of the works cited here offers precisely the same interpretation as that presented in this book, each is interesting and helpful.

The following books by Hockett and McLaughlin reveal a politically conservative outlook, but the objectivity of their works is not damaged:

---

13. Max Farrand, ed., *The Records of the Federal Convention of 1787.* (Yale University Press, 1923), vol. III, p. 85.

Homer C. Hockett. *Political and Social Growth of the American People, 1492–1865.* Macmillan, 1941. Hockett's excellent work puts the period of interest in a longer time perspective than McLaughlin's.

Andrew C. McLaughlin. *The Confederation and the Constitution, 1783–1789.* Collier Books, 1962; original edition 1905.

A short book that accomplishes the subtle task of historical reconstruction—seeing the facts of history from the perspective of the time at which they occurred—with remarkable facility.

More specialized studies of considerable interest include three classics:

Charles A. Beard. *An Economic Interpretation of the Constitution.* Macmillan, 1913.

Carl L. Becker. *The Declaration of Independence—a Study in the History of Ideas.* Vintage, 1958; originally published in 1942.

Clinton Rossiter. *Seedtime of the Republic—the Origins of the American Tradition of Political Liberty.* Harcourt, Brace, 1953. Covers the period up to 1780.

For an interesting brief study, see:

David G. Smith. *The Convention and the Constitution: The Political Ideas of the Founding Fathers.* St. Martin's Press, 1965.

For a provocative and stimulating examination of political thought in America since the Revolution, and its relation to the Europe from which America was escaping, see:

Louis Hartz, *The Liberal Tradition in America.* Harcourt, Brace, 1955.

Finally, two excellent and stimulating analyses will be found in the same volume:

Roger H. Brown's "Politics and Ideology: The American World Mission" and Harry N. Scheiber's "America in the World Economy: A Retrospect." *America: Power and Purpose.* Edited by Gene M. Lyons. Quadrangle, 1965.

Chapter 3
The Democratization of the Republic

It is difficult to avoid the paradoxical conclusion that the great expansion of the republic during its first half-century both preserved it and changed it. As we have seen, even the formation of the first government was accomplished by avoiding and excluding the opponents of national ruling power. In fact, had it not been for a constant expansion of the republic, it is doubtful whether any national government could have survived a clash of those opposing camps. And yet, while expansion proved a means of incorporating dissident elements into the structure of ruling power, it also caused the undoing of the original basis of ruling power, and was instrumental in democratizing the republic. We shall trace these developments through their successive stages.

The Ruling Elite

With a few Anti-federalists represented, the new federal government organized itself along lines that already had been established in the governments of the states. The only novel organizational development was the emergence of the cabinet, which resulted from Washington's practice of seeking advice from the heads of the departments (who were called secretaries) of the administration he established. During Washington's administration (1789–1797), disputes between two members of the Cabinet, Alexander Hamilton and

Thomas Jefferson, afford a useful focus upon the politics—the disputes over authority—which attended the exercise of ruling power.

The Federalists at once set about to establish relations and negotiate treaties with the several foreign powers that were still intent on maintaining their colonial interests on the American continent. The skill of the United States' agents combined with the competitive difficulties of the European powers to produce important diplomatic successes for the new political society. But, of course, their permanence necessarily hinged on the ability of the United States to exercise effective ruling power at home.

No man in America (and probably few in the world) possessed so thorough an intellectual grasp of the principles of mercantilism (see Chapter 2, p. 29) as Alexander Hamilton, whose influence was strongly felt among the Federalists. Hamilton had made his feelings about democracy plain in a speech at the Constitutional Convention: "All communities divide themselves into the few and the many. The first are the rich and well born, the other the masses of the people . . . . The people are turbulent and changing; they seldom judge or determine right . . . . The British Government was the best in the world."[1] He concluded that government should exercise ruling power to foster the development of resources and industry, which in turn would permit heavy taxes to strengthen the government. Taxes would support a strong navy, which would further far-flung commerce and trading, which, in turn, would strengthen the nation with more tax monies.

Hamilton, as the first secretary of the treasury, proposed that the United States should assume the debts that the states had incurred under the Articles of Confederation. Many objected because speculators had bought much of this currency at below face value, and stood to make fortunes if it was redeemed at face value for new, sound bonds. But Hamilton prevailed with his unanswerable argument that the government must establish its credit with an act of good faith. Moreover, in Hamilton's view it was desirable for the central government to have men of wealth looking to it as a source of investment. To provide a sound currency, Hamilton proposed a bank of the United States, which would be pri-

---

1. Homer Cary Hockett, *Political and Social Growth of the American People, 1492-1865* (Macmillan, 1941, 3rd ed.), p. 320.

vately owned and managed (subject to conditions prescribed by Congress); only its notes (or specie) would be receivable in payments to the United States. "The establishment of a great central bank, pledged to the redemption of its notes on demand," he argued, "would . . . make it useless for unsound institutions to put out their paper."[2] Finally, to supplement and improve a hastily passed system of import duties, Hamilton advocated a policy of protective tariffs (high duties on those imports that would compete with domestic products) to promote crucial domestic manufactures. This proposal generated little enthusiasm, but an excise tax on liquors that he also proposed did pass Congress.

Each of these programs would constitute an exercise of ruling power. Each would benefit some people directly, and disadvantage others. In general, Hamilton's plans promised to benefit a "money class," a strong central government, and commercial and manufacturing interests. The same plans would not please the friends of states' rights, state banks, and the interior farmers who distilled whiskey to make their surplus grains portable (to the coast) and thus a source of income. Inevitably, then, as ruling power was actually exercised—and especially in consonance with Hamilton's program—the ranks of the opposition grew and a split developed in the Federalist coalition as disaffected members cast their lot with the Anti-federalists.

But by this time, "Anti-federalist" did not quite describe the opposition, since many of the opponents had been, and remained, "Federalists" of some sort. The Hamiltonian Federalists clung to their name and branded the opposition as "Democrats." For their part, the opposition took the name "Republicans." (To avoid confusion with later parties, we will call them "Democratic-Republicans," as many historians have.) The dividing line between the two groups was not the Constitution they had all helped to construct and ratify, but the proper way to *interpret* the Constitution. And, as we shall see, the judiciary and its power to interpret the Constitution soon became a major area of contention between the two groups.

James Madison was an important figure among the opponents of the Federalists, but the leadership of the opposition fell eventually to Thomas Jefferson. Jefferson had supported the Bill of Rights, and if his theory of government

---

2. Ibid., p. 316.

was not as detailed as Hamilton's, it was nevertheless buttressed by a strong faith in the common agrarian man and an aversion to the emerging alliance between the government and the capitalists. Jefferson strongly opposed the creation of a United States Bank, arguing that the "general welfare clause" of the Constitution (Article I, Section 8) did not empower the Congress to do "anything they please . . . but only to lay taxes . . . for the general welfare." Hamilton responded with his doctrine of "implied powers." "If the end be clearly comprehended within any of the specified powers, and if the measure have an obvious relation to that end, and is not forbidden by any particular provision of the Constitution, it may safely be deemed to come within the compass of the national authority."[3] Washington was convinced by Hamilton's reasoning (much to Jefferson's chagrin), as were most of the Federalists, and the bank was chartered for twenty years.

The same basic dispute over claims to authority—in this case, authority to interpret the Constitution, an important part of ruling power—also arose in the case of the excise tax on liquors. It appears that Hamilton wanted the tax not only to help raise needed revenues, but also to give the frontiersmen a taste of the ruling power they might otherwise be able to ignore because they were so remote from the seat of national government. Jefferson thought the law "infernal," infringing as it did upon the activities of the small farmers in whom he set so much store. Indeed, the farmers were mightily aroused by the law and saw in it precisely the kind of thing they had hoped to eliminate with the overthrow of the English king. Many of them gathered under arms to thwart the tax-collectors, and Washington, at Hamilton's urging, sent 15,000 men summoned from state militia to quell the disturbances. As it turned out, it was another great success for Hamilton. Armed opposition melted with the news of the approaching army. The leaders were convicted of treason, and then (the threat to national supremacy being over) Washington pardoned them. To Hamilton (and many Federalists), the important principle of national ruling power had been demonstrated; to Jefferson (and a growing opposition), the government was "fast galloping into monarchy."

Thus, political disputes were developing with the exercise of ruling power, but the disputes were contained within

---

3. Ibid., pp. 322–323.

a definite ruling elite. At the end of Washington's first term, Hamilton, Madison, and Jefferson joined to urge the reluctant president to take a second term. Washington agreed, and the members of Congress were able to effect their decision to back Washington with a second unanimous election. For all practical purposes, the election of the president did happen in Congress. In most states, the presidential electors were chosen by the legislatures; as political leaders in the respective states, the representatives to Congress had only to report their deliberations to their state legislatures as to the Congress' choice for president. It was not just Washington's general popularity that made this unanimity possible, as the contest for vice president shows. The Democratic-Republicans refused to support John Adams for the vice presidency, and, in a separate caucus, chose instead to back George Clinton. The results came back from the several states, exactly along caucus lines: Washington won a unanimous vote; Adams was given seventy-seven votes, and Clinton fifty. (See Article II, Section 1 of the Constitution for details of electoral procedure.)

The subtlety and importance of this authority dispute between Hamilton and Jefferson can hardly be overemphasized. From our vantage-point, it may appear academic; a dispute in terms of democratic and constitutional philosophy. But, in fact, the very existence of the political society, and its effective external representation, turned on the outcome of these disputes. In the first rounds, Hamilton emerged with greater authority as his policies were put into effect. Jefferson thought him a virtual dictator of his party, which he became, as time went on. Jefferson's policies also became crucial for external representation, as we shall see presently. First, however, we must examine the relation of Hamilton's policies, which were dominant in these early years, to external representation.

It is easy to see the importance for external representation of Hamilton's fiscal policies. This was the era of mercantilism, and a nation without good credit and the ability to attract and hold gold and silver within its borders was simply not to be taken seriously in the diplomacy of the day. Moreover, during the late eighteenth and early nineteenth centuries there were a series of "economic wars" between the great powers of Europe, in the course of which the belligerents would ban trade with one another in sometimes complicated strategies designed to weaken or discourage an opponent. One result was the development of a very lively "carrying trade" for the United States. By means of the "broken voyage," ships forbidden by, say, England to carry goods to European ports would dock in the United States. The goods then would be reexported to Europe from the neutral United States. American merchants and shippers grew rich, and the nation profited (due to artificially high import volumes) from its import duties. To take advantage of this situation, a sound currency and a flourishing commercial economy were required, and Hamilton's policies promoted both of these.

The quarreling among the European powers, however, did not make things easy for the United States. At sea, there was the problem of "impressment." The British, especially, constantly stopped American carriers to look for English sailors who had deserted their warships because life was unbelievably hard on British warships. Since Americans were English-speaking, it was natural for English deserters to seek cover on American ships. Conversely, it was natural for British warships to "find" deserters who were, in fact, bona fide citizens of the United States. To put a stop to this practice was a long and delicate diplomatic undertaking for the United States. It required that the status of American citizens be recognized by all parties, including the citizens themselves. Usually, American citizens were happy enough to acknowledge their status; but sometimes they were ready to join in on these European wars, especially on the side of the revolutionary French against the English. This could not be tolerated by a government enjoying the fruits of neutrality, so it was very important that its requirement of its citizens not to involve themselves be observed. The situation was even more delicate on the interior frontier, where the remaining English settlers and Indians combined to threaten the American settlers living there. It was not easy to keep American citizens from engaging in war against the British, who still held outposts there and encouraged the hostility of the Indians against the encroaching settlers from the United States. Thus Hamilton's idea that the force of national ruling power be brought home to the interior dwellers was doubtless important, for harsh necessity and European belligerents competed constantly for the loyalties of those settlers and tried to use them to achieve their own ends.

At the same time, the exercise of ruling power continued to swell the ranks of the opposition. By the end of Washington's second term, Jefferson had left the cabinet and openly assumed leadership of the Democratic-Republicans. Meeting in caucuses, the Federalists recommended John Adams for president and Thomas Pinckney for vice president. Hamilton was the most powerful Federalist, but by very reason of this power and its tendency to make enemies, he was not considered a good presidential candidate. The Democratic-Republicans, meeting in separate caucus, chose Jefferson and Aaron Burr. Adams won the election, and under the rules of that time, Jefferson became vice president (see Article II, Section 2 of the Constitution).

With the opposing factions increasingly at odds, and each represented in the executive branch, it became more difficult to exercise ruling power. This fact had external repercussions. The revolutionary French government had hoped for a Democratic-Republican victory because the Federalists were decidedly more pro-English than Jefferson's party. The French ministers insulted the American agents so badly that a state of limited war between the nations was provoked. It was settled by treaty eventually (France could not risk a British-American alliance in war), but the domestic effects were fateful. Because the split between the Federalists and the Democratic-Republicans in Congress mirrored the enduring hostilities between Britain and France, the measures taken by the Federalists to stifle antigovernmental policies (such as pro-French propaganda) during the limited war with France were also virtually measures to stifle the political opposition of the Democratic-Republicans. Four laws known as the "Alien and Sedition Acts" were passed by the Federalists in 1798. The first lengthened the naturalization period from five to fourteen years for people wishing to become American citizens; the second authorized the president to deport "undesirable aliens"; the third gave the president power to deport any subject of a country at war with the United States; and the last, and most infamous, provided for punishment of any person (foreign or not) who wrote, printed, or uttered any "false, scandalous and malicious statement against the government of the United States, or either house of the Congress . . . or the President . . . with intent to defame . . . or bring them . . . into contempt or disrepute." There were arrests and convictions under this last law, with Federalist-appointed federal judges upholding the law. For their part, the Democratic-Republicans sponsored denunciatory resolutions in state legislatures where their party dominated. Federalist state legislatures replied with resolutions upholding the law. The resolutions are significant because Virginia and Kentucky, in resolutions secretly authored by Jefferson and Madison, set forth the doctrine that a single state may *nullify* the force of a federal act within its borders, if it deems the act unconstitutional. Once again, the authority of the central government was challenged, and this fierce political dispute proved to be a harbinger of things to come. The doctrine of nullification was not to die easily.

The uproar surrounding the Alien and Sedition Acts cost the Federalists their power. As new, more democratically minded states were added (discussed in the following section) the Democratic-Republicans gained electoral strength, while the Federalists lost strength, partly because of particular policies they fostered, but also partly because as the ruling party they inevitably antagonized those who preferred their autonomy to the extension of central rule.

The electoral college system had failed to foresee and take account of the emerging party competition, and the election of 1800 was thrown into the House of Representatives. (This necessitated the passage of the Twelfth Amendment, below.) Jefferson won, as he would have anyway, had the system worked properly, and the reign of the Federalists was over.

During the twelve-year Federalist era, treaties had been negotiated with Spain, England, and France; the good credit of the United States had been established; and ruling power by the national government had been exercised directly upon the citizens. The result was the one the Federalists intended: effective external representation had been established in relations with the major European powers.

At the same time, however, unintended results also followed. The politics of ruling power had regularized an opposition within the ruling elite that had a different image of actual and ideal reality and came to claim the authority necessary to implement it. While Hamilton thought ruling power should center in the national government, and should be based on the judgments and interests of the rich and well-born, Jefferson thought ruling power could not infringe upon the sovereignty of the states, where power should be based on the judgments and interests of the modestly propertied small farmers. And thus politics were born in the new American ruling elite—politics that rapidly filtered down to those outside the elite, setting the terms for contests for office and authority that would shape the politics of the American republic throughout its lifetime.

Early Amendments to the Constitution

While the Bill of Rights consisted of amendments that represented a compromise with opponents of the Constitution of 1787, they were not corrections. During the Federalist years, however, certain confusions concerning the authority of the federal judicial branch led to the early passage of the Eleventh Amendment. And as we have seen, the Twelfth Amendment was also the rectification of error or oversight in the original Constitution that first became evident in the election of 1800, which ended the Federalists' rule.

AMENDMENT XI
Ratified 1795

The Judicial power of the United States shall not be construed to extend to any suit in law or equity, commenced or prosecuted against one of the United States by Citizens of another State, or by Citizens or Subjects of any Foreign State.

AMENDMENT XII
Ratified 1804

The Electors shall meet in their respective states and vote by ballot for President and Vice-President, one of whom, at least, shall not be an inhabitant of the same state with themselves; they shall name in their ballots the person voted for as President, and in distinct ballots the person voted for as Vice-President, and they shall make distinct lists of all persons voted for as President, and of all persons voted for as Vice-President, and of the number of votes for each, which lists they shall sign and certify, and transmit sealed to the seat of the government of the United States, directed to the President of the Senate;—The President of the Senate shall, in the presence of the Senate and House of Representatives, open all the certificates and the votes shall then be counted;—The person having the greatest number of votes for President, shall be the President, if such number be a majority of the whole number of Electors appointed; and if no person have such majority, then from the persons having the highest numbers not exceeding three on the list of those voted for as President, the House of Representatives shall choose immediately, by ballot, the President. But in choosing the President, the votes shall be taken by states, the representation from each state having one vote; a quorum for this purpose shall consist of a member or members from two-thirds of the states, and a majority of all the states shall be necessary to a choice. And if the House of Representatives shall not choose a President whenever the right of choice shall devolve upon them, before the fourth day of March next following, then the Vice-President shall act as President, as in the case of the death or other constitutional disability of the President.—The person having the greatest number of votes as Vice-President, shall be the Vice-President, if such number be a majority of the whole number of Electors appointed, and if no person have a majority, then from the two highest numbers on the list, the Senate shall choose the Vice-President; a quorum for the purpose shall consist of two-thirds of the whole number of Senators, and a majority of the whole number shall be necessary to a choice. But no person constitutionally ineligible to the office of President shall be eligible to that of Vice-President of the United States.

Jeffersonian Democracy

It is important to understand the major source of the growing strength of the Democratic-Republicans, as well as the contribution of Jeffersonian principles to external representation. As we have seen in Chapter 2, policies were established during the period under the Articles of Confederation that set the pattern for expansion. Had these policies not been in existence, trouble would have ensued because the Federalists were so jealous of their power that they omitted any provision for adding new states in the Constitution of 1787.

Early in the 1780s, when the ex-colonies were struggling to find a way to join in a common government, Maryland served notice that it would never agree to the Articles until the several states that claimed vast territories stretching away from their own western borders should fix their western boundaries, reserving the western territories for future states. Finally, all of the states ceded their territorial claims to Congress, creating the problem of what to do with these vast territories. Thomas Jefferson had been the author of an early plan for expansion, the Ordinance of 1784, and several Jeffersonian features reappeared in the Ordinance of 1787. This ordinance provided that the Northwest Territory be governed by congressional appointees, but that as soon as there were 5,000 free inhabitants of age in the territory, mechanisms of self-government might be established. Then state governments (not less than three nor more than five) might be organized (with governments like those of the original thirteen). When a state achieved a population of 60,000, it would be admitted into the Union on terms of equality with the other states. Following Jefferson's earlier lead, slavery was forbidden in the Northwest Territory after 1800. An orderly system of townships was included, with the provision for lots to be set aside for schools and religious institutions.

There were two main reasons that the admirable and orderly provisions for the Northwest Territory were not followed so well in the southwestern territories. First, settlers already had been moving there, and their claims antedated orderly arrangements. Second, the antislavery provision favored by Jefferson and most Northerners was unacceptable to the Southern states near the lower territories. However, settlers in those regions (especially the growing settlements in Tennessee and Kentucky) took for granted that the heart of the Northwest Territory ordinances applied to them as well—that organization into republican state governments would eventuate in admission to the Union with the full rights of the original states.[4] Indeed, all during the Confederation period three territories—Vermont, Kentucky, and Tennessee—agitated for statehood, but Congress was so weak with respect to the existing states that only unanimous consent (a virtually impossible condition) could have brought them in.

Once the Constitution of 1787 was established, the ruling Federalists generally were hostile toward admission of the new states. Universal manhood suffrage was characteristic of those states, and the Federalists tended to distrust the judgment of the masses. In addition, the economic interests of the settlers were not quite like those of the neomercantilistic Federalists, which provided the latter with another reason for doubting the wisdom of welcoming the western states into the Union. However, there was need to

4. See Andrew C. McLaughlin, *The Confederation and the Constitution, 1783-1789* (Collier Books, 1965), chap. 7. Also see Benjamin H. Hibbard, *History of the Public Land Policies* (Macmillan, 1924).

stabilize these outlying regions, and if statehood was put off it might result in the petitioning states' turning to a foreign power. Thus Vermont (1791), Kentucky (1792), and Tennessee (1796) were admitted. Had the predilections of some Federalists held sway, and the territories been kept in sub-sovereign status, the United States would have been saddled with the same problem that eventually ruined England's American empire—how to govern from afar independent-spirited people with ambitions for full political representation. As it was, however, the dangerous frontier lands were stabilized by strong state governments, which had been made loyal to the national government by the effective expedient of including them as full partners in the federal arrangement. Nonetheless, the old-line Federalists eventually lost national ruling power as the new states joined the Union because these democratically minded states fell into line with the Jeffersonian party.

When Jefferson assumed office, he promised a significantly different kind of government: "A wise and frugal government, which shall restrain men from injuring one another, shall leave them otherwise free to regulate their own pursuits of industry and improvement, and shall not take from the mouth of labor the bread it has earned. This is the sum of good government." These principles were implemented by reliance for national defense on the militia (citizen soldiers of the states) rather than a national army and navy, abandonment of the excise tax, the encouragement of agriculture (with industry as "its handmaiden") and the avoidance of public debt (through frugal government). In the next section we shall examine the extent to which Jefferson, and the Democratic-Republicans who succeeded him, were able to curtail the exercise of ruling power. First, however, to understand the character of politics in the era, we must consider the immense expansion that occurred during this period.

The victory of the Democratic-Republicans in 1800, which might have signalled the beginning of a divisive struggle between the then-dominant factions, actually resulted less than twenty years later in the "Era of Good Feelings"—an apparent (but false) end of factional disputes and a seemingly complete vindication of Jeffersonian concepts.

No event was more responsible for this curious trend than the Louisiana Purchase of 1803. Spain had acquired the huge Louisiana Territory in the French and Indian War, and the Americans, especially Jefferson, were content for Spain to hold this possession because Spain was by 1800 a relatively weak European power that was unable to establish strong colonial government in North America. This was an important fact, because possession of Louisiana included control of the mouth of the Mississippi River, the only practical route of transportation for commercial purposes out of the entire, vast interior valley. Were a strong power like England to acquire Louisiana, the United States would be trapped: inferior to the major powers at sea, and cut off on its interior side. When France under Napoleon virtually stole the territory from a helpless Spain, by means of a broken treaty, Jefferson (despite his pro-French feelings) was alarmed: "There is on the globe," he wrote for the benefit of Napoleon, "one single spot the possessor of which is our natural and habitual enemy. It is New Orleans, through which the produce of three-eighths of our territory must pass to market. . . . [Spain's] possession of the place would hardly be felt by us . . . . Not so can it ever be in the hands of France . . . ."[5] Accordingly, and in consideration of the frenzied anxiety of the West over these developments, Jefferson instructed his minister to Paris, Robert Livingston, to negotiate for the purchase of a tract of land at the mouth of the river. (Monroe was later sent as well). In the meantime, however, Napoleon was losing interest in Louisiana. The great value of Louisiana for Napoleon's prospective colonial empire lay mainly in the fact that it could be exploited to provide sustenance for the French-held island of Santo Domingo, which was not self-supporting but was a rich source of sugar. However, the black slaves of the island had risen in revolt during the French Revolution, under the leadership of Toussaint L'Ouverture. Napoleon sent an army to Santo Domingo and L'Ouverture was captured; but the attempt to reinstitute slavery produced yet another rebellion. The unexpectedly tough resistance of the island's blacks, combined with the ravages of yellow fever, decimated Napoleon's army. Without firm control of Santo Domingo, the Louisiana Territory held little glamour for Napoleon. And so it was, that despite his promise to Spain never to dispose of the territory to any country other than Spain, Napoleon decided to sell it to the United States.

On April 11, 1803, Talleyrand, discussing with Livingston the sale of the Isle of Orleans, suddenly asked, 'What

---

5. Hockett, *Political and Social Growth of the American People,* p. 380.

would you give for the whole of Louisiana?' Livingston, surprised beyond measure and somewhat deaf, could hardly trust his ears. Once convinced that the First Consul was in earnest the only question to be decided was the price. Although Livingston conducted the negotiations, he would not conclude them until Monroe arrived, and both signed the Treaty . . . which for 80,000,000 francs more than doubled the area of the United States. Livingston may be pardoned for exclaiming, 'This is the noblest work of our lives!'[6]

"Noble" though it may have been, this work of diplomacy, as we shall soon see, raised interesting, indeed critical questions, about the exercise of ruling power. The purchase was a decided turn of fortune for the Democratic-Republicans because one provision of the treaty was that Louisiana should be "incorporated into the Union," with the inhabitants to be admitted to the privileges of citizenship. There was hardly any question that the expanding West would be in the Democratic-Republican fold, and the practice of manhood suffrage in the West only increased the likelihood that the champion of agriculture, Jefferson, would reap the political benefits.

Meanwhile, pending the establishment of state governments in the West, the Ohio Territory was ready to join the fold. By 1821, ten new states had been added to the original thirteen, and full (white, manhood) suffrage was common in them. Two states were northern, eight "Western," and in all of them the relatively egalitarian practices drew settlers from the conservative East, where the more well-to-do still dominated political representation. That old Federalist tactic of winning a major dispute over authority by excluding much of its opposition from full participation in the contest was now proving counterproductive. The Anti-federalists were eagerly taking advantage of the unanticipated new opportunities for the farmers and settlers opened up by the Louisiana Purchase.

In a pattern that was to be repeated, the issues that had been won by the conservatives in one context reemerged in a new and larger context created by the expanding frontier. And the frontiersmen won their final victory over the Federalists as their egalitarian practices eventually were emulated even in the East. In 1810, Maryland and South Carolina changed their constitutions to enfranchise all adult, white

6. Ibid., p. 383.

males; Connecticut did likewise in 1818, Massachusetts in 1821, New York in 1826; and other states made changes as well. The main reason for these changes, which enfranchised the previously voteless laboring class, was that migration to the new states was having economic as well as political repercussions in the East. Where labor was scarce and needed, men could work long enough to gain a small stake, and then head for the West. There land could be had for one or two dollars per acre and full political participation was expected. Thus few were tempted to stay the rest of their lives in the dismal sweatshops as second-class citizens.

Thus the fortunes of the Democratic-Republicans improved with the growth of the idea that the common man could and should participate in the selection of his political representatives. In 1804—the first election in which the majority of states (including Kentucky, Ohio, and Tennessee) had selected their electors by popular vote—Jefferson won by a landslide. The Democratic-Republican juggernaut continued as Madison won successive terms in 1808 and 1812; then in 1816 James Monroe won in a contest virtually devoid of opposition, and in 1820, during the "Era of Good Feelings," he became the second president (Washington had been the first) to win every electoral vote cast.

Despite superficial appearances, however, politics had not disappeared. If the ominous disputes over ruling authority did not manifest themselves in the electoral outcomes of the period, it was because the means of political expression for the common man had been only partially articulated thus far. For the period under discussion saw the growth of sectional politics, where the inhabitants of different sections of the vast and expanding political society interpreted reality in very different ways. For a time, the deep disagreements between North and South were overshadowed by the continuous growth of the West, which rendered the older political divisions politically irrelevant. Moreover, although the tension between the external demand on the representative for effective ruling power and the internal demand on the representative for freedom from ruling power (now usually expressed as "states' rights") was ameliorated by means of expansion, the issue was by no means solved. A fortuitous sequence of circumstances allowed the Democratic-Republicans to uphold the principles of limited government while exercising considerable ruling power; and the same circumstances helped produce an independent judiciary.

The Sons of the Ruling Elite

What the Democratic-Republicans tried to undo with one hand, they nevertheless then did with the other. Among the many, necessarily precedent-establishing works of the Federalists had been the establishment of the federal judicial system, as authorized by the Constitution of 1787. The federal judiciary was the most visible and effective instrument of national ruling power, and the means by which the hated Alien and Sedition Acts were applied. Moreover, in the opinion of the Democratic-Republicans, the Federalists had swelled the judicial system beyond necessity (reflecting the Federalist belief in the vigorous exercise of national ruling power) by the addition of a set of circuit judges to the existing federal system in 1801. On Jefferson's recommendation, that act was repealed to shrink the judiciary. But what really irked Jefferson was the series of events culminating in the now-famous case of *Marbury* v. *Madison* (1803).

In February 1801, during the very last days of the Federalist majority under President John Adams, forty-two justices of the peace were authorized for the District of Columbia. Adams filled those positions with Federalists at the last moment (midnight, it was said, on his last day in office), and when Jefferson assumed office he instructed his secretary of state, Madison, not to deliver the signed commissions. The Federalists' Judiciary Act of 1789 provided for an original hearing in such a case by the Supreme Court, and Marbury, one of the "midnight judges," sought an order from the Supreme Court directing Madison to deliver the commission. In a memorable, precedent-setting, and extremely shrewd decision, Chief Justice John Marshall ruled that, while Marbury was indeed entitled to the commission, the Court could not rule for him because the law that gave the Court original jurisdiction (a Federalist law) was unconstitutional as the Constitution plainly specified the classes of cases where the Supreme Court had original jurisdiction, and this was not one of them. (For the specific wording see Article III, Section 2, paragraph 2 on page 41.)

The decision let Jefferson's action stand, then, but it also established the precedent of judicial review of the constitutionality of acts of Congress, which infuriated the Democratic-Republicans. Indeed, the latter were moving at Jefferson's suggestion with impeachment proceedings against a Federalist judge, who (despite an apparently unsound mind) was found guilty by the Senate. Then the House impeached a second Federalist judge, Samuel Chase, who had assailed what he called the "mobocracy" of the Democratic-Republicans from the bench. Chase escaped conviction in the Senate by a narrow margin when some of Jefferson's party had second thoughts about the wisdom of such a vindictive policy. After all, it had been just such excessive zeal that had cost the Federalists their power when they were in a position to exercise it—and the impeachment of Chase was part of a move to impeach almost all of the Federalist judges. At the top of the hierarchy was Marshall, who may have been saved when the impeachment movement lost impetus during the Chase affair. As Robert McCloskey points out, "Marshall's alarm can hardly be exaggerated. Apparently despairing of the chances for full independence, he privately suggested that Congress might be given appellate jurisdiction over Supreme Court decisions, as àn alternative to impeachment . . . the suggestion is a measure of his fear for his precious tribunal . . . ."[7]

However, the same administration that was finding it necessary to find in the Constitution certain "implied powers" in order to acquire Louisiana, would not at the same time wish to impeach John Marshall for holding similar views. In fact, some Democratic-Republicans may already have had an inkling of what was to come, namely, that the party of Jefferson would rely upon the Federalist judges to uphold the national authority of the DemocraticRepublicans. (See next section).

Jefferson, who had contested so bitterly Hamilton's readiness to interpret constitutional powers that were not explicitly stated could hardly find a constitutional warrant for the Louisiana Purchase and its promise of citizenship for the inhabitants of the territory. Accordingly, Jefferson drafted a constitutional amendment, which he proposed to submit to Congress and then to the states. But the Democratic-Republicans were unwilling to risk the uncertain outcome of the amendment when treaty ratification by the Senate was certain, given the benefits to the country and their party that would flow from ratification. Thus they adopted Hamilton's doctrine of implied powers, holding that the powers of declaring war and treaty-making implied the power to acquire territory.

---

7. Robert G. McCloskey, *The American Supreme Court.* (University of Chicago Press, 1960), p. 46.

At any rate, the Louisiana Purchase was a clear exercise of ruling power made more or less exclusively by the "second generation" of ruling elites. Of course, the western states did not complain, and neither did the South, which was already looking for fresh, fertile soil for cotton. But in the Northeast, the Federalists were thoroughly alarmed. Indeed, a definite sentiment for secession developed there, and Aaron Burr, the vice president, was approached as a possible leader. The plans were scotched when Hamilton's advice was sought: "Dismemberment of our empire will be a clear sacrifice of great positive advantages, without any counterbalancing good."[8] (When Burr learned that Hamilton had advised the Federalists to avoid him, he challenged Hamilton to a duel, which cost the latter his life.)

The War of 1812 was another instance of the exercise of national ruling power by the Democratic-Republicans, in which the fruits of actual and anticipated expansion ameliorated the tensions that otherwise might have surfaced. The expansion of the United States had precipitated considerable hostility among the Indians, especially in the Northwest. Curiously, the Americans blamed the British for the Indians' hostility; and, although it was not an official cause for war (impressment was), it is clear that the feeling among the Democratic-Republicans that the British were aiding and abetting the hostile Indians was an important cause (and excuse) for war. And there was also the greed for land. Some Democratic-Republicans were naively confident that they could occupy Canada, and that once this was accomplished the Federalists of New England might accede more willingly to the acquisition of Florida in the South.

As the War of 1812 ran its course, it became clear that each side miscalculated: the United States was unable to seize Canada, and almost lost a considerable portion of the Northwest as the British carried the war into Ohio, Baltimore, and Washington. On the other hand, the vaunted British Navy had great difficulty with America's small but well-made vessels. Nevertheless, the war went badly for the United States, partly because of inept management by a party with little taste for the vigorous exercise of ruling power. The Democratic-Republicans had refused to build up the navy, they had lowered taxes, and they had relied on militia (which the Northeastern states would not supply). The Unit-

---

8. Hockett, *Political and Social Growth of the American People*, p. 386.

ed States almost lost the war. Only Admiral Perry and a surprisingly good navy (and armed merchant ships employing quasi-guerrilla tactics), plus the campaign successes of Andrew Jackson and his makeshift army of backwoods marksmen marching toward New Orleans in the Southwest saved the United States. The War of 1812 ended in a virtual draw. Neither side was able to take and hold the territory of the other; and the alleged issues—the rights of neutrality at sea and in commerce for the United States—were never settled.

After the war ended in 1814, the Democratic-Republicans never returned to their prewar ways. They maintained the navy at full strength, kept up a small national army, retained a direct tax and, most humiliating of all, had to resort to the establishment of a second national bank (the charter of the first having expired in 1811) because the issuance of unregulated currency by the states had resulted in chaos by 1815.

To add insult to injured pride, it was the Supreme Court —still headed by the redoubtable Federalist John Marshall— that saved the Democratic-Republican Bank of the United States. In several southern and western states, laws were passed taxing the branches of the new United States Bank, with the intent to destroy its functioning in those states. Marshall's court ruled in the case of *McCulloch* v. *Maryland* (1819) that a state may not tax an agency of the federal government (the power to tax being the power to destroy). Supporting the constitutionality of the bank, Marshall quoted Hamilton's original, "implied powers" justification almost word for word: "Let the end be legitimate, let it be within the scope of the Constitution, and all means which are appropriate, which are plainly adapted to that end, which are not prohibited, but consist with the letter and spirit of the constitution, are constitutional."

The war had also taught the Democratic-Republicans to encourage domestic industry because reduced shipping had resulted in privation at home. In 1816, protective tariffs were established, putting the party of Jefferson in the neomercantilist camp.

Thus did expansion ameliorate the tensions caused by the exercise of ruling power. Each new state that joined the Union was, in comparison to the original thirteen, a "people's state," a victory for the principle of self-determination and full (white) manhood suffrage. The "democratic" Republicans gained strength despite their exercise of ruling power because expansion added constantly to their ranks, while the Federalist strongholds underwent a process of democratization that diminished their strength. However, it strikes us as curious that the works of the Democratic-Republicans turned out, in the somewhat longer run, to be quite similar to those of their predecessors, the Federalists. Why did not these great infusions of democracy wreak either havoc or fundamental changes in governmental ruling power? The answer seems to be that the democratization of the states was manifested only indirectly in the chambers of ruling power, the Congress. As Hamilton had predicted when he advised his fellow Federalists to give up their stranglehold on the House election of 1800 (allowing Jefferson to win), the opposing faction would have too much sense to wreck the sound works of the Federalists.

Although much of the ruling power of the first quarter of the nineteenth century was exercised in the *name* of the people, it was still done by a ruling elite, original participants (and their protégés) in the coup d'état of 1787. All through the reign of the Democratic-Republicans, nominations for president were accomplished by means of the congressional caucus, where party leadership would determine the best candidate to be recommended to the states. And since the state governments constituted the only organization of the electorate, it is not surprising that opposition candidates simply did not, and could not, arise.

However, this period of expanding suffrage saw the quickening of political consciousness among the plain people, and it would not be long before their influence would be felt more directly. Indeed, the origins of a number of democratic and egalitarian popular movements can be traced to the end of the first quarter of the nineteenth century. In 1827 the lectures of a visiting Scotswoman, Frances Wright, touched off controversies and organizations that bloomed as the American women's rights movement; the spread of democracy stimulated the spread of agitation for free public schools, a movement that became a force to be reckoned with around 1830; the first organized movement against the use of intoxicants began in 1826; in 1828 the American Peace Society was organized; and the early 1830s saw the rise of organized antislavery movements.[9]

9. Ibid., chapters 26 and 27, for more on these movements and for bibliographical references.

These and other similar movements are evidence that politics as we understand it—disputes over claims to the authority to determine or interpret the nature of reality—pervaded much of the population by the 1830s; there was lacking only the *means* by which these disputes could manifest themselves in the chambers of national ruling power. But at about the same time the means were discovered and profoundly affected the nature of ruling power in America.

The beginning of the end of the old system of nomination by congressional caucus occurred in 1820, in the middle of the "Era of Good Feeling." James Monroe became the de facto nominee for president when the congressional caucus, which was very sparsely attended since there was no opposition caucus at all, failed to make nominations. Then in 1824 several state legislatures submitted their own nominees for the presidency: Tennessee nominated its popular war hero, Andrew Jackson; Kentucky put forward the great Henry Clay; Massachusetts named John Quincy Adams; and a congressional caucus attended by only 66 of the 216 eligible members named William Crawford (who, having suffered a paralytic stroke five months earlier, was practically eliminated from serious consideration). In other words, the caucus system was being abandoned because it produced a false consensus: the real differences among the sections of the country were worked out and compromised in caucuses, and the electorate was presented with a fait accompli—"their" nominee.

Once the sectional differences emerged through nominations by state legislatures, the false consensus broke down quickly. No candidate received a majority of electoral votes (Jackson got the most, then Adams, then Crawford, then Clay), and Clay, being eliminated from the House election (by the Twelfth Amendment), was "kingmaker." Since Clay regarded Jackson as a mere "military chieftan," he supported Adams, who won. But when Adams subsequently appointed Clay as secretary of state, the charge of "bargain and corruption" was raised, and in 1828 Andrew Jackson swept to a victory many felt he had been cheated out of four years earlier. In 1828, all presidential nominations had been made by state legislatures; a development, which coupled with Jackson's adaptation of the "spoils system" to national party organization, spelled the end of the congressional caucus system of nomination and the beginning of national, popularly based political parties.

Jacksonian Democracy

The election of Andrew Jackson, and the events of the succeeding three decades, were truly momentous for American political representation. So chaotic was the period that it is difficult to describe it while at the same time showing the steady, even logical, articulation of political society that took place. We must briefly chronicle the fortunes of the new Democratic (Jacksonian) Party and those of their erstwhile rivals, the Whigs, and show how the next wave of territorial expansion of the United States fanned fierce intersectional controversies in the nation. Then, in the next section, we shall return to the crucial organizational developments of the period, for this is the key to understanding the form of political representation that came to characterize the fully articulated American republic.

Considering the divisive sectional struggles of the day, and the three "panics" (general bank failures associated with unstable currencies and overextended speculation) that occurred before the Civil War, the Democratic Party fared remarkably well at the polls. First came Jackson (1829–1837) and then Martin Van Buren (1837–1841). The Whigs (about whom more presently) then came to power for four years with William Harrison (1841) who died after thirty-one days in office and his successor, John Tyler (1841–1845). Next came the Democrat, James Polk (1845–1849) and then another four years of Whig rule as President Zachary Taylor (1849–1850) died in office and was succeded by Millard Fillmore (1850–1853). Then Democrat Franklin Pierce served four years (1853–1857), as did James Buchanan (1857–1861).

Considerable expansion occurred during this period, but the usual effect of ameliorating tensions associated with ruling power was tempered by the intrusion of the slavery issue into the question of expansion. This transformed the process that formerly had buffered political disputes into a source of political controversy.

The issue of slavery actually had emerged in 1818, during debates over the admission of Missouri to statehood. A representative from New York proposed an amendment prohibiting slavery in the state, and a fierce debate ensued. Indeed, mass meetings occured throughout the North, protesting any admission of another slave state. After two years of debate and struggle, the "Missouri Compromise" of 1820 admitted Missouri on an unrestricted basis, but fixed a line above which slavery "shall be and is hereby forever prohibited." These debates were the "firebell in the night" that startled the aging Jefferson, causing him greater concern for the Union than he had felt ever before.

The debates quieted down for a time after that, mainly because the Democrats and the Whigs tried every means to avoid the explosive issue. But when the question of annexing Texas (which had won independence from Mexico) came up, the slavery controversy reemerged. Andrew Jackson avoided the issue, contenting himself with displacing Indians from the Southwest. In 1845 Texas was annexed during a "lame-duck" session under the Whigs. But the nation's real expansion occurred under President James Polk. First he settled a treaty with England concerning the huge Oregon country, thus fixing the present northern boundaries of the United States. Then in the years 1846 to 1848, during what was in fact a war of expansion with Mexico, the United States won all of Mexico's northwest provinces—in present-day terms, everything north of the United States southern boundaries as they are now drawn.

The acquisition of territory was always popular with the land-hungry Americans, but the slavery issue quickly transformed such acquisitions into political liabilities. Indeed, controversies over the delicate matter cost the Democrats victory in 1849, but the Whigs fared no better in office, because the discovery of gold in California virtually necessitated the admission of that state, and a furious battle ensued. The Compromise of 1850 admitted California as a free state, and this upset the old balance in the Senate between free and slave states. In return, a drastic fugitive slave act was passed.

The sectional compromise was an uneasy one, and ten years later the nation was at the brink of civil war. But as the historian Hockett put it, "Had the South seceded in 1850, it may well be doubted whether the northern people were as yet sufficiently united in opinion to wage a war to preserve the Union."[10]

The answer to why the North could not in 1850 have waged a war for union—as well as the answer to why the tactic of expansion this second time produced more controversy than calm—is to be found in the organizational developments that began with Jackson's election.

10. Ibid., p. 659.

The Ruling Organization

The election of Andrew Jackson was a landmark in democratic representation; not until the election of Abraham Lincoln would a purer form of democratic representation occur. Jackson was himself a "common man," and enormously popular with the people. His background and attitudes were in sharp contrast with those of his relatively aristocratic predecessors in the presidency, and his conduct and especially that of his followers were horrifying to the old guard politicians.

This contrast did not stop at superficialities. On the question of internal improvements, such as roads and canals, where even the Democratic-Republicans had supported limited federal activities to open the vast continent, Jackson was adamant: the federal government should stay out of the field of public improvements. When he encountered a Supreme Court ruling he did not like (Chief Justice Marshall had ruled that the Cherokee Indians in Georgia were a nation, upon which Georgia could not infringe), Jackson said, "John Marshall has made his decision; now let him enforce it!" He vetoed congressional action to recharter a third United States Bank, and ruined the existing one. And he nationalized the "spoils system."

The spoils system had been used in some states, especially New York and Pennsylvania, to build "political machines." The idea was simple and effective: the winner of elective office, especially executive office, can under law appoint persons to various nonelective, official positions—not only positions such as department heads, but, technically, all of the aides and office-help as well. The postal service, military positions, and so on offer a number of choice opportunities for the spoils system. Using it, the successful politician rewards those who have worked for his election by giving them public jobs (and pay); in turn, a portion of their pay is "kicked back" into the treasury of the party organization. Over time, a well-disciplined party can be forged because the same people who authorize the expenditures of public money can finance their own campaigns for reelection and, as their success grows, their opposition (deprived of this source of money) weakens. In other words, the strong get stronger, and the weak grow weaker.

Martin Van Buren, who was experienced in machine politics in New York, brought Jackson considerable expertise in the system, and together they forged the first national, popularly based party. To gain a national basis, the practice of nomination by means of national convention was inaugurated. Party members from every state would meet together to elect their nominee, and the Democrats adopted a rule requiring a three-fourths majority to select their candidate, making for consensus and much bargaining (especially for patronage) among party professionals.

The Whig Party, or coalition, was formed during Jackson's term in opposition to the imperious ways of "King Andrew." The Whigs, who were not agreed upon much besides their opposition to Jackson, illustrate more than anything the potency of the Democratic Party's organization. At first, the Whigs tried to divide the electoral vote by supporting nominations in several states, hoping to throw the election of 1836 into the House of Representatives. They fared miserably against the national organization behind Van Buren. In 1840 they were forced to assume the style of the Democrats, and held a national convention. Their candidate (Harrison) was successful, largely as a result of the Panic of 1837. Moreover, the Whigs found themselves appealing to the "log cabin" image in the population, further evidence of the power of the Democratic Party's style. But, because they never represented a genuinely popular base, the Whigs could only exploit the occasional failures of the Democrats, and eventually passed from the scene.

The Democrats, on the other hand, were better at wresting ruling power from the ruling elite than they were at exercising it. To be sure, Jackson was a fearless political representative. When South Carolina tried to "nullify" a hated tariff law within its borders, Jackson pushed through the Force Bill, which authorized him to employ armed forces against the state. South Carolina then backed down. But, in general, Jackson was fearlessly (and in the name of the people) dismantling the power of the national government, rather than building it. And, when the durability and power of his Democratic Party succeeded in returning Democrat after Democrat to the presidency, it turned out that they had to avoid the increasingly dangerous problem of sectional controversy over slavery in order to preserve their party unity. This was possible until the emergence of the Republican Party because the Whigs usually neglected to frame a "platform"—a statement of policy intentions—since they lacked a positive consensus. Consequently the Democrats, who always had stated a platform, were spared the necessity of taking a stand on "everything."

It eventually became obvious to everyone that the form of *organization* devised by the Democrats would inherit ruling power. As we have seen, even the Whigs finally had to resort to the Democrats' organizational techniques, but they could do so only half-heartedly, since the original basis for their party was their opposition to Jackson and his kind of organization.

In the minds of most Whigs, a national organization of the Jacksonian sort rendered the presidency too powerful in relation to the Congress, and there is no doubt that such an effect accompanied the democratization of the office. The potential strength of the presidency always had resided in the fact that the president is nationally elected, while congressmen are not. But until Jackson, the organization initiative had rested in Congress, which functioned rather like a nominating committee, with the states and the people having to wait to find out whom the congressional caucuses would name. When the initiative fell to the states' legislatures, enterprising politicians gathered around Jackson's popularity to forge the granddaddy of national political organizations, the Democratic Party.

Once the Jacksonians had appeared on the scene, political parties of that type sprang up every election year, often around rather quixotic themes. One of the first was the Anti-Masonic Party. In 1826, a man who had published a pamphlet revealing Mason secrets was abducted and, presumably, murdered. With amazing rapidity a surge of feeling against secret societies spread across the country (churches even expelled Masons from membership), and Anti-Masonic parties sprang up in several states. So vigorous was the movement that some anti-Jacksonians tried to nationalize the Anti-Masons in 1832, in order to field a contender against Jackson.

The Anti-Masons and subsequent parties (the Know-Nothings, for instance) showed surprising strength, but they could not be turned into true competitors of the Democrats. The Democrats were the "party of the people" and, owing to their success, they enjoyed not only their original legitimacy as a people's party, but the huge advantage of relatively well-disciplined and well-financed national organization. After the "sectional truce" of 1850, the Democrats won in a huge landslide with Franklin Pierce in 1852. Barring some major disaster such as an economic panic, the Democrats always won. But this time, the issue of national ruling power could no longer be avoided through the technique of territorial expansion, which previously had been used to postpone the final settlement to some future time. For now, the continent was filled, and while the Democrats openly coveted Cuba and parts of Mexico, the vast, virgin reaches of the continent were no longer available. Thus, in 1854, when the time came to organize the territory of Nebraska, Americans found themselves squabbling over scarce resources, and the slavery issue thrust itself forward again.

Now the full ambiguity of the Democratic Party's organization with respect to the issue of ruling power revealed itself. Spawned in the name of popular sovereignty, the Democrats returned to this theory in the face of the slavery issue. In its final form, the Kansas-Nebraska Act of 1854— written by, and maneuvered through Congress by Senator Stephen Douglas with the backing of President Pierce and his patronage machine—provided for two territories, with the question of slavery left to the territorial legislatures. As for national authority in the matter, questions involving title to slaves should be appealed to the Supreme Court.

The latter point is the key to the ambiguity. Remember that Jackson, the first Democratic president, had scorned the authority of the Supreme Court when it ruled against his intention to displace the Cherokees; and Jackson's attitude was consistent with the local-sovereignty tendencies of his party, inasmuch as the Supreme Court was one of the enduring legacies of national ruling power under the Federalists. Now, however, the Democrats were trying to foist the unavoidable issue of national ruling power onto the Supreme Court: "We're for local sovereignty," they seemed to be saying, "but where that presents problems, let the Court decide."

It was now just a matter of time before the issue would be fully joined. In 1856 the Republican Party, which had been founded just two years earlier, made a strong showing against the Democratic candidate, Buchanan. But in that year, the issue swirled about the question of slavery; next time, it would be focused quite clearly on the question of national ruling power.

Just after Buchanan's inauguration (at which time Buchanan again appealed to the Supreme Court), the Supreme Court ruled in *Dred Scott* v. *Sanford* (1857) that Congress could not deprive persons of their property, including slaves.

The Missouri Compromise was declared unconstitutional. The decision was widely discussed, acclaimed in the South and denounced in the North. By means of it, Abraham Lincoln was to shed cold light on the Democratic Party's dilemma. In 1858 the Republicans, who were building a national organization like that of the Democrats, ran Abraham Lincoln against Stephen Douglas in the United States Senate race in Illinois. The rivals appeared in a series of debates, during which Lincoln quoted Douglas' position on popular sovereignty. Douglas had said, "If Kansas wants a slave-state constitution, she has a right to it; if she wants a free-state constitution, she has a right to it . . . . I care not whether it is voted down or up." But then Lincoln juxtaposed the Dred Scott decision, which had made the abolition of slavery in the territories unconstitutional, and asked Douglas to reconcile the two positions. Douglas replied with the "Freeport Doctrine" (so-called because the debate was held in Freeport, Illinois): if a territory failed to adopt a "slave code," then no master would go there, where the right of slavery was not fully upheld. Therefore, although in theory slavery was legal in all the territories, it would be in practice excluded where popular opinion was against it. This answer pleased the people in Illinois, but it became known as the "Freeport Heresy" in the South. As a result, in 1860, Douglas was unable to command the three-fourths majority required for nomination by the Democratic Party because eight southern delegations withdrew rather than accept him as their candidate. The convention adjourned and Douglas later was nominated at a special meeting, under special rules. Meanwhile, the Republicans selected Abraham Lincoln, whose relative obscurity was an advantage for a party with a fine prospect of victory because of the deep troubles within the Democratic Party and the lingering effects of the Panic of 1857.

In 1860, when President James Buchanan was delivering his last State of the Union address, saying, in essence, that the South had no right to secede and the government had no right to prevent secession, Lincoln and the Republicans were defeating a divided opposition. For the first time, a truly national political party, organized similarly to the Democrats, had emerged to contend for authority directly with the Democrats on the issue of national ruling power. A voter in 1860 had a choice between candidates representing "states' rights" on one side, or "national supremacy" on the other.

Government of the People, By the People

With the articulation of competing, nationally organized, popularly based political parties, the issue of national ruling power finally was drawn inside the political society. Prior to 1860, a certain ambiguity had always attached to the question of ruling power. In the early days of the republic, the issue had been drawn between those contending for national ruling power out of concern for effective external representation, and those contending for states' rights out of concern for legitimate (nonmonarchical) internal representation. When the Democratic-Republicans arose in the name of the plain people and states' rights, their exercise of ruling power was ameliorated through the constant acquisition of new territories and the constant addition of new, egalitarian states. Then when the Democratic Party seized the presidency through a nationally organized, state-based political organization, the principle of popular control was in its ascendancy. However, the question now was raised anew: if the people had the power (and the means) to prevent the exercise of ruling power by the government, how would ruling power be exercised at all?

In 1860, the people were organized to provide the answer: it was to be government *of* the people, *by* the people. As Lincoln wrote, "I consider the central idea pervading this struggle is the necessity of proving that popular government is not an absurdity."[11] For Lincoln, it was a question of relations between national authority and citizens in insurrection. For the South, it was a question of the right of self-determination—the same right that had been demanded by the colonists in the Declaration of Independence. It was thus that the tragic consciousness of political ruling power devolved upon the people themselves. Centuries earlier, William Shakespeare had written words to the effect that the low-born were happy, while the head that wore the crown was uneasy, knowing as the latter did the tragic burdens of political rule. But in 1860, a plain backwoodsman and hundreds of thousands of Americans would face and know that same tragic burden.

The fact of the Civil War, which began in 1861, is often referred to as a "breakdown" of our democratic government. But the Civil War was not a breakdown of civil order, in

---

11. Quoted in ibid., p. 725.

the sense of a general, violent disintegration. Rather, it was the *result* of a degree and kind of social integration never before achieved, wherein it was possible for the pro-Union and secessionist elements in the sprawling population to be so well-organized that a state of war could exist between them, like two sovereign nations. Indeed, some European powers, including England and France, hovered like vultures, ready to grant recognititon to the Confederacy—England because its ruling minority cherished the hope of seeing popular government discredited, and France because Napoleon III thought an American empire might be possible if the United States collapsed. But the Union forces finally proved themselves equal to the task of the war at the Battle of Antietam in September, 1862, and the Europeans reconsidered. Externally, the representative of the political society remained intact; internally, the mechanisms of popular government had brought the issue of representation into ultimate focus, and national ruling power was established once and for all. Appropriately, the institution of slavery, which was so incompatible with popular sovereignty, was abolished as Union was affirmed.

Suggested Further Reading

Among the more readable general histories covering the period in this chapter are the following:

Homer C. Hockett. *Political and Social Growth of the United States: 1492-1865.* Macmillan, 1941.

Richard Hofstater. *The American Political Tradition.* Knopf, 1948.

Samuel Eliot Morison. *The Oxford History of the American People.* Oxford University Press, 1965.

A classic account of the transition from Federalism to Democratic-Republicanism is found in:

Henry Adams. *A History of the United States During the Administration of Jefferson and Madison,* 2 vols. Spectrum Books, 1963.

The presidencies of Jefferson and Jackson are described in readable fashion in the following two volumes:

Claude G. Bowers. *Jefferson in Power: The Death Struggle of the Federalists.* Houghton, Mifflin, 1936.

Claude G. Bowers. *Party Battles of the Jackson Period.* Houghton, Mifflin, 1922.

The following is a concise, descriptive account of the Jacksonian period:

Henry Steele Commager and Richard Morris, *The Jacksonian Era: 1828–1848*. Harper Torchbooks, 1963.

For another interesting examination of the impact of Jacksonian Democracy and the new form of political party organization, based on an extensive analysis of voting patterns before and after the rise of the Democratic party, see:

Lee Benson. *The Concept of Jacksonian Democracy: New York as a Test Case*. Atheneum, 1963.

For an account of the Monroe Doctrine from its inception to modern times, see:

Dexter Perkins. *A History of the Monroe Doctrine*. Little, Brown, 1963.

Relevant interpretations of the emergence of an independent Supreme Court and its conduct during the ascendancy of the Democratic Party will be found in:

Robert McCloskey. *The American Supreme Court*. University of Chicago Press, 1960.

On the two major leaders of the Civil War, see:

Carl Sandburg. *Abraham Lincoln: The Prairie Years and the War Years* (condensed). Dell, 1963.

Jefferson Davis. *The Rise and Fall of the Confederate Government* (abridged). Collier Books, 1961.

Chapter 4
The Republic Articulated

Although the Union survived, the Civil War was a deeply divisive experience for the American people. The polarization of the period left its permanent imprint upon the structure of American government, and it is not just a curious irony that the same polarization that threatened to split the political society asunder came to stabilize it during the turbulent period of America's advanced industrial revolution. It will be helpful if we outline the argument in advance of its more detailed presentation.

After the Civil War, a radical and vindictive Republican Congress strongly reasserted its historic claim to supremacy in national government. As we shall see, both the Supreme Court and the president were intimidated and temporarily weakened. But the characteristic tendency toward monopoly by the winning political party was offset by the emotional polarization that lingered after the war. This condition at first made the checks and balances system an instrument for obstructionists in both parties. But by 1869 the Supreme Court was asserting its independence by protecting the rights of the (not altogether reconstructed) southern states against congressional control. And by the 1880s, a dynamically competitive two-party system was beginning to force America's people and institutions toward a painful, difficult encounter with a new and different threat to popular government, advanced capitalism and monopoly.

The protracted struggle that followed between advocates of political reform, governmental regulation of monopolists and various radical movements on the one side, and political "standpatters," big business and states' rights advocates on the other (to oversimplify rather drastically), occurred in a separation of powers, checks and balances context. Until the outbreak of World War II, Congress never completely lost its post-Civil War eminence; but it had to share its power with the Supreme Court and an increasingly independent presidency.

Postwar Development

There was no way to deal with Civil War and its aftermath in "normal" fashion. The key question, therefore, deals with the effects of the particular abnormalities that occurred as a result of the war.

In the longer view, two things stand out. First, the extraordinary powers seized by President Lincoln to deal with the war situation and the impending problem of reestablishing normal state governments in the South after the war; and second, the fierce reaction of a Congress dominated by the Radical Republicans. The situation, basically, came to this: Lincoln, who had assumed unprecedented powers while prosecuting the war for Union, also began to execute his own plan for reestablishing loyal state governments in the South. Despite congressional attempts to intercede, Lincoln was beginning to enact his moderate plans just before he was assassinated in 1865. Consequently, his successor, Andrew Johnson, bore the brunt of congressional reaction to Lincoln's policies. As Johnson was himself a plain and stubborn man (rather after the fashion of Andrew Jackson), the tensions between Congress and the presidency degenerated into an irreconcilable struggle. After the Radical Republicans won large majorities in Congress in the 1866 elections, they proceeded to pass a program of "Reconstruction" for the South that was thoroughgoing and frankly vindictive. Veto after veto came back from the president, only to be overridden by the Congress. The political and social structure of the South was "turned on its head" and Johnson, who resisted the radical program in favor of his predecessor's more moderate one, was impeached. He escaped conviction in the Senate by one vote, but the presidency was saddled with the Tenure of Office Act, which prohibited a president from removing any official from office—even in his own cabinet. Congress, in other words, intended to run the whole show, even the president's cabinet.

Postwar Amendments to the Constitution

The role of Congress was further underlined in three postwar amendments to the Constitution, which attempted to make all citizens more nearly equal under the law.

AMENDMENT XIII
Ratified 1865

Section 1. Neither slavery nor involuntary servitude, except as a punishment for crime whereof the party shall have been duly convicted, shall exist within the United States, or any place subject to their jurisdiction.

Section 2. Congress shall have power to enforce this article by appropriate legislation.

AMENDMENT XIV
Ratified 1869

Section 1. All persons born or naturalized in the United States, and subject to the jurisdiction thereof, are citizens of the United States and of the State wherein they reside. No State shall make or enforce any law which shall abridge the privileges or immunities of citizens of the United States; nor shall any State deprive any person of life, liberty, or property, without due process of law; nor deny to any person within its jurisdiction the equal protection of the laws.

Section 2. Representatives shall be apportioned among the several States according to their respective numbers, counting the whole number of persons in each State, excluding Indians not taxed. But when the right to vote at any election for the choice of electors for President and Vice President of the United States, Representatives in Congress, the Executive and Judicial officers of a State, or the members of the Legislature thereof, is denied to any of the male inhabitants of such State, being twenty-one years of age, and citizens of the United States, or in any way abridged, except for participation in rebellion, or other crime, the basis of representation therein shall be reduced in the proportion which the number of such male citizens shall bear to the whole number of male citizens twenty-one years of age in such State.

Section 3. No person shall be a Senator or Representative in Congress, or elector of President and Vice President, or hold any office, civil or military, under the United States, or under any State, who, having previously taken an oath, as a member of Congress, or as an officer of the United States, or as a member of any State legislature, or as an executive or judicial officer of any State, to support the Constitution of the United States, shall have engaged in insurrection or rebellion against the same, or given aid or comfort to the enemies thereof. But Congress may by a vote of two thirds of each House, remove such disability.

Section 4. The validity of the public debt of the United States, authorized by law, including debts incurred for payment of pensions and bounties for services in suppressing insurrection or rebellion, shall not be questioned. But neither the United States nor any State shall assume or pay any debt or obligation incurred in aid of insurrection or rebellion against the United States, or any claim for the loss or emancipation of any slave; but all such debts, obligations, and claims shall be held illegal and void.

Section 5. The Congress shall have power to enforce, by appropriate legislation, the provisions of this article.

AMENDMENT XV
Ratified 1870

Section 1. The right of citizens of the United States to vote shall not be denied or abridged by the United States or by any State on account of race, color, or previous condition of servitude.

Section 2. The Congress shall have power to enforce this article by appropriate legislation.

Postwar Changes in the American Political Scene

In the South, the largely disenfranchised whites (prevented from holding office or even voting under the strict reconstruction laws) turned in large numbers to secret, terrorist organizations like the Ku Klux Klan to reassert their power. In the North the Radical Republicans "waved the bloody shirt" (the bloody shirt of a flogged "carpetbagger," a Northerner gone South, was actually shown to an incensed House of Representatives) to prove how recalcitrant the Southerners remained. Thus the basis for an enduring, emotion-laden cleavage was laid. For generations thereafter, the South would never support the hated Republicans, and for years, at least, the Democrats would not escape identification with brutality and bigotry. The fact that such a cleavage did not lead to accurate impressions is neither surprising nor did it prevent the Republicans from dominating national government for twenty years. And during that twenty years of domination, the Republicans were able to build the kind of patronage machines that had served the Democrats so well prior to the Civil War. This is the key to the stability of the two-party system in the years of the republic.

A political party built on the spoils (or patronage) system grows more powerful with success. With electoral victories, the coffers of the party and its professional, fulltime membership grows because electoral victories bring control over public offices; and, as the party treasury and professional membership grows, so do its organizational advantages and prospects for future victories. There is a tendency, in other words, toward monopoly. But in the United States, the polarization of the Civil War produced a basis for a two-party monopoly. The so-called "solid South" and the border states accounted for about one-third of the nation's electoral votes after the war, and this core of electoral strength enabled the Democratic Party to survive the twenty years of Republican ascendancy.

Withal, it was a surprisingly short time before the even, competitive balance between the major parties, so characteristic of the republic, was struck. Between 1876 and 1896 the competition was evenly balanced. Republicans held a majority in the Senate for eighteen of those twenty years, while Democrats held the House majority for sixteen years. In all five presidential elections the popular vote margin of the winner was very small. Because the major parties were so closely balanced, the last quarter of the nineteenth century was a period when third parties could exert an influence on national politics that was considerably greater than one would imagine on the basis of their size and durability. The popular movements that had sprung up before the Civil War, with the democratization of political life, continued to manifest themselves in various forms. Not only could they influence the outcome of a presidential election, they could, as we shall see, introduce important policy changes as well.

By holding the pattern of party organization to the polarized theme of the Civil War, that great conflict actually stabilized the political system during the dizzying, dislocating national experience that was the industrialization of America. Between 1860 and 1890, America's population doubled. Its wealth tripled. Railroads crossed, then crisscrossed the nation. Telegraph and telephone lines multiplied. A veritable orgy of invention and ingenious application filled the whole, vast continent with Western civilization. At the same time the original populations—the Indians, as they had been termed by the European immigrants—were decimated. And even before the last Indian was slain in combat, America's industrial wealth began to exceed its astonishing agricultural output. Quite suddenly, America was dotted with cities—scores of large ones, several huge ones, and all of them growing.

The growth of cities meant the necessary growth of public utilities—water, garbage disposal, electricity, and so on, with a similar increase in police and fire-protection facilities. The rapid expansion of these public works and services meant the equally rapid growth of "machine politics" in the cities, for the patronage opportunities that arose from these increased government activities were stupendous. Powerful and corrupt political machines provided all the ballast necessary to keep the organizational clout in the major parties substantially decentralized, for city "bosses" and their cohorts in state government could easily command the major resources of the state parties when they worked in concert. Before long, in many a city and state, the difference between political organization and organized crime was difficult to discern.

But this very decentralization of party organization, and the blatant corruption so often associated with the parties, also served to give much of the population a first-hand knowledge of the palpable evils of their system. In the growing cities, the voters and taxpayers walked muddy streets and shuddered at the sight of pauperized immigrants, while their tax dollars, which allegedly had been collected to alleviate such problems, lined the pockets of the grafters. Thus the spirit of political and moral reform took solid root in the country's population, providing a basis for the great Progressive movement that was to come.

This capacity of the American people for moral action

is of immense importance, for it underlay their successful response to the greatest challenge to popular government since the Civil War itself: industrialization. During the first half of the nineteenth century, when the chief problem had been how to extend a system of republican representation over almost unbelievably vast and sparsely populated territories, the unique American federal system had succeeded beyond every hope. Not only was a republican form of government maintained and extended, but it had been further democratized in the process.

But after the war, the forces of industrialization—particularly immigration, urbanization, and the concentration of capital—presented grave challenges to the federal system (including the party system). On the one hand, the patronage-supported parties, whose mode of organization had made possible the unification of a diverse and scattered population, in many places became a means of domination as populations were more concentrated through growth (without territorial expansion) and urbanization. (Indeed, the parties came to be known as "third governments," over which the people had little control.) On the other hand, the concentration of capital removed the source of economic power from many local and state scenes, while the national government lacked the constitutional and administrative powers to regulate the economy on a national basis. Thus party control fell more and more into the hands of well-entrenched local chieftains, who in turn dictated national office nominations at conventions of party regulars. Before we examine the people's response to this situation, however, we shall need to look more closely at what they had to work with. For it was not until after the Civil War that the fully articulated American republic became a way of life for Americans, as well as an indisputably established political society among the other major nations of the world.

Checks and Balances

We have been told so often that "ours is a system of checks and balances," when nothing like it seems to obtain, that we are apt to believe the idea of a balance of powers in the government is no more than just an idea which, when set against our actual experience, proves to be illusory. But the checks and balances of the American republic were no illusion; what is illusory is the assumption that we still live in the republic.

During the second half of the nineteenth century, Americans struggled with the problem of the proper balance of power in government, and this very struggle was the essence of the balance. If we try to see these disputes from the perspective of the context in which they actually occurred, we can see the republic adjusting its federal system to the new demands of industrialization. Our tendency may be to succumb to the viewpoint of the nation-state, and therefore to see certain nineteenth- and early twentieth-century developments as being of a piece with our present form of government. But as the next chapter shows, it was not the changes made in the governmental organization of the republic that produced the American nation-state, but rather the unanticipated confluence of external and internal developments. It is most important not to assume that the disputes in nineteenth-century America foretold the shape of twentieth-century America; rather, we should think of the republic as trying to adjust its form of government to new kinds of problems brought on by industrialization.

A balance of powers in the republic's system of government could be located at several different points. There were the separated and shared functions of the national and state levels of government, resulting in one kind of "balance of powers." There was, of course, the separated national government, where each branch could (and did) exercise checking power over the others'. There was the intracongressional separation, wherein one house could (and often did) nullify the effects of the other. Finally, there was the Constitution itself, which was interpreted as an instrument limiting absolutely the powers of any level or branch of government. In addition, the two-party system that had developed and was now firmly entrenched, also served to balance the exercise of ruling power. Now, this entire system of checks and balances had served the republic well and in a generally positive way for a full century; and parts of it had grown through time during that century of development. But as the twentieth century approached and industrialization proceeded apace, this venerable system became more obstructionist than developmental. Consider, for example, the balance of powers between the states and the national government. As has already been shown, the development of substantially self-governing states prior to their admission to the Union was an important and useful feature of the American system of expansion, and it is highly doubtful that the United States could have extended its borders to the western shores of the continent with a fully centralized government. During the long period of economic development on the continent, the division of powers worked well that permitted the states to regulate their own commercial and industrial activities, while the federal government undertook to regulate (mainly through tariffs) international trade. But by the end of the nineteenth century, industrialization and urbanization had produced a situation where the states lacked powers they needed, and the federal government lacked powers it needed. Giant financial combinations had nationalized the economic life of the nation, and the federal government had neither the laws nor the constitutional precedents to regulate such activities. And urbanization had removed from the hands of the people the control they needed over the newly relevant areas of public works—hospitals, utilities, etc.—since the party machines spent more time lining their members' pockets than serving the urban public.

The balance of powers between the federal branches of government became a labyrinth of obstructionism. In the uncertain climate of new demands on federal powers, the Supreme Court was forever checking national legislation to curb the increasing abuses of concentrated capitalism; the Congress was unable to unite on policy goals; and the presidency was beset by the problems of patronage disputes and inadequate administration. The question became whether the republic could adjust its elaborate system of checks and balances to the new demands of an industrialized society.

The "Kept Republic" and Reform

Franklin's "republic, if you can keep it," became, in time, kept indeed. On the one hand were the corrupt party bosses who had gained a stranglehold on the mechanisms of nomination. On the other hand were the "robber barons," whose monopolistic practices in railroads, heavy manufacturing, and corporate finance gained them immense power that was virtually untouched by legal restraints. But successive waves of popular sentiment for reform eventually went far to redress the situation.

In 1881, President Garfield was shot by a man who thought he should have received a patronage office. The assassin was no doubt insane, but the fact that he was a disappointed patronage-seeker and that Garfield was a successful machine politician, was enough to galvanize the disparate reform movements that had been rumbling throughout the land. In 1883 the Pendleton Act was passed, providing a legal basis for subsequent civil service reform. (In essence, the law provided for limited use of an impartial examination system for civil service jobs.) But more important at the moment was the impetus given to the fortunes of such "reform politicians" as Grover Cleveland, who became the first Democratic president since the Civil War in 1885. Although his two (nonconsecutive) terms of office were marked by struggle and frustration, it was nevertheless a period of realignment in the balance of governmental powers.

Now the parties began to compete with one another in terms of political reform, and if progress was slow, it was nevertheless real because the question of honesty in government had now assumed the status of a national issue in the electoral process. Indeed, Cleveland's first victory came as a result of critical defections by Republican leaders (called "mugwumps" by party regulars) who took up Cleveland's slogan, "Public office is a public trust."

Cleveland's election sent reverberations through the stagnant system. He discovered that the highly protectionist system of tariffs was producing huge surpluses in the Treasury at a time when business was threatening to stagnate. Accordingly, he began a vigorous campaign to steer a new, less protectionist tariff bill through Congress, with several interesting results. First, the seriousness of obstructionist tactics in Congress were revealed in sharp focus, with important results that we will examine presently. Second, such a stir was created that the next presidential election was conducted with the issue of protectionism clearly in the forefront. Betrayed by several machine politicians in his party (notably the Tammany machine of New York); confronted by blatant vote-buying by Republicans in several states; and facing a Republican campaign that was financed in unprecedented quantities by big-name manufacturers, Cleveland was defeated. But the light thrown on this electoral corruption resulted in the widespread adoption of the so-called "Australian" ballot, requiring secret voting on uniform official ballots.

In 1892, an aroused electorate was able to make itself heard in two important ways. First, Grover Cleveland was again elected to the presidency, and he set out to achieve the kind of tariff law he thought should be instituted. Second, populist movements, which had sprung up in western, agrarian states, coalesced in the People's Party, which polled over a million popular votes and twenty-two electoral votes in the 1892 election.

Prairie farmers who were economically hard-hit by their own productivity and the turn to industrialism in the nation, had combined in their financial distress and moral outrage to forge mass, popular movements for reform and "free silver"—that is, a return to the free coinage of silver (now abundant and no longer used by major nations to back their currency), which would have been a little like the issuance of "paper money" unbacked by specie of an earlier time (see Chapter 2). The People's Party platform of 1892 called for paper money, free silver, a graduated income tax, the popular election of United States senators, government ownership of railways and telegraphs, a shorter workday for urban laborers, and other reformist measures.

Thus the drawing of major party lines on an economic policy issue (which had resulted from the election of a reform candidate for president) in time produced a situation in which the Populist movement could have an impact on national policies by holding a crucial balance of power. In return for Populist support for his tariff bill, Cleveland was forced to support a graduated income tax as a means to offset revenue losses from the reduced tariff. And while an obstructionist Senate amended Cleveland's bill beyond recognition, the income tax stayed in.

But the reverberations of reform continued. In 1895 the Supreme Court declared the income tax unconstitutional, which, in turn, triggered the passage of the Sixteenth Amendment (see the next chapter). In the meantime, the disastrous Panic of 1893 resulted in such serious depletions of the nation's gold reserves that Cleveland, a "sound-money" man, was forced to turn to the financial syndicate of J. P. Morgan to bail out the faltering Treasury. Morgan's syndicate loaned the government $65,000,000 worth of gold in return for government bonds. Now the Populists could charge Cleveland with helping the capitalists to make huge profits. The Supreme Court decision against the income tax only further fed the fires of suspicion in the public.

The upshot of these and other reverberations of reform was not, as is often erroneously asserted, a drift toward centralization and the undoing of the balance of powers. Rather, what occurred over a period of a decade or more was a realignment of the checks and balances system that brought the articulated institutions of the republic more in line with the actual disputes over claims to authority concerning the nature of reality that prevailed in an age of industrialism. We can trace this realignment right up to the outbreak of World War I, but there we must stop, because it is at that point that the transformation of America into a nation-state began and interrupted the historical continuity of the American republic.

The Panic of 1893—a very severe one—ruined President Cleveland's chances to make the kinds of gains he had expected with the recent electoral fortunes of the Democrats. Indeed, the Republicans swept back into power in 1896 with the election of William McKinley. At the same time, partly in reaction to the recent panic, corporations continued and even accelerated their processes of combination, to the point that plutocracy (rule by the rich) came to seem a grave threat. Moreover, the United States under the leadership of the triumphant Republicans moved quickly into the field of imperialistic competition with the great European powers. Reversing Cleveland's aversion to imperialism, McKinley declared that annexation of the Hawaiian Islands was the "consummation" of American destiny. Then the United States divided the Samoan Islands with Germany. In 1898 war against Spain was declared, as a result of which the United States acquired Cuba (which was to be granted independence), Puerto Rico, Guam, and the Philippines.

Nevertheless, a readjustment in the system of checks and balances had occurred during the preceding twenty years, which permitted the people to become more directly involved in the fateful decisions facing the republic. Most importantly, the vitality of the American presidency had been reawakened as it became the focus for national reform movements. Now presidential elections were marked by platforms that presented important issues to the public, issues reflecting the new realities of industrialization. In the election of 1900, the issue of imperialism was pressed by the Democrats as being of overriding importance, while the Republicans defended the "destiny" of America, and waved "the full dinner pail" of Republican prosperity.

In the judicial branch, an important shift had also occurred. In 1883, the Supreme Court interpreted the Fourteenth Amendment (guaranteeing all citizens equal protection under the laws) to confer upon Congress only the power
to enforce the Constitutional prohibition of state laws that
violate the letter of the Fourteenth Amendment. "It does not
invest Congress with power to legislate upon subjects which
are within the domain of state legislation. . . ." In other
words, federal authority seldom could interfere with the activities of the states. But shifting public opinion and the constant pressure on the national government to deal with the
new forces of industrialization produced a decided shift in
Supreme Court decisions toward the end of the 1880s. Along
with changes in Court personnel came a series of decisions
in which the Supreme Court reviewed state and local legislation affecting the rights of property: "That its influence generally favored the great corporate interests is less important
[here] . . . than the fact that the court . . . assumed the high
function of arbiter and censor of the national economic
order."[1]

Congressional organization also was affected by the reverberations of reform. Also in the late 1880s, the Speaker
of the House Thomas B. Reed, a Republican from Maine,
greatly increased the powers of the Speaker by reinterpreting
Constitutional provisions and securing crucial rules changes.
Reed, ruling House procedures with an iron hand, found the
means to prevent a plethora of obstructionist tactics that previously had paralyzed the slim Republican majority. Later,
when the Democrats got control of the House, they adopted
similar measures to prevent Republican obstructionism.

These and other developments neither constituted a centralization of power, nor did they upset the checks and balances system. On the contrary, the struggles between the
various branches and levels of government were, if anything,
intensified at the turn of this century. But now, instead of
missing the point or confusing the issues, these struggles
began to reflect the disputes of the industrialized republic.
As we have seen, Supreme Court decisions became the occasions for great public controversies and criticism—which, at
least, meant that the decisions were relevant. And the dominating leaders of Congress were now obliged to place their

---

1. Arthur M. Schlesinger. *Political and Social Growth of the American People,
1865–1940* (Macmillan, 1941), p. 249.

parties on record before the public, along with the president.

However, the problems of industrialization could not be solved easily, if at all. As we have said, the turn of this century saw even greater monopolization by "money trusts," advancing imperialism, and outright disregard of such antitrust legislation as had been passed. (The greatest business leaders were not particularly impressed with antitrust legislation: "Law! What do I care about the law? Hain't I got the power?" Such was the response of Cornelius Vanderbilt, while the phrase, "The public be damned!" is attributed to William H. Vanderbilt.)[2] By 1900, it began to look as if the public would share the cynicism of their de facto bosses: A "full dinner pail" and the acquisition of far-flung territories suited the voters fine, and McKinley was reelected easily.

Still, the stage was set for the great issues of industrialization to be fought out in the unique framework of the American republic. Could the republic cope? The Progressive movement of the early twentieth century was America's response; whether and how it would have worked can be seen but dimly, for World War I interrupted its climax (see Chapter 5).

The Progressive Era: "Golden Age" of the Republic, Or Seedtime of the Nation-State?

If public opinion seemed bland and unconcerned enough on the surface at the turn of this century, there was a deep vein of moral indignation waiting to be tapped. The United States was by now a relatively old fashioned form of political representation (in Europe, the modern nation-states, such as Germany and England, had emerged), but its people were modern. Its leading universities were now important centers of learning and culture in their own right and its industry led the world in output. Its labor struggles were as fierce and radical as those of any European nation. Its common people were the most literate in the world. It was a public, in other words, quite capable of responding to the call of the "muckrakers."

---

2. Ibid., pp. 130–131.

The muckrakers were (mostly young) journalists who undertook, just after the turn of this century, to expose the American plutocracy and assorted other evils. The Standard Oil Company, the Chicago meat-packing houses, the inner workings of the stock-market syndicates, the railroad monopolies, the "bought" United States Senate, the city machines, child-labor abuses, "white slavery," the perils faced by industrial workers, and many other dreadful features of industrialization and urbanization were exposed to the public, with names named and accusations detailed.

The realignment of the balance of powers and the galvanizing effect of the muckrakers' exposés produced a groundswell of reform in the nation. In several major cities, reform politicians led movements to gain public control of utilities, reorganize city governments, and so on. These reform movements, in turn, revealed the extensive control exercised by the parties, and movements aimed at toppling the bosses of state party machines gained momentum, especially in the newer states.

One reform technique, which spread rapidly after its origin in Wisconsin, was the state primary election, a system of "direct nominations" by general vote of the party membership in advance of the regular election. Another reform technique attacked the power of state legislatures (where party organizations were firmly entrenched) by passing "reform laws" requiring the legislatures to support for United States Senator the man who won popular endorsement in state primary elections. Thus the Seventeenth Amendment, which provided for popular election of senators, only reflected a practice that had been instituted in most states by the time of its ratification in 1912. It was also state reform movements that produced the Nineteenth Amendment (giving women the vote), for women's suffrage had proved a valuable aid to the reform movements in several states where it was instituted.

In the states where reform was successful, social welfare laws and laws regulating railroads and industry were enacted. However, the real targets of such laws were beyond the effective reach of the states because the great industrialists and money trusts occupied that "no man's land" between state and federal authority. Plainly, national action would have to be taken to buttress and support the reform movements at the state and local levels. Naturally, such a widespread movement was not ignored at the national level. At first, it seems clear in retrospect, the Progressive movement was more exploited than really heeded by national political leaders. But time proved that the public had indeed gained a firm grasp of the issues, and a remarkable series of elections finally resulted in fundamental responses by the national government.

President McKinley was assassinated shortly after his second term began, and Theodore Roosevelt assumed office. Roosevelt's flamboyant personality, and his energy and zeal for office, have led many historians to call him our first "modern" president. In the light of the analysis that follows in Part III, we cannot agree. But no one can deny that Theodore Roosevelt was a vigorous, forward-looking president who knew how to dramatize his own actions and give voice (if not depth) to the people's aspirations. He said of himself that he was able "To put into words what is in their [the people's] hearts and minds but not their mouths."

During his first term, he made much of the newly aroused clamor for trust-busting, and the like. However, he accepted increasing business concentration as inevitable, even while pressing for stricter enforcement of the inadequate antitrust laws then on the books. Nevertheless—and with more personal action than sound, basic reform to recommend him—Roosevelt stormed to reelection in 1904. His great victory seemed to embolden him further, and he now took up the cause of reform with a more serious set of proposals. Stronger regulatory measures for railroads were sought, along with government inspection of meat-packing plants, and so on. Conservation became a pet project, as well as trust-busting. But when William Howard Taft, the man Roosevelt picked as his successor, took his term in the presidency, the weaknesses in the new "progressive" Republican Party began to show. Many progressives of both parties had won congressional offices along with Taft's victory, and their devotion to basic reform soon pointed up the essential conservatism of Taft. Not only did Taft accept compromise bills that were quite unacceptable to the progressives, but he refused to aid the Progressive Republicans' efforts to curtail the powers of the House Speaker, the "standpatter," Joseph Cannon. Progressive Democrats joined the Progressive Republicans to curb the Speaker's powers, and the cause of liberal Democrats was strengthened. Surprisingly to old-guard politicians, the Democrats won decisive victories in the congressional elections of 1910 by pressing those once-esoteric issues (like the power of the Speaker) on the voters. The upshot was a serious split in the Republican ranks in the presidential election of 1912, with the Progressive Party emerging in support of Theodore Roosevelt (who now found Taft a traitor to his goals). What was left of the Republican Party went with Taft, while the Democrats, seeing their chance for victory, came up with the impeccable candidate, Woodrow Wilson.

With a bit of luck (both good and bad), with an electorate capable of a good deal more perseverance and intelligence than many observers had expected, and with the full panoply of American institutions in "high gear," the American republic had at last produced an electoral outcome that promised to cope with the deep-seated evils of uncontrolled industrialization. The two-party system found its party bosses falling under the assault of the state and local reformers and the primary system. Its national monopoly was threatened by the Progressive Party and Eugene Debs' Socialist Party. But it kept its stability and, under pressure, returned a true reform politician in the person of Wilson.

Wilson, who had championed an energetic executive during his outstanding academic career, proceeded to lead his majority in Congress in a "triple assault on privilege." First came the Underwood Tariff Act in 1913, the first really new tariff since 1846, which drastically reduced the protections afforded vested economic interests in the past, and thus lowered the price of cost-of-living items. Second came the Federal Reserve Act, a major overhaul of an inflexible banking system, which had contributed to panics and left economic control in the hands of great private bankers. Finally, the Federal Trade Commission was established in 1914 to regulate trusts more effectively.

Now, each of these basic laws was the product of progressivism and the reform movement that had grown and culminated in the republic. Yet we cannot evaluate them in their own terms, for scarcely had they passed than war broke out in Europe. Although the United States did not enter the war until 1917, it became increasingly involved after 1914. Thus, as we shall see in the following chapter, many of these progressive products of the republic dovetailed with the new demands of the nation-state, altering their impact and meaning fundamentally. Wilson himself, after resisting United States entry into the war, finally turned with vigor to the task of transforming the nation.

In the last analysis, then, our commentary on the American republic must be a question unanswered. Did the republic, indeed, manage to cope with industrialization? Would a limited, democratic government have had the power to curb the possibly greater power of the monopolists? As we shall see, a nation-state, by virtue of its structure, possesses such power. Whether the republic did or did not cannot positively be judged, because the United States emerged from the crucible of world war as a political society that was fundamentally, if not at first quite visibly, changed.

Suggested Further Reading

For a good, general treatment of this period see either of the following:

Arthur Meier Schlesinger. *Political and Social Growth of the American People.* Macmillan, 1941.

Samuel Eliot Morison. *The Oxford History of the American People.* Oxford University Press, 1965.

An attempt to provide a balanced view of the many currents and problems characteristic of the Reconstruction era will be found in:

John Hope Franklin. *Reconstruction After the Civil War.* University of Chicago Press, 1961.

For a brief overview of the tremendous growth and transformation of the nation's economy after the Civil War, see:

Lance E. Davis. *Growth of Industrial Enterprise: 1860–1914.* Scott, Foresman, 1964.

A readable treatment of the evolution of the office of the president is:

Clinton Rossiter. *The American Presidency.* Harcourt Brace Jovanovich, 1956.

For a specific account of one aspect of the history of the presidency, see the standard work on the subject of Johnson's impeachment:

D. M. DeWitt. *The Impeachment and Trial of Andrew Johnson,* 1903, reproduced by Russell, 1967.

For a well-received account of the important third-party movement that spurred major reforms, toward the end of the last century and at the beginning of this one, see:

John D. Hicks. *The Populist Revolt.* Bison Books, 1964.

More information about the muckrakers will be found in:

David Mark Chalmers. *The Social and Political Ideas of the Muckrakers.* Citadel, 1964.

A quite complete picture of the pre-"Red Scare" struggle in America will be found in:

Ray Ginger. *Eugene V. Debs: A Biography.* Collier Books, 1962.

For an account based on the idea that the Progressive era presaged our own (which the authors believe requires modification), see:

George Mowry. *The Era of Theodore Roosevelt and the Birth of Modern America.* Harper Torchbooks, 1962.

Part III
The American Nation-State

Introduction

The form of political representation chosen by the United States in the eighteenth century, was a radical break from the then-dominant form of representation in Europe. Curiously, by the early twentieth century the form of political representation of the United States was relatively conservative, compared to that of many European states. "Conservative" may not be quite the right word, because it means so many different things; "traditional" may come closer to the meaning we wish to convey, because during the nineteenth century in America, as we have seen, a fierce and bloody civil war was waged in which the viability of the form of political representation established in the late eighteenth century was the principal issue. In a sense, the victory of the Union forces was a conservative one, inasmuch as the form of representation established and articulated during the previous half-century was conserved.

But, if the nineteenth century saw the preservation of America's (relatively modern) form of political representation, it saw the rather thorough destruction of many European political traditions. The Napoleonic conquests of the early 1800s destroyed or seriously weakened many of the traditional representatives of European political societies. By the mid-nineteenth century a wave of revolutions in Europe had toppled all but a few of the remaining ancient regimes. World War I saw the collapse of the last representatives of the ancient ruling houses in east and central Europe—the Habsburgs in Austria, the Romanovs in Russia, and the Hohenzollerns in Germany. As the old forms of political representation in Europe were destroyed, where conditions were appropriate for their articulation, modern nation-states emerged.

Not only the first theoretical conceptualization of the modern state, but its first concrete manifestation as well, can be found in the nineteenth century development of Germany. However, we need not concern ourselves here with the history of the German-speaking people's long struggle for unification and statehood. It will suffice to state the preconditions for the emergence of the modern nation-state, and compare these preconditions with the actual situation in the American republic in order to see the chief differences in the forms of political representation. The modern nation-state has three main characteristics:[1]

1. It possesses a monopoly of the means of domination and administration; this monopoly is based on a centrally directed and permanent system of taxation, and a centrally directed and permanent (standing) military force in the hands of a central govermental authority.

2. The central authority monopolizes legal enactments and the legitimate use of force to execute its laws.

3. The central authority directs a rationally oriented officialdom, a burecauracy (defined and discussed in Chapter 5), which administers the legal enactments of the central authority on a continuous basis.[2]

While the republic had some of the elements of the modern state, it was nevertheless constructed in a way that distinguished it clearly from a nation-state. First, the republic was a *dual* government; the national government by no means "monopolized" the means of domination and administration. The several states collected and spent far more tax monies than did the national government; and the national government relied on state militia for its permanent military strength, which was limited by Constitutional mandate and custom. Second, the governmental power of the republic was separated so that power was distributed among its branches.

---

1. Here, and in our later discussion of bureaucracy, we follow closely the analyses of Max Weber. Weber's work is drawn together and interpreted in a work we rely upon extensively, Reinhard Bendix, *Max Weber: An Intellectual Portrait* (Anchor Books, 1962).
2. Ibid., p. 183.

The courts, the executive, and the legislature could and did check the exercise of power by each other. Finally, the officialdom of the republic was not primarily rationally oriented (that is, it was not primarily oriented to the execution of legal enactments by rational, efficient means). Rather, the spoils system prevailed, with the bulk of administrative officials oriented to political party considerations. Many of them were directed less by a central authority than by state-based bosses.

Today, the situation in the United States is much different. The chapters in this section will show that the United States today is more like the modern nation-state than it is like the republic of the nineteenth century. Since this is the twentieth century, that should not be surprising. However, Americans persist in talking about their government as though it were still the republic of old. Whether the nation-state is good or bad, desirable or undesirable, is a question that we reserve as far as possible to the conclusion of this book. Here in Part III we shall first discuss (Chapter 5) the process by which America was transformed into a nation-state as the conditions for modern statehood were realized here. Then in Chapter 6 we shall discuss the modern presidency, the office that has come to monopolize the means of domination and administration in the United States. Chapter 7 considers the transition of the legal system of the United States, with its increasing application of positive law in place of a reliance on natural law doctrines. Chapter 8 discusses the curious fate of the Congress of the United States, and explains how the exercise of the vast powers granted to Congress by the Constitution has fallen under the control of the presidency. Finally, in Chapter 9, we return to the problem of democracy in America, discussing political participation. In part, the power of the people in the republic was limited by the fact that the power of their national government was limited; but in the nation-state, it is the very power of the national government that limits the power of the people.

Chapter 5
The Transformation
of America

It is very difficult to acquire perspective on the American nation-state, but without such perspective on the whole entity, any analysis of it will seem boring and meaningless. This is because it is a *system* that we must analyze, and we are only parts, or functioning elements, of that system. Our minds are wary of stepping out of this system to see how it is coordinated and what makes it work. As long as the mind is secure in its slot in the system, it will tolerate strange dislocations of bodily experience: men have stood on the cold moon, and watched the life-bearing earth rise above the horizon, a thing apart. But the men who experienced that dramatic physical perspective on our planet did not thus automatically acquire a perspective on the system that produced the event. On the contrary, their minds and actions were but parts of a vast and intricate system of coordinated thoughts and activities capable of well-nigh incredible administrative outputs. It is a perspective on this system itself that we seek—a perspective on the modern nation-state.

To get a perspective on the nation-state—and to understand modern American government—we need to understand the transformation of America from the republic described and analyzed in Part II to the nation-state that shall be described and analyzed here in Part III. First, we will try to clarify *what* happened: what did the United States "turn into," anyhow? Second, we will suggest *why* the transformation occurred at all. Third, we will show *when* the transformation occurred (a surprisingly recent event). Fourth and finally, we will then consider *how* the transformation occurred, and this will bring us to a more detailed examination of the processes and institutions of the American nation-state.

Assembly Lines of Thoughts

The American republic did not and could not put a man on the moon (nor, for that matter, could most of the countries of the world do it today, even if they had the desire and the money to do so). The reason that the republic would have been incapable of putting a man on the moon was *not* only that the scientific knowledge was lacking. To be sure, the twentieth century has seen the development of scientific knowledge that was unknown in the nineteenth century ("relativity theory" is a good example), but, in scientific terms, placing a man on the moon was a practical application of Newtonian physics, which, of course, was well known in the nineteenth century. It is more accurate to say that what was lacking in the nineteenth century was an adequate technology—the organizational and technical means of applying scientific knowledge to practical ends. Unfortunately, "technology" is one of those much abused terms that often obscures more than it explains; but if we can get a clear idea of what a "technological society" is, then we will be closer to a clear idea of what a nation-state is. The central idea is that in a technological society, human thoughts and communications are themselves coordinated in the manner of assembly-line production:

In the nineteenth century, factories and railroads required accurate coordination of complex sequences of human actions—a requirement that became central in the assembly-line methods and flow charts of modern mass production. The same age saw the rise of general staffs, and of intelligence organizations for diplomatic as well as for military purposes. These staffs and organizations, just as the modern large-scale industrial research laboratory itself, *represent in a very real sense assembly lines of information, assembly lines of thoughts . . . .* the increasing division of intellectual labor between different human minds preceded today's divisions of intellectual labor between different human minds and an ever-growing array of electronic or other . . . equipment.[1]

1. Karl W. Deutsch, *The Nerves of Government: Models of Political Communication and Control* (The Free Press, 1966), pp. 75–76 (emphasis added).

This quotation from the work of Professor Karl Deutsch usefully points up both the similarities and differences between mass production and the modern communications networks of nation-states.[2] Mass production features: The production of standardized commodities, continuous plant operation, use of specialized equipment, and division of labor to the point where most production workers repetitively perform short and simplified operations. Thus the output is "depersonalized," because no one person produces it alone. Continuous plant operation is another indication of the depersonalized aspect because, of course, people must rest. Perhaps most important, however, is the extensive division of labor. What this means for the experience of the production worker is that he is, in a sense, "doing something he cannot do." That is, if he works in an automobile manufacturing plant, then he is said to be building automobiles— although, in all likelihood, he does not know the first thing about building a complete automobile. In mass production, the coordination of the various physical acts required to produce an automobile takes place outside the worker's experience. Yes, he coordinates his own actions, but *his* actions do not, of themselves, produce automobiles. His actions and those of many others are coordinated with machines so that the final product is a finished automobile. A different category of personnel, management or administrative personnel, must plan and coordinate the production workers' actions and the machine outputs.

The situation becomes rather more difficult to understand when the actions of the management or administrative category are similarly subdivided and coordinated from outside the experience of the administrator. Yet, in order to achieve very large administrative outputs, this is what must happen. When the actions of many workers are specialized and coordinated from the outside, rather than each worker performing all of the tasks of production, the output is increased geometrically. In the same way, administrative outputs that could not have been achieved otherwise are possible when administrators' tasks are specialized and coordinated.

---

2. The analogy between bureaucratic organization and machine mass production was employed extensively be Max Weber as well. See Reinhard Bendix, *Max Weber: An Intellectual Portrait* (Anchor Books, 1962), pp. 426ff.

When administration is subdivided into specialized tasks, and coordinated as assembly-line operations are coordinated, we have *bureaucracy.* (This term is used in different ways—often as a term of abuse; here we intend the definition given below.) The details of bureaucracy are discussed below, but several points are quite significant here. First, there are important similarities between bureaucratic organization and mass production. Administrative output is substantially *standardized,* instead of varying with the personal idiosyncrasies of the administators. Administration is *continuous.* A project does not "die" with its planner or director because the administrative organization continues, just as a modern factory continues, beyond the time frames of individuals. And the activities of the bureaucrats are *specialized.* But this brings us to an important difference between mass production and bureaucracy.

In mass production, the planning and supervision of the production workers' activities are performed by a separate category of personnel, the management. But when management itself is subdivided and coordinated, who plans and coordinates *its* separated activities? This coordination and supervision is accomplished by means of a *hierarchical structuring* of the organization, with each bureaucrat, or officer, reporting to a superior, who in turn answers to a superior. Ideally, all communications, "up" or "down," travel through fixed channels, which allows a central coordination of all of the parts of the system, and assures reliable control from the "top" or "center" of the bureaucracy. The ability to control the organization thus tends to be concentrated at the top of the structure, because it is only there that the various parts of the system can be coordinated. And just as the assembly-line worker is not making a car, neither is the bureaucrat actually executing policy; rather, he is performing a function that is *part* of the administration of policy.

The reason that a nation-state can, with sufficient resources, place a man on the moon is that it is capable of an administrative output of such great scope and reliability, whereas societies that are differently organized are not capable of such a coordinated effort. To put a man on the moon, a great deal of coordination of very different sorts of activities was required over time. For more than a decade, the activities of all sorts of specialists—computer experts, engineers, accountants, financiers, pilots, and so on—had to be coordinated with machines and specialized equipment of all sorts. Factories had to be financed and built or redesigned; special personnel had to be trained; different problems had to be identified and solved—all of this, and more, had to happen in a coordinated way. This whole complex of activities had to be coordinated further with other major undertakings of the government—such as its military, diplomatic, and economic policies. This kind of long-range planning and coordination can only be accomplished by means of the bureaucratic administrative apparatus, which is peculiar to the modern nation-state.

What has happened, then, in the United States is the *bureaucratization* of the society. Our jobs, our thoughts, and our lives have been organized into "assembly lines of information, assembly lines of thoughts." In terms of our *experiences,* this means that the coordination of our thoughts and actions occurs outside of our personal experience. This is a difficult idea to accept, in a way, because most of us feel that we are going about our own business, and that we are not being "coordinated" by the government at all—or, at least, only in limited ways. Nevertheless, it is only this coordination, or "steering" of the system, which makes possible the tremendous administrative outputs of the United States. We must examine *how* this process operates before we turn to a discussion of *why* America was transformed.

Principles Governing Bureaucratic Organization[3]

In its "pure form," in a nation-state under the rule of law, bureaucratic organization is governed by the following six principles:

1. *Official business is conducted on a continuous basis.*

Under different modes of authority, administration of government is more or less *discretionary.* But a bureaucracy is permanent and continuous in the sense that its officials are full-time, career bureaucrats, and the administration of law is impersonal and continuous as well.

2. *Official business is conducted in accordance with stipulated rules.*

---

3. Adapted from the account of Weber's analysis in R. Bendix, *Max Weber,* pp. 424ff.

An official (bureaucrat) possesses the authority to perform his assigned functions, but this authority is limited to these functions only. Moreover, the sanctions and means of coercion at the disposal of the official are limited to specified instances—all stipulated in written rules of procedure that govern the exercise of authority and the administration of sanctions in impersonal terms.

3. *A hierarchical, authoritative communications net connects the activities of every official.*

An official's activities and his performance of them are supervised by a superior; and problems or disagreements concerning a superior's decisions regarding a subordinate are appealed through specific channels to a superior in the hierarchy.

4. *Officials do not own the appurtenances of their offices nor do they own any of the resources necessary for the performance of their assigned functions.*

Physical accomodations, materials and supplies, and so on, are not owned by officials, but they are responsible for their use and disposition. In other words, the private person (and his property) is strictly separated from the official role he performs (and "its" property). By contrast, under traditional rule, administrative functionaries (tax collectors, and the like) are part of the ruler's household or personal property. Or consider the practices of the American Civil War, where officers were chosen (expecially in the South) on the basis of family position and their ownership of the necessary appurtenances of military office (a horse, weapons, etc.). In a modern, bureaucratic military organization, soldiers and officials do not own the vehicles or weapons they use.

5. *Offices, cannot be appropriated by their incumbents to be sold, inherited, or given to personal favorites.*

Under the spoils system, official positions were often appropriated by their incumbents and passed on in recognition of personal loyalties. But bureaucratic offices are filled according to impersonal criteria (such as competitive examinations) and cannot be owned in any sense by the incumbents of those offices.

6. *Official business is conducted on the basis of written documents.*

"Orders" lack official status except as they are in writing and recorded; by contrast, oral communication and personal encounter may be preferred under traditional or charismatic regimes, partly because what is reliable or trustworthy under such systems is personal loyalty, not impersonal rules.

The Confluence of Internal and External Demands

It is not clear what the course of America would have been had it not been for the confluence of two major developments in political representation, one that took place inside the republic and one looming on the European continent. It is doubtful that either development by itself would have effected such a fundamental transformation in our form of political representation.

The internal development was Progressivism, that complex of movements discussed in Chapter 4. Gathering national strength during the 1880s, Progressivism peaked at about the turn of this century and reached "flood tide" with the election of Woodrow Wilson, who was not only the last of the Progressives but the first president of the nation-state. It was during his administration that the confluence of internal and external forces occurred.

Progressivism was a great *moral* movement in the republic. It is extremely important to grasp this point (unlikely as it may seem to some of us), otherwise we may see an apparent but misleading continuity between certain developments in the republic and the emergence of the nation-state. What with the unheard-of riches of the plutocracy on the one hand, and political patronage machines glutted with spoils and graft on the other, the movement for political reform during the Progressive Era of the republic had a strongly moralistic flavor. (This same period saw the rise of the temperance movement, which culminated in the ill-starred Eighteenth Amendment.) "Throw the rascals out" was very much the mood of the day, and a call for economy and efficiency in government easily complemented the call for honesty and integrity. Very few men in government, let alone the general voting public, could have grasped the possibility of, or necessity for, a vast bureaucratic apparatus in governmental administration. To be sure, the need for economy and efficiency was plain to many, but the scale of administrative output that was anticipated did not require a modern bureaucracy; rather, the demand for an extension of the merit system in the civil service was a demand to end the abuses and gross unfairness of the spoils system.

The legal basis for the extension of the merit system in the civil service actually had its origins in the wave of revulsion touched off by the assassination of President Garfield in 1881 by a disappointed office-seeker (the fact that the assassin was also insane did not get much press at the time).[4] Thus in 1882 Congress reversed its previous recalcitrant position and quickly passed, in rather hypocritical earnestness, the Pendleton Act. Shortly thereafter, a statute creating a new Civil Service Commission was also passed. During the decades that followed, reform politicians riding successive waves of public sentiment, added more and more civil service jobs to the classified list, which meant that those jobs were to be filled by competitive examinations on a merit basis. Typically, these limited moves were made in the name of honesty, integrity, and efficiency in public office, and were followed closely by an aroused electorate.

Civil service reform proceeded during the Progressive Era with political reform in general, including the decisive weakening of the party system that thrived on patronage. Chapter 4 has detailed the successes of the Populists and Progressives during the 1890s and early 1900s in their efforts to eliminate the convention system of nominating candidates for public office and replacing it with primary elections. This movement, which also was strongly moralistic and reformist in its origins, never really achieved its goal of placing control over nominations in the hands of the people. However, it substantially weakened the party organization of the republic in several ways. First, it weakened party control over nominations by undermining the convention system. Second, it weakened the hold of party leadership over its nominal nominees, again by undermining the convention system. Third, the primary system often produced divisions in the parties by pitting party leader against party leader in contests for nomination.[5] This same movement for primary elections led, as we have seen, to the adoption of the Seventeenth Amendment, providing for the direct election of senators.

4. Paul P. Van Riper, *History of the United States Civil Service* (Row, Peterson, 1958), pp. 88ff.
5. Frank J. Sorouf, *Political Parties in the American System* (Little, Brown, 1964), pp. 101-102.

Finally, the curious admixture of Progressivism and Populism also led to a fateful constitutional change, the Sixteenth Amendment, which established the income tax. As we saw, the Populists could never really seize control of national government, but their strong, if somewhat naive, demands did produce effects. Thus, the Sixteenth Amendment, like the other basic changes that occurred at the turn of this century, was not made in anticipation of the needs of the nation-state. Rather, it was in the belief that the source of new revenues required by tariff reductions should be borne by those people most able to pay that led the Populists to demand, and ultimately to win an income tax.

The Progressive movement, then, was a set of demands on the representatives of American political society born of popular disgust with political corruption and a related desire to curb the power of the great economic combinations of the day. By itself, Progressivism would not have altered fundamentally the form of political representation of the republic. However, Progressivism was enjoying its heyday when a new and ominous threat to the external representation of all Western political societies emerged in Europe, culminating in World War I.

World War I was a different kind of war. The reason that it developed into a worldwide conflict, and the reason that the United States could not enjoy its accustomed security from European wars behind the protective expanse of the oceans, was that imperial Germany was capable of making war on a scale and with an efficiency previously unknown to mankind. Just as the methods of mass production differentiate and recombine human actions in such a way as to increase geometrically the material output of a given number of workers, so did bureaucratic organization differentiate and recombine the activities of the German population to increase geometrically their administrative output. Gradually, those few nations that were capable of it began to pit their total resources in the war effort, and the United States was at last drawn into the war.

Suddenly, the modest income tax was put to use in earnest. It had been 1 percent on family incomes over $4,000, with surtax rates on taxable incomes over $20,000; but in 1918, progressive rates from 6 to 12 percent were introduced, with the surtax on incomes over $20,000 jumping from 1 percent to 65 percent! Incomes over $1,000,000 were now taxed at a rate of 77 percent. But this unprecedented taxation of the wealthy was not resisted as much as one might suppose. The war in Europe was of enormous economic benefit to America—especially to the businessmen: "From 1917 to 1920 the ranks of American millionaires grew from sixteen thousand to twenty."[6] Suddenly huge amounts of money were being funnelled through the government (the war expenditures were almost three times as great as the total outlay of the government for all purposes during its first century of existence),[7] and the economy was expanding as never before.

Thus the Progressivist and Populist developments of the republic meshed perfectly with the new demands of war among nation-states. Just a few years after its inception, the income tax was used to raise unprecedented sums for the war. The civil service, by now passably reformed, was expanded under new recruiting and personnel techniques and was relied upon to undertake the huge administrative tasks of the war. Furthermore, the populist, progressive moods in the country were exploited to stimulate as much individual, direct involvement with this great national effort as possible.

Before twenty years had passed, the United States, now fundamentally altered in its structure, would again experience a dual demand on its form of representation, sealing once and for all the transformation. After World War I, the country eagerly returned to "normalcy" (in the charming term of President Warren G. Harding), and a sort of Indian summer for the republic followed. The great armies were dismantled, the civil service shrank in size, the tax rate dropped again, and prosperity seemed widespread. Then, in 1929, the longest and by far the worst depression in America's history began.

Actually, the great prosperity of the 1920s was not a "normal" prosperity. Like previous booms, it had been marked by speculation that finally got out of hand; but much of the expansion was in new industries—radio, chemicals, motion-picture, rayon, and so on—that had been developed in the "assembly lines of thoughts" of the new nation-states. Indeed, the United States had entered some manufacturing and development fields directly (shipbuilding, for instance), because no private enterprise could coordinate and supply

6. Arthur Meier Schlesinger, *Political and Social Growth of the American People, 1865–1940* (Macmillan, 1941), p. 441.
7. Ibid., p. 458.

these critical undertakings. So great had become the interconnections between different levels of government, industry, and other modern nations, that the economic debacle of the 1930s soon became worldwide, and bewildered and desperate populations turned to their government for help. As we shall detail later, the measures taken by the inevitable new administration, the Democrats under President Franklin Delano Roosevelt, were extraordinary indeed. Not only were unheard of new programs inaugurated in Roosevelt's first term, but the traditional check on the Congress and the executive—the Supreme Court—was devastated when it tried to stand in the way (see Chapter 7).

So again it happened. The extraordinary demand from the inside was reinforced and made permanent as World War II brought America into deep and mortal combat with Germany and the Axis powers.

AMENDMENT XVI
Ratified 1913

The Congress shall have power to lay and collect taxes on incomes, from whatever source derived, without apportionment among the several States, and without regard to any census or enumeration.

AMENDMENT XVII
Ratified 1913

The Senate of the United States shall be composed of two Senators from each State, elected by the people thereof, for six years; and each Senator shall have one vote. The electors in each State shall have the qualifications requisite for electors of the most numerous branch of the State legislature.

When vacancies happen in the representation of any State in the Senate, the executive authority of such State shall issue writs of election to fill such vacancies: *Provided,* That the legislature of any State may empower the executive thereof to make temporary appointments until the people fill the vacancies by election as the legislature may direct.

This amendment shall not be so construed as to affect the election or term of any Senator chosen before it becomes valid as part of the Constitution.

AMENDMENT XVIII
Ratified 1920

After one year from the ratification of this article, the manufacture, sale, or transportation of intoxicating liquors within, the importation thereof into, or the exportation thereof from the United States and all territory subject to the jurisdiction thereof for beverage purposes is hereby prohibited.

The Congress and the several States shall have concurrent power to enforce this article by appropriate legislation.

This article shall be inoperative unless it shall have been ratified as an amendment to the Constitution by the legislatures of the several States, as provided in the Constitution, within seven years from the date of the submission hereof to the States by Congress.

AMENDMENT XIX
Ratified 1920

The right of citizens of the United States to vote shall not be denied or abridged by the United States or by any States on account of sex.

The Congress shall have power by appropriate legislation to enforce the provisions of this article.

The Two Stages of the Transformation

World Wars I and II placed great external pressures on the American political representation, and these external pressures coincided almost uncannily with the peaks of internal demands on the representation. Moreover, the chief executives during those two critical moments of history were almost ideally suited to seize the opportunities thereby presented to turn the nation in the direction of nation-statehood. Since the basic transformation occurred in the form of political representation, we can place the time of the transformation at the points where effective representation shifted decisively to the office of the president—the logical point in the institutional structure of the republic to assume the mantle of representation for the nation-state.

Woodrow Wilson's term of office extended from 1913 to 1921, a period that saw the introduction of the income tax as well as the beginning and conclusion of World War I. Wilson was very much a representative of the Progressive movement in the country. At a time when "an honest politician was hard to find," Wilson fit the bill calling for a candidate whose personal integrity would come across to the voters. Indeed, his background was less that of a politician than an academician, for he had been a professor of jurisprudence and political economy at Princeton, and later president of Princeton University. He had written several books and articles on government and history, and was an acknowledged expert on congressional government and public administration.

Wilson's impact on American government doubtless would have been substantial had there been no war, for he was a reformer at heart, with the ability to make permanent and effective reforms. But the war—which Wilson tried to keep America out of with particular earnestness—required finally that he turn his unusual administrative ability to the task of transforming, not reforming, the government. This was necessary because, as was noted, World War I was a different kind of war, a war that not only pitted the military forces of one country against another, but a war that pitted the whole, coordinated resources of nations against one another. "However remiss the administration may have been in forearming against the war, it sought now to make up for lost time by organizing the nation with a thoroughness and on a scale unparalleled in American annals."[8] Not only was universal conscription of males adopted, but the country's material and human resources were organized and mobilized in totally new ways. As Secretary of War Baker put it, "Under modern conditions, wars are not made by soldiers only, but by nations . . . . The army is merely the point of the sword."[9] We shall detail some of the measures taken in the next section. Here it should be stressed that Wilson, unlike the presidents who had preceded him during periods of national emergency, did not arrogate to himself extraordinary powers. His was not a charismatic leadership, but one grounded in law. With unusual and perceptive thoroughness, he sought and acquired the necessary laws from Congress to execute the business of the nation-state at war. This is why, perhaps, the pendulum did not swing back toward con-

8. Ibid., p. 419.
9. Quoted in ibid., p. 420.

gressional dominance as it had after the Civil War. For Congress had itself participated in the construction of the nation-state. To be sure, the government was notably quiescent after the war—perhaps too quiet, as it turned out—but the fundamental changes were allowed to stand in law.

Wilson's presidency, then, was the first stage of America's transition, and it was the decisive one. A second, much more obvious and dramatic stage was yet to come, but the second stage was built upon and, in many ways, necessitated by the first stage. As we have observed, the second stage coincided with the emergence of an extraordinary president, Franklin Delano Roosevelt.

If the first stage of the transformation required a president who would attend to the underlying legal structure of the transformation, the second stage required a president who could ignite the popular imagination in terms of the nation-state. Roosevelt was just the man—a charismatic personality, extremely skilled at utilizing the now-developed national radio broadcasting systems, hungry for the power that could only be exercised by the chief executive of the nation-state, and singleminded to the point of ruthless disregard for precedent when he was challenged. Roosevelt's term of office lasted from 1933 to 1945; he was the only president to serve more than two terms (now limited by Constitutional amendment). During his first, famous "Hundred Days" in office, he blitzed Congress with a huge package of legislation which, in effect, made him the administrative director and coordinator of the nation's economic life. Roosevelt was a "doer" and an experimenter, which was the perfect attitude in the situation. In response to the devastation of the Great Depression, Roosevelt's proposals were aimed at relief for the thirteen millions who were unemployed, at recovery from economic stagnation, and reform of the system that permitted such a breakdown.[10] Like a few men who had preceded him in the presidency—especially Theodore Roosevelt—FDR took naturally to the idea that he could and should exercise such power as he could get in order to do what was good for the country. Now, however, the structural reformations wrought during the first stage of the transformation, coupled with the possibility and necessity in the public's mind for drastic action, made Roosevelt's experimentations

10. Ibid., p. 523.

more than a personal interlude in the nation's history: instead, it was an epoch-making period.

This time, when world war again broke out, the United States was able to enter it in the full capacity of a nation-state—and to emerge as by far the premier power of the world. The same year that Roosevelt took office, Adolf Hitler became Chancellor of Germany, and the next year he acquired total power. In 1939, Hitler invaded Poland and World War II was underway. This time, however, people knew what to expect of the nation-state at war, and few knowledgeable people anticipated safety behind the Atlantic. Acting under the authority of Wilson's statute of 1916, Roosevelt created an Advisory Commission on National Defense to plan America's greatest war effort, which was to seal the transformation once and for all, and to produce the nation-state we live in today. Almost overnight, the tax that had been a "rich man's tax" was converted to one that reached down to the great majority of workers. Exemptions were lowered, and a progressive tax on all taxable income ranged from 23 to 94 percent. By 1943, the withholding system was introduced, which made compliance automatic for most people. (Later we shall discuss the means by which the population was socialized, or "conditioned," to an acceptance of this new mode of experience.) During the protracted second stage of the transformation, the bulk of the population was drawn into the assembly lines of thoughts, which is the nation-state, producing what Max Weber called "a form of power relation . . . that is practically unshatterable."[11] At this point we can consider in more detail the "how" of the transformation by bureaucratization.

Attributes of Bureaucracy [12]

1. Bureaucracy is *technically superior* to other forms of organization in terms of speed; precision (reliability and predictability); lack of equivocation; continuity (reliability over

11. Max Weber, "Bureacracy." In Albert Rubenstein and Chadwick Haberstroh, eds., *Some Theories of Organization* (Richard Irwin and The Dorsey Press, 1966), p. 79.
12. Adapted from the account of Weber's analysis in R. Bendix, *Max Weber*, pp. 426ff.

time, with no breaks in performance); reliability of information and documentary records; ability to maintain confidentiality or secrecy; uniformity of operation; and maintenance of authority relationships. Notice that these advantages parallel the advantages of mass production (standardization, continuity, speed, and so on); the disadvantages are not dissimilar, either. Because the system standardizes output, the individual case is often overlooked or treated as though it were like all others. Reliability and calculability (rationality) are bought at the price of rigidity.

2. Bureaucracy is *centralized;* it is characterized by a "concentration of the means of administration." Just as mass production concentrates the means of production in the hands of a few (the factory owners), so does bureaucracy concentrate the means of administration in the hands of a minority. This is a corollary of the feature of hierarchy in bureaucracy.

3. A third attribute of bureaucracy is its *levelling effect* on social and economic differences. In nonbureaucratic administration (such as the spoils system), rank in the organization depends on social, economic, or personal considerations, and administrators exploit their positions to further enhance their social and economic status. But bureaucracy provides set pay scales for its officials, and impersonal rules and merit procedures tend over time to diminish the significance of, and even effect the eradication of, personal privileges based on social and economic distinctions. The expert, not the cultivated man, is the educational ideal of a bureaucratic age.

4. Finally a system of *authority relationships,* which is practically indestructible, is implemented. As Weber puts it, " . . . the professional bureaucrat is chained to his activity by his entire material and ideal existence. In the great majority of cases, he is only a single cog in an ever-moving mechanism . . . . normally the mechanism cannot be put into motion or arrested by him, but only from the very top. The individual bureaucrat is thus forged to the community of all the functionaries who are integrated into the mechanism. They have a common interest in seeing that the mechanism continues . . . . "[13]

---

13. Weber, "Bureaucracy," pp. 79–80.

New Deal and Related Constitutional Amendments

AMENDMENT XX
Ratified 1933

Section 1. The terms of the President and Vice President shall end at noon on the 20th day of January, and the terms of Senators and Representatives at noon on the 3d day of January, of the years in which such terms would have ended if this article had not been ratified; and the terms of their successors shall then begin.

Section 2. The Congress shall assemble at least once in every year, and such meeting shall begin at noon on the 3d day of January, unless they shall by law appoint a different day.

Section 3. If, at the time fixed for the beginning of the term of the President, the President elect shall have died, the Vice President elect shall become President. If a President shall not have been chosen before the time fixed for the beginning of his term, or if the President elect shall have failed to qualify, then the Vice President elect shall act as President until a President shall have qualified; and the Congress may by law provide for the case wherein neither a President elect nor a Vice President elect shall have qualified, declaring who shall then act as President, or the manner in which one who is to act shall be selected, and such person shall act accordingly until a President or Vice President shall have qualified.

Section 4. The Congress may by law provide for the case of the death of any of the persons from whom the House of Representatives may choose a President whenever the right of choice shall have devolved upon them, and for the case of the death of any of the persons from whom the Senate may choose a Vice President whenever the right of choice shall have devolved upon them.

Section 5. Sections 1 and 2 shall take effect on the 15th day of October following the ratification of this article.

Section 6. This article shall be inoperative unless it shall have been ratified as an amendment to the Constitution by the legislatures of three-fourths of the several States within seven years from the date of its submission.

AMENDMENT XXI
Ratified 1933

Section 1. The eighteenth article of amendment to the Constitution of the United States is hereby repealed.

Section 2. The transportation or importation into any State, Territory, or possession of the United States for delivery or use therein of intoxicating liquors, in violation of the laws thereof, is hereby prohibited.

Section 3. This article shall be inoperative unless it shall have been ratified as an amendment to the Constitution by conventions in the several States, as provided in the Constitution, within seven years from the date of the submission hereof to the States by the Congress.

AMENDMENT XXII
Ratified 1951

Section 1. No person shall be elected to the office of the President more than twice, and no person who has held the office of President, or acted as President, for more than two years of a term to which some other person was elected President shall be elected to the office of the President more than once. But this Article shall not apply to any person holding the office of President when this Article was proposed by the Congress, and shall not prevent any person who may be holding the office of President, or acting as President, during the term within which this Article becomes operative from holding the office of President or acting as President during the remainder of such term.

Section 2. This article shall be inoperative unless it shall have been ratified as an amendment to the Constitution by the legislatures of three-fourths of the several States within seven years from the date of its submission to the States by the Congress.

The Centralization and Monopolization of Authority

The crucial development for a modern nation-state is the centralization of the means of domination and administration, based on a centrally directed and permanent system of taxation and a centrally directed, permanent military force. The ability to administer these crucial areas of activity generalizes itself as an ability to administer all other areas of activity, owing to the greater efficiency of bureaucracy.

As we have already indicated, ratification of the Sixteenth Amendment and the adoption of an income tax law in 1913 paved the way for the centralization of authority in the nation-state. But the way this actually happened requires some elaboration. Under the Constitution, "Congress controls the purse strings." In the republic, this virtually was the case. The various agencies and departments of the executive branch, which executed the laws, would request appropriations of money from Congress, where these requests would be reviewed by different committees, and then would be acted upon by Congress. The system was not particularly efficient. On the one hand, all of the requests for appropriations could hardly be acted upon by Congress as a whole; on the other hand, dealing the load out to different committees produced rather poor coordination of monetary outgo with income. Nevertheless, the system was workable for the republic, and was principally instrumental in maintaining the balance of power between Congress and the executive. But the huge expenditures and income of the World War I years quite outstripped the capacity of Congress to keep track of and properly administer the country's finances. Therefore Congress simply had to approve a Budget and Accounting Act that would create a Budget Bureau in the Treasury Department to prepare estimates of revenue and to recommend expenditures. However, Congress was reluctant to part with its exclusive authority over the budget. Consequently, the bill was amended to provide that the director, the comptroller general, could be removed by Congress alone and without presidential concurrence.[14] In retrospect, it is clear that Congress's jealousy was well-placed. But Woodrow Wilson was astute as well, and he vetoed this much-needed bill because of that offending provision. The bill came around again, with that provision removed, the year after Wilson left office, and the honor of signing into law the Budget and Accounting Act of 1921 fell to President Harding.

Although the occasion of apparent, pressing need for a Budget Bureau had passed with the war, its establishment soon had important effects. It turned out that the preparation of a budget was practically impossible because of the chaotic situation in the civil service. Careful estimates of personnel and personnel costs required the standardization of federal wages and functions, and this necessity finally tipped the balance in favor of a law (the Classification Act of 1923) that was an important step toward the rationalization of the civil service. Although limited in its application, the law established occupational divisions ("services") on a functional

14. Van Riper, *History of the United States Civil Service*, p. 297.

basis, subdivided the services by "grades," established uniform compensation schedules by grades, established allocation procedures for placing persons in grades, removed sex discrimination in order to promote uniformity of schedule applications, authorized "classes" of positions within grades, established a central classifying agency, and fixed lines of authority.[15]

In other words, the establishment of full, central taxing authority and its extensive utilization during World War I necessitated the establishment of a central budgeting office. The efficient utilization of the Budget Bureau, in turn, necessitated the passage of laws rationalizing and standardizing the administrative agencies of the government, that is, bureaucratizing those agencies. During the interlude after World War I, it was possible for Congress, and particularly Senator Reed Smoot (an influential opponent of governmental expansion), severely to limit the scope of these changes, but the die was nevertheless cast. If the tools were not effectively wielded at first, during this period when "economy in government" had first priority, it was still true that the government had now enacted into law new personnel procedures of modern, bureaucratic form.

The important legacy of the first stage of the transformation was to be dramatically augmented during the second stage, but before that happened the impact of the nation-state on politics would have to manifest itself. This new kind of politics—what we have called the "politics of knowledge"—began to take form during Franklin Roosevelt's first campaign in 1932. With a keen insight into the nature of politics in the nation-state, Roosevelt separated "in a way that had not been so thoroughly done before in American history intellectual policy-making from politial policy-selling."[16] What he did was to put one man in charge of the vote-getting organization, and another man in charge of the policy-making organization. This arrangement bloomed first into the "Brain Trust," a group of advisers brought together mainly from the nation's universities in 1932. The Brain Trust and the "Kitchen Cabinet"—an informal but important group of advisors to whom Roosevelt really turned, in contradistinction to the formal cabinet, for advice and assistance—were responsible for much of the New Deal legislation that was

15. Ibid., p. 299.
16. Ibid., p. 324.

to reform the nation. During the "First Hundred Days," Congress received (and passed) legislation that for the first time in the nation's history had already been fully drawn up by the White House's "assembly lines of thoughts." Congressional politicians were no longer at the center of policy-making because FDR had found the means of utilizing the assembly lines of thoughts of the nation-state.

Roosevelt had tapped the centers of differentiated and specialized knowledge in the nation, the universities, and he had drawn these specialists into the new center of government. However, a gap between the policy-making and policy-executing abilities of the government soon showed itself. If the legal basis for a modern bureaucracy existed, the bureaucracy itself was still in disarray. Roosevelt put a staff of his experts to work on this problem, forming the President's Committee on Administrative Management (headed by Louis Brownlow and Luther Gulick, the two top experts in the then-new science of public administration, along with Charles Merriam, the founder of the behavioral revolution in political science). The Brownlow Committee, as it was called, came up with a complete proposal for the reorganization of the executive branch. As it turned out, the proposal came out at the same time that President Roosevelt, enraged at the Supreme Court for declaring most of his main legislative packages unconstitutional, presented his notorious "court-packing scheme" to Congress. (This plan would have allowed the president to place a liberal majority in the Court by greatly expanding its size.) The scheme failed amid great controversy (though the Court got the message and promptly did an about-face, as described in Chapter 7). As a result, the impact of the Brownlow report was, if not lost, at least greatly delayed.

However, Roosevelt finally got the heart of what he needed—a reorganization law that let the president do the reorganizing when and as he found it necessary. Despite certain limitations, the main idea was to let the executive branch reorganize itself, with the Congress given a sort of veto power. The president's executive orders would go into effect within sixty days unless revoked by concurrent action of Congress. Here and elsewhere, then, the initiative had moved to the executive.

We shall detail the main developments in governmental administration in the next chapter. For the moment it will suffice to point out that the Bureau of the Budget became more and more the principal instrument of presidential power. By means of the Bureau, the president could exercise control through his exclusive ability to coordinate an increasingly complex and differentiated budget and administrative apparatus. As a body, Congress was in no position to control the policies it enacted into law because they were complexly related to a total policy coordinated by the executive branch. In a world of increasing expertise and reliance upon experts, only the office that coordinated these assembly lines of thoughts could retain control.

The states, in the meantime, were simply preempted. The great administrative efficiency of the national government soon put it in effective control of the economic life of the nation, as well as the taxing policies. Starting in 1913, and growing enormously in more recent times, the technique of federal grants-in-aid enabled the national government to steer and control state policies of concern to the central government.

Finally, the great military establishment of World War II never shut down. Straight from victory in the war, the United States continued a "preparedness" policy in the "cold war" with the Soviet Union and, as we know, states of undeclared war in one place and another, involving enormous expenditures, have continued since then.

World War II also ushered in for all the population the era of the impersonal authority of scientific and technical expertise. World War I and its aftermath had outlined in no uncertain terms the power potential of the nation-state organized in bureaucratic terms and administering the application of the natural sciences to military and economic ends. World War II then became the dramatic setting for the emergence of the scientist as crucial actor in the battle between nation-states. In 1939, Roosevelt received a letter from Albert Einstein on behalf of physicists who now saw the possibility of developing a nuclear fission bomb. Within a few months the administrative machinery to produce such a bomb was set in action, and by the time Harry Truman succeeded to the presidency upon Roosevelt's death in 1945, a successful test of the atomic bomb was imminent. By now, all, not just the well-born or well-educated, lived in a world where science and the state were welded into ultimate authority. World War II and its aftermath saw the atomic bomb, television, proliferating automation, and universal compulsory education woven in a seamless web.

The cold war, which followed the complete but necessarily precarious victory of the Allied forces in 1945, instituted the continuing dominance of the form of representation characteristic of the nation-state. Not only were large, standing armies maintained by the United States and the Soviet Union, but the educational systems of both countries were put increasingly to national purposes, thus extending the assembly lines of thoughts throughout the populations. In 1950 the National Science Foundation (NSF) was created "to promote the development of new scientific knowledge and new scientific talent." Governmental grants to scientific research projects, often worth millions of dollars, were made available through NSF to scientists working mainly in the large and growing universities of the nation. Money to support science-related scholarships was also made available. During the late 1950s, partly in reaction to the Soviet Union's apparent technological coup in launching an orbiting satellite, and partly in general recognition of the key place of science in the nation-state, substantial federal monies were made available to various levels of the educational system to further stimulate and promote science-related education and research.

Our interest in the relevance of the educational system for the bureaucratized society goes beyond its contribution to scientific expertise because the educational system is the primary "training ground" in bureaucratic discipline.

"Industrial discipline" refers to the special requirements of the individual laborer where the production process is organized "externally" to his experience, outside of his own person. He has to adjust his actions to the assembly line—to machines, shifts, and so forth. "Bureaucratic discipline" refers to the requirement made of the individual where bureaucratic organization prevails. He must respond to impersonal authority legitimized by law and universal rules; he must participate in a hierarchy of roles; typically the incumbents of these roles and offices hold them by virtue of expertise; and he must separate his bureaucratic status from his private or personal status. Universal schooling segregates the population into industrial labor and bureaucratic strata (primarily by means of examination), and also trains the individual to norms and habits appropriate to his role. Especially since World War II, examinations and educational procedures have been extensively standardized across the nation. The compulsory aspect was nationalized during Wilson's tenure, as child labor laws and the culmination of Progressivism in education coincided. Although we will discuss these developments in greater detail in Chapter 10, they are mentioned here to give an idea of how the norms of bureaucracy are instituted throughout our society. The center of our modern nation-state, however, is the presidency. It is to this crucial office that we now turn our attention.

Suggested Further Reading

The best analyses of the modern nation-state are still those of Max Weber; Weber's work is also a good source of relevant historical background on the emergence of the modern state. Not all of his works are translated from the German, but there is an excellent overall interpretation and summary of Weber's writings in:

Reinhard Bendix. *Max Weber: An Intellectual Portrait.* Anchor Books, 1962.

A useful book containing translations of several of Weber's most important essays, and an introduction to his work is:

H. H. Gerth and C. Wright Mills. *From Max Weber: Essays in Sociology.* Oxford University Press, 1949.

An analysis of the modern political system, from which we draw our emphasis upon the "steering" function of the Presidency will be found in:

Karl W. Deutsch. *The Nerves of Government: Models of Political Communication and Control.* The Free Press, 1966.

For a readable, summary history of the emergence of twentieth-century America, see:

Arthur Meier Schlesinger. *The Rise of Modern America, 1865–1951.* Macmillan, 1951.

For an interpretation of modern America, which is different from the one we are presenting, see:

Seymour Martin Lipset. *The First New Nation: The United States in Historical and Comparative Perspective.* Anchor Books, 1967.

A recent analysis of bureaucracy will be found in:

Anthony Downs. *Inside Bureaucracy.* Little, Brown, 1967.

A sweeping study of bureaucracy on a worldwide scale will be found in:

Henry Jacoby. *The Bureaucratization of the World.* University of California Press, 1973.

Scholarly and theoretical interest in modern organizations has concentrated on forms of organization other than bureaucracy. For the most authoritative collection of studies (with extensive bibliographies) on various aspects and topics of organization theory, see:

James G. March, ed. *Handbook of Organizations.* Rand McNally, 1965.

A good, general public administration text (a field of study that has partially separated itself from political science) that relates to this chapter is:

John M. Pfiffner and Robert V. Presthus. *Public Administration.* Ronald Press, 1960.

Finally, for an excellent study placing (philosophical) political theory in the context of modern science and the emerging nation-state see:

Arnold Brecht. *Political Theory: The Foundations of Twentieth-Century Political Thought.* Princeton University Press, 1959.

For history and analysis of the cold war, see:

Warren I. Cohen, "The United States and the Cold War." General Learning Press, 1973.

The concept that the "frontier society of America"—the expansion phenomenon discussed in Part II—reopened after World War II in a new frontier, the "metropolitan-technological frontier" is discussed in:

Daniel J. Elazar, "The Metropolitan Frontier: A Perspective on Change in American Society." General Learning Press, 1973.

Chapter 6
The Bureaucratic Presidency

When President John Kennedy was assassinated in 1963, there was grief among the many who loved and admired him, there was concern among many who saw the event as another instance of a rising tide of violence in the United States, and there was—and still is—a suspicion among some that a wider conspiracy has gone undetected. Some or all of these elements were present when three other presidents were assassinated; but Kennedy's tragic death spurred a reaction that had not followed earlier assassinations: the Twenty-fifth Amendment. In the 1960s, the American nation-state was a fully articulated fact, and two generations of Americans had never known a different form of government. Quite suddenly, the precariousness of the situation confronted responsible persons in and out of public life. If the office of the presidency were to fall vacant, or be inadequately manned, the nation would be in crisis. Steps were taken, then, to constitutionalize a set of procedures designed to assure the continuous incumbency of this now utterly indispensable office.

AMENDMENT XXV
Ratified 1967

Section 1. In case of the removal of the President from office or of his death or resignation, the Vice President shall become President.

Section 2. Whenever there is a vacancy in the office of the Vice President, the President shall nominate a Vice President who shall take office upon confirmation by a majority vote of both Houses of Congress.

Section 3. Whenever the President transmits to the President pro tempore of the Senate and the Speaker of the House of Representatives his written declaration that he is unable to discharge the powers and duties of his office, and until he transmits to them a written declaration to the contrary, such powers and duties shall be discharged by the Vice President as Acting President.

Section 4. Whenever the Vice President and a majority of either the principal officers of the executive departments or of such other body as Congress may by law provide, transmit to the President pro tempore of the Senate and the Speaker of the House of Representatives their written declaration that the President is unable to discharge the powers and duties of his office, the Vice President shall immediately assume the powers and duties of the office as Acting President.

Thereafter, when the President transmits to the President pro tempore of the Senate and the Speaker of the House of Representatives his written declaration that no inability exists, he shall resume the powers and duties of his office unless the Vice President and a majority of either the principal officers of the executive departments or of such other body as Congress may by law provide, transmit within four days to the President pro tempore of the Senate and the Speaker of the House of Representatives their written declaration that the President is unable to discharge the powers and duties of his office. Thereupon Congress shall decide the issue, assembling within forty-eight hours for that purpose if not in session. If the Congress, within twenty-one days after receipt of the latter written declaration, or, if Congress is not in session, within twenty-one days after Congress is required to assemble, determines by two-thirds vote of both Houses that the President is unable to discharge the powers and duties of his office, the Vice President shall continue to discharge the same as Acting President; otherwise, the President shall resume the powers and duties of his office.

The aftermath of the Kennedy assassination casts light upon the changed nature of political representation in America, and the point should stay with us as we examine the details of the presidency: This office is the indispensable *center* of the system.

There is another, even more recent event that must concern us here, troublesome and uncertain as its lessons still are: the "Watergate" investigations and trials which dramatized a permanent danger for the modern nation-state—a danger that Max Weber called "bureaucratic absolutism." (The following account follows very closely Bendix's summary of Weber's argument.)[1]

The same conditions that make bureaucracy the most efficient large-scale organization may also lead to a subversion of the rule of law, transforming the bureaucracy from a *policy-implementing* to a *decision-making* body. Because of their organizational know-how, acquired through day-to-day experience in the bureaucracy, and because their appointments to office typically reflect certified technical knowledge, bureaucratic officials become virtually indispensable to their superiors, and consequently quite powerful. Officials tend to protect and enhance their superior expertise by treating official business as confidential, which makes outside inspection and control quite difficult. Secrecy and concealment, of course, are typical of organizations (governments, political parties, corporations) in contest with hostile organizations, but secrecy in bureaucracy tends to exist even where no such justification makes sense. (Weber found that bureaucracies will even simulate hostile conditions to justify concealment.) Thus, "a bureaucracy that uses its capacity for concealment to escape inspection and control jeopardizes legal domination by usurping . . . decision-making . . . that ideally should result from the political and legislative process."[2] These tendencies in bureaucracy developed into bureaucratic absolutism in the first modernized nation-state, Germany, at the turn of the century:

Bureaucratic absolutism is the consequence of such usurpation as in imperial Germany. . . . the parliament was excluded from participation in the political leadership of the country. The result was a species of 'negative politics' that reduced the parliament's power to the rejection of budgetary authorizations and legislative proposals originating in the administration. Under such circumstances the parliament and the bureaucracy became hostile powers. Officials would give the legislature only the barest minimum of information, because they regarded it as an assembly of impotent grumblers . . . and a drag on efficient operations. In turn, members of the legislature as well as the people at large regarded the bureau-

---

1. Reinhard Bendix, *Max Weber: An Intellectual Portrait* (Anchor Books, 1962), pp. 450–454.
2. Ibid., p. 452.

cracy as a caste of careerists and policemen who treated the people as mere objects . . . political leadership went by the board; appointments, promotions and patronage were handled by the bureaucracy, which had no responsibility to outside authority, while the highest positions of government were filled on the basis of personal connections by capable officials who possessed no trace of political ability. Such men remained in office until some intrigue led to their replacement by men just like themselves. Weber maintained that under bureaucratic absolutism the evils of personal influence and the personal struggle for power that exist under all systems of domination occur in exaggerated form because they are perpetuated behind closed doors and without any possibility of control.[3]

The Watergate affair did not prove decisively that a condition of bureaucratic absolutism exists in the United States, but they certainly dramatized the tendency that is inherent in bureaucracy: the pervasive secrecy and consequent possibility of subversion of the rule of law; the hostile atmosphere between the bureaucracy and the legislature and the bureaucracy and the public; the enormous scope of patronage and promotions drawn inside the White House offices, which is uncontrolled from without; the ousting of highly placed men due to "some intrigue" and their replacement "by men just like themselves." That these problems are inherent in our modern form of representation cannot be ignored. Neither will it do to accept the soothing blandishments of commentators who seemed to find in Watergate a redress of the governmental balance of powers, as though, because of Watergate, Congress had resumed its rightful control over governmental affairs. As we shall see, the very structure of the bureaucratic presidency and the consequent relations of Congress to the bureaucracy render the situation deeply resistant to fundamental change.

Bureaucracy and Power

In a modern, bureaucratic nation-state, day-to-day power is in the hands of administrators. The law is impersonal, and its application upon individual members of the society is continuous. The laws that are and have been passed by

---

3. Ibid., pp. 453–454.

Congress, and the judicial rulings handed down by the courts, are constantly and continuously being applied. Because no other form of administration is as efficient or capable of as great administrative output, the centralized bureaucracy assumes progressively more of the exercise of day-to-day power. In the days of the American republic, the details and specifics of legislation were written in Congress, and the president was charged with the duty of executing laws, which were usually fairly specific. Moreover, the money that would be required to execute the laws was budgeted by Congress. In other words, a great deal of the day-to-day power of the government was effectively exercised by the Congress. But today, in the American nation-state, all such details are handled by the executive branch of government. Typically, Congress will pass broad laws that then are transformed into specific details and budgeted by the executive branch.

With the emergence of centralized, continuous means of mass administration, effective day-to-day power passed into the hands of administrators. With the transformation of the United States into a modern nation-state, the presidency fell heir to this new distribution of power in the society. However, we should not think of this power in the personal terms more characteristic of the republic. The *presidency* is enormously more powerful and salient in the nation-state; the *president,* by contrast, becomes personally less powerful, in an important sense. As Clinton Rossiter has put it, ". . . the office has a kind of prestige that it did not know under Washington and lacked as late as the turn of this century. Washington, after all, lent his prestige to the Presidency, but today quite the reverse process takes place when a man becomes president. He becomes the great figure in our system because the office is the great institution."[4] Not only is the power and prestige of the office conferred upon the individual, rather than the other way around; it is also the case that the power of the presidency inheres in the institution—in the great bureaucracy that comprises it—rather than in the individual who is president. To be sure, the individual who is president enjoys great power as a result of his incumbency, but it is not all of the power of the presidency as such. To see this, let us look at how the presidency exercises the great day-to-day power that it has.

---

4. Clinton Rossiter, *The American Presidency* (Harcourt, Brace & World, 1960), p. 83.

Bureaucracy is a system of control. By integrating a large number of specialized human activities, great organizational output is effected—and the organization can be adapted to many different kinds of human outputs. Essentially, the power of the head of a bureaucratic administrative apparatus is the capacity to *coordinate* the myriad specialized activities of the bureaucrats. The capacity of the head of the apparatus to coordinate these activities is virtually exclusively his own —no one else is in a position to do it—because he has a monopoly on the *reliable* communications required to coordinate all of the activities in the bureaucracy. As we shall see, the power of coordination is tantamount to a monopoly over the society's *expertise,* that peculiar human resource so characteristic of and vital to the modern nation-state.

The analogy of bureaucracy to mass production, which we used in Chapter 5, can now be made more explicit. When we focus on the patterns of communication within bureaucracy, we find in the process of communication the bureaucratic counterpart of the assembly line in mass production. Communications are used to coordinate the outputs of the numerous individuals and functional groups of individuals (subunits of the organization) that comprise the bureaucracy. In the military, for example, it is by means of communications that air attacks are coordinated with (perhaps several) ground attacks, while supplies of the appropriate kinds are delivered to the appropriate places and while, at the same time, the entire military operation is pursued in concert with related diplomatic and political efforts. In other words, communications are necessary to prevent one's own airplanes from bombing one's own troops, or to prevent one's own military from attacking one's ally. Moreover, such communications occur in a *net* that is hierarchically structured. By means of the hierarchy, control over the various elements of the organization is possible: just as the various subunits in the military will be coordinated from a central office, so a particular superior office will coordinate the military and diplomatic operations that are occurring separately. The American nation-state constantly undertakes an enormous variety of tasks and operations, internally and externally and, to the extent that these activities are coordinated, it is by means of communications in a hierarchial net—at the top of which is the president.

Clearly, only the ability to receive from and send to *all* subunits of the bureaucracy would constitute "control" of the bureaucracy. If the total system is functionally differentiated—if the different subunits have specialized tasks and activities—then by definition it is the total system, the subunits in integration, which achieves intended goals. There is no person or single sector of the American nation-state that "put man on the moon," or "produced" the nuclear fission explosion at Hiroshima, Japan. The historical uniqueness of man on the moon or nuclear explosions is due to the emergence of bureaucratic administration, which made possible the coordination of the numerous human and mechanical activities necessary to the production of such relatively prodigious social output. To be sure, other conditions must be present as well, but no amount of wealth or science could produce such outputs without bureaucracy. Being able to produce *part* of what is necessary is not the same as producing the totality. And neither is control over part of the communications net the same as control of the bureaucracy. That is why, for example, a highly placed general officer in the United States Army could not "take over" the country by means of military force. In fact, the military output of the armed forces is possible only in coordination with the educational system of the nation, with numerous specialized industrial organizations, and with numerous other governmental agencies. Control over communications between a specialized part of the nation-state system and the "center" or "top" of the system can serve only limited, probably destructive, purposes.

We see, then, that only the capacity to control all information is the capacity to control bureaucratic output, and we see that a hierarchical communications net places such capacity in the presidency alone. The presidency is thereby in a relatively good position to monopolize expertise in a specialized society such as the United States. It is important to remember that we are describing a modern nation-state characterized by what can be referred to as "assembly lines of information, assembly lines of thoughts."

Just as the typical automobile assembly-line worker cannot make an automobile by himself (his labor is useless unless coordinated from the outside with other people's activities), neither is the specialist an "expert" unless his activities occur in a context coordinated from above such that his activites are a working part of the total system. An experimental physicist, for example, works in a material and intellectual environment replete with "black boxes," as they are called. The "black box" may be (as the term originally developed) a piece of equipment the technical properties of which are not, and need not be, known to the experimenter—even though the equipment functions crucially in his own work. Indeed, expertise and what is usually referred to as "technology" both occur in bureaucratically administered contexts. Technology is not strictly speaking merely material, or physical; generally, technology is the application of science and engineering by means of coordinating scientific and engineering expertise with mechanized and automatic systemic components. Both the humans and the equipment are but parts of a system. Without the other parts of the system they cannot function.

The president gets his power—or, rather, the presidency is the most powerful office in the American nation-state—due to the monopoly that the office has on the means of control of the bureaucracy. That monopoly is the organizationally specific location of communications coordination in the office of the presidency. But the American nation-state is not an ideal, perfect bureaucracy. And thus far, we have described the *formal* properties of bureaucracy as though actual bureaucracies were just like that. In fact, the federal bureaucracy is not nearly the unified, fully rationalized apparatus we have discussed—but it is now more like an ideal bureaucracy than anything else, and this fact explains the unique power of the modern presidency. We must remember this as we turn to a description of the actual structure, which contains many discontinuities from the basic bureaucratic pattern, of the American presidency.

Power and Persuasion in the Presidency

The power of the modern president, as we have seen, is the power to "steer" bureaucracy owing to his monopoly of communications. But it is only in a "perfect" bureaucracy that the head has an actual monopoly over communications. In the case of the American presidency, this potential monopoly is severely attenuated by the breakdown of hierarchy at the cabinet level of administration. The cabinet still consists of the heads, called secretaries, of the several departments of the federal bureaucracy. There are presently eleven of them, and in a proper bureaucracy they might constitute the next-to-highest level of the communications net, with the president as their superior. Indeed, the secretaries do answer to the president, but not in the mode of bureaucrat. As a rule, the heads of the bureaus that make up the departments do not, in fact, respond to the secretaries and undersecretaries as their bureaucratic superiors. The main reason for this state of affairs is that the cabinet is a carryover from the days of the republic, and the secretaries are not fully functional in a modern bureaucracy. The secretaries and most of their immediate subordinates, the undersecretaries, are political appointees, recalling the spoils system of the republic. This does nothing to assure their expertise in the areas administered by their departments (although experts sometimes are appointed), nor does it assure the obedience of the bureau chiefs to these, their nominal superiors. The latter fact is due to the incompatibility of the spoils system with the merit system characteristic of bureaucracy. For the bureaucrat, bureaucracy is a career; his income, expertise, and authority are part and parcel of the administrative apparatus, which is continuous and impersonal. The spoilsman, by contrast, is tied to the personal fortunes of his political patron; it is the person, not the office, to whom the spoilsmen owe their obedience.

There are well over three-hundred bureaus in the executive branch, many with thousands of employees (there are over two-and-one-half million civilian employees in the federal bureaucracy, plus approximately three million military personnel). Obviously, the president could not effectively oversee directly so many bureau chiefs—and neither would the operation of the bureaus be effective without coordination from above. In fact, it was mainly a concern with this problem—known as "span of control"—that led to the major reorganizations of the executive branch and its further bureaucratization. During the first stage of American transformation, the legislative basis for bureaucratic proliferation was laid, and the unprecedented taxation and expenditures necessitated by World War I stimulated bureaucracy's growth. However, a substantial gap between the effective heads of various bureaus and agencies and the president's office soon manifested itself. It was during Franklin Roosevelt's administration, the second stage of the transformation, that decisive action was taken. Roosevelt's Brownlow Committee criticized the huge span of control of the president, finding about one hundred separate agencies "presumably reporting to the President."[5] The committee proposed a sweeping reorganization of the executive branch, arguing that it had to be completely overhauled "and the present 100 agencies reorganized under a few large departments in which every executive authority would find its place."[6] The reorganization that followed was not so streamlined, however, because (among other factors) President Roosevelt had just stirred substantial criticism and hostility in Congress with his "court-packing scheme" (see the next chapter), and Congress intended to limit him. Nevertheless, it was not possible by this time to ignore utterly the analysis of the Brownlow Committee. Basically, the executive branch was already bureaucratized, and Congress as much as any other group or person depended on the effective functioning of that bureaucracy. Congress especially depended upon the bureaucracy for budget preparation—see Chapter 8—and of course, for the execution of laws passed by Congress. Threatened by the crippling chaos of an uncoordinated bureaucracy, and faced with the unequivocal Constitutional instruction that the president execute the laws, there was little choice but to authorize executive reorganization. However, nineteen agencies were exempted from the authority granted to the president to reorganize the executive branch. This practice of limiting reorganization by exempting certain agencies under law has continued through subsequent reorganizations; but again, as we shall see in more detail later, such practices by Congress are limited in their effectiveness, except as they are merely obstructionist.

In September 1939 Roosevelt issued Executive Order 8248, described by the public administration expert, Luther Gulick, as a "nearly unnoticed but none the less epoch-making event in the history of American institutions."[7] This executive order created the Executive Office of the President, a collection of organizations and individuals formally subordinate to the president which, taken together, constitute his means of coordinating the entire bureaucracy. The problem of span of control is partially dealt with, and partially struggled with, in the Executive Office. Reorganized and expanded since 1939, the Executive Office nevertheless remains continuous, comprised largely of specialists of various sorts

---

5. John M. Pfiffner & Robert V. Presthus, *Public Administration* (Ronald Press, 1960), p. 207.
6. Rossiter, *The American Presidency*, p. 129.
7. Quoted in ibid., p. 129.

and personal go-betweens and assistants of the president. The lack of bureaucratic perfection, particularly the still over-large and inconsistent span of control of the president, is "struggled with" in the White House office, which contains the president's personal staff, go-betweens, personal advisors, trouble-shooters, and the like. These persons have a lot to do with the president's role as *persuader*—that slightly unbureaucratic skill that the successful president must command, either personally or through his staff. As we have already indicated, it is the high incidence of bureaucratic discontinuities that necessitates a goodly measure of persuasion on the part of the president. Depending upon how successful he and his personal staff are at acquiring and disseminating the communications that do not flow in a coherent, hierarchical communications net, the president will be more or less successful at realizing the full power of his office.

Entirely too much has been made of an important but definitely incomplete analysis of the presidency that holds, in effect, that such *power* as the president holds is the "power to *persuade.*" Richard Neustadt's useful book, *Presidential Power,* quotes President Truman's prediction about Eisenhower's fate in office: "He'll sit here and he'll say, 'Do this! Do that!' *And nothing will happen.* Poor Ike—it won't be a bit like the army. He'll find it very frustrating."[8]

Analyses of American government frequently cite Neustadt in this respect, and talk about how the president can exercise power mainly by persuading, not commanding. There is something to this, but it ought not to obscure the fact that the president has, if he is capable of exercising it, enormous power. In general, if you walk up to a machine (an automobile, say) and tell it to "go," nothing will happen. You have to know how to operate it, by coordinating several actions; similarly, the bureaucracy will not "work" unless it is properly steered, or coordinated. But the point that must not be overlooked is that *nowhere* but in the office of the presidency is the vast machinery of government and the entire nation-state itself coordinated. The fact that it can, to an extent, "run by itself" even when the president (as often happens) does not know how to run it effectively, may be likened to the fact that there are automobiles that can be driven by people who do not know how to shift gears because the shifting process is automated. Similarly, as we shall discuss fur-

8. Richard Neustadt, *Presidential Power* (Wiley, 1960), p. 9.

ther in this chapter and in Chapter 8, much of the coordinating processes of the office of the presidency are "automated" —they occur as a part of the normal functioning of the bureaucracy—in the activities of the Office of Management and Budget.

The *power* of the presidency is the institutionalized leverage that enables the president and his staff to be relatively successful (even if they are not very good at it) in the role of persuader. We refer now to the more fully bureaucratized agencies and organizations within the Executive Office. At the heart of this bureaucracy is the Bureau of the Budget, now the Office of Management and Budget (OMB), which was created when the administrative tasks associated with budget preparation got well beyond the ability of Congress to cope with them. Located in the Treasury Department in 1921, it was transferred, under Executive Order 8248, to the Executive Office, where it has remained. Here the communications net is classically bureaucratic, and the power thus disposed to the presidency is virtually incalculable. The OMB prepares and administers the budget of the United States of America (the enormity and scope of which requires little discussion), and this is the president's chief means of maintaining executive supremacy. The departments and agencies of the bureaucracy submit budget estimates (i.e., how much money will be required for their existence—employee salaries, and so on—and operations) to the OMB, which reviews them and approves or alters such estimates. In perfect bureaucratic form, the agencies and departments can appeal decisions by the OMB to the president. Requests for budgets also often entail requests for legislation authorizing new programs or new forms of expenditure, which are also reviewed by the OMB.

Now, most legislative reference work is performed by the OMB, including the consultations and clearances with other agencies and departments directly or indirectly concerned with the proposed legislation. Even legislation passed by Congress is reviewed and coordinated with existing and proposed legislation by the OMB, and recommendations for passage or veto—along with veto messages if need be—are prepared and passed along to the president. The OMB also investigates and recommends changes and improvements in management and administrative practices throughout the bureaucracy, determining the need for and rationale of reorganization. As a generalized means of control, the Office of Management and Budget could hardly be improved upon, which accounts for the formalization of the Bureau of the Budget into its fully generalized control function.

The OMB provides the president with the means to coordinate and, thus, steer and control the bureaucracy; but the OMB cannot "direct" itself, which means that the president must (and does) instruct the OMB as to broad policy objectives to be effected by the budget, and with which specialized legislative recommendations it must conform. Not only the White House staff, but several other more specialized agencies of the Executive Office assist the president in formulating feasible, coordinatable policies. The Council of Economic Advisors (CEA) consists of three professional economists selected by the president (with the consent of the Senate) to advise him on broad economic policies. Other agencies (as shown in the figures)—most notably the National Security Council and the Domestic Council—provide further sources of advice and means of planning at the policy level for the president.

Functions of the Presidency

To see clearly the extent to which bureaucratization has centralized power in the presidency, we can compare the performance of presidential functions in the American nation-state with those same functions in the republic. Most discussions of the presidency list six functions, or roles, of the president; we shall continue the practice in order to highlight the shift of power to the executive in the twentieth century.

1. Chief of State. Usually considered of limited significance, this function is nevertheless of considerable interest in terms of political representation. The Articles of Confederation failed to provide for adequate political representation, internally or externally. The Constitution of 1787 provided for "kingless representation," but the presidency fulfilled certain king-like functions for external representation. As the head of state, he could send his agents to negotiate treaties; and he could receive visiting rulers and

Figure 1. The Government of the United States*

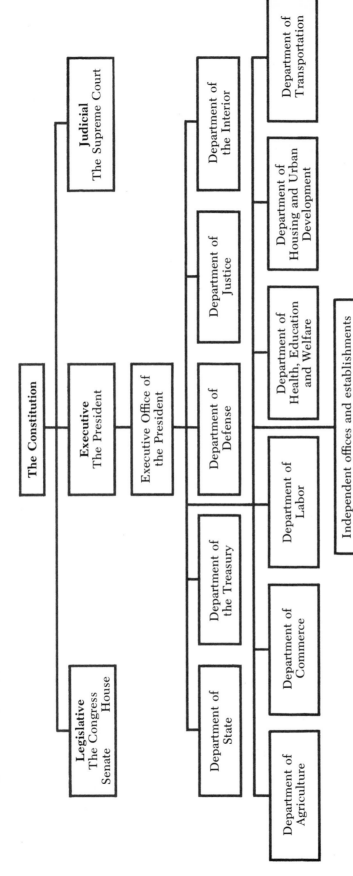

*Adapted from the *United States Government Organization Manual, 1972-73* (U.S. Government Printing Office, 1972), p. 25.

their agents. But constitutionally and in practice, Congress was always at least corepresentative of the United States. The balance of powers was no fiction, and more often than not Congress was the acknowledged representative of the political society.

World War I saw the shift of representative power to an increasingly centralized executive branch—and it also saw the establishment of precedents in the exercise of the president's role as chief of state. Woodrow Wilson was the first of seven presidents to visit Europe while in office, and the first of five to visit England while in office. When abroad, the president (as head of state) ranks with kings (above prime ministers, who are heads of governments, not of states); when at home, as we have mentioned, he enjoys in the era of the nation-state a prestige lacking in the office at the turn of this century. Nowadays, in other words, the president acts out, more or less exclusively, the role of chief of state in a way he could not and did not in the republic. Why this is so becomes clearer when we compare the other functions of the presidency then and now.

2. Chief Executive. The Constitution of 1787 specifies that the president "shall take care that the laws be faithfully executed . . . ." Since the Constitution cannot be read to require that the president personally collect tariffs or to apprehend federal law-breakers and incarcerate them in his basement, we understand this role to be that of administrator, or manager of the processes of law execution. The president has always performed this function, but, as we have already seen, the difference between bureaucratic administration and other means of administration is as night to day. Bureaucratic administration is so much more efficient, predictable (rational), and therefore controllable, that its output is astronomical compared to other means of administration. This great efficiency, centered in the presidency, has a tendency over time to preempt and displace other, competing sources of power. This is true both with respect to the other branches of the national government, as well as to federal-state relations. In the republic, Congress was the great center of power, not least because of its constitutionally granted power to control governmental spending. But to spend is to budget, and complex budgeting requires management. No means of large-scale management can compete with the pres-

Figure 2. Executive Office of the President*

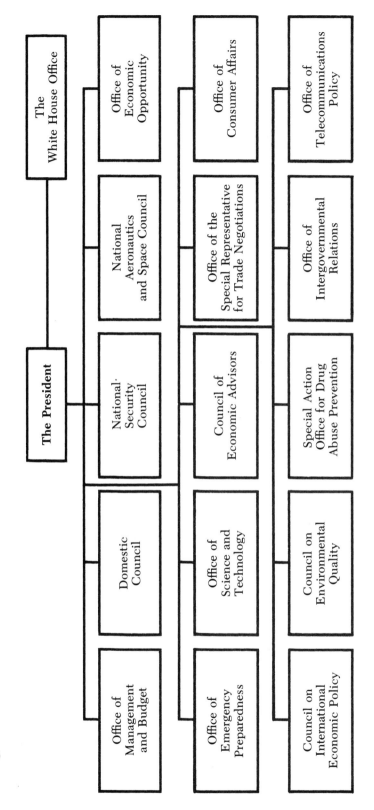

*Adapted from *United States Government Organization Manual, 1972-73*, p. 68

ident's bureaucracy, and it has come to pass that *effective* control of the budget has fallen to the presidency, where the administrative wherewithal to collect and disburse huge amounts of money resides. In the republic, the several states of the Union collected the most taxes, and did the most spending. But with the rise of the federal bureaucracy, and its administrative capacity to tax individual incomes, the states have come more and more to rely upon the national government to provide laws and services they once provided themselves. The states simply cannot match the national government's efficiency and output.

Some political scientists have found in the bureaucratization of the presidency more limitations than enhancements of the president's power to execute the laws. A president's control over his subordinates, so the argument runs, rests on his ability to appoint and remove them at his will. Bureaucratization tends to limit such authority, since appointment is increasingly by competitive examination (controlled by the Civil Service Commission and protected by legislation from presidential overhaul), and removal is permitted only "for cause," limited by strict regulations. Therefore, the president's power is limited because he cannot control many of his subordinates with the power of appointment and removal. There is something to this argument. It directs our attention to the difference in the nature of the power of the bureaucratic presidency—which is impersonal and based in law—from the more personal power of the president in the republic. However, two points are most important: first, the president *does* have appointive and removal powers over most higher positions in the bureaucracy (subject in many instances to consent of the Senate for appointment). Second, and more importantly, the impersonal relationships characteristic of bureaucracy actually confer *more* power on the presidency. For it is the reliability and predictability of the bureaucrats that is the key to the president's power, *not* their personal loyalty to him. After all, among the millions of bureaucrats in the national government, only a very few perform coordinating roles at the level of general policy (and these *are* appointive roles). What is required of bureaucrats is not that they will "obey the president" (who is not their immediate superior anyway), but rather that they will conform to the rules and expectations of their specified roles. They do the president's bidding not by following his direct wishes, but by reliably performing their specialized functions. Their activities are transformed into planned or calculated administrative outputs by the *coordination from above* of all these activities. For example, the war in Asia was an administrative output of the government, and through most of its duration it was a policy opposed, sometimes bitterly, by as much as a majority of the adult population of the nation-state and a majority of Congress. Nevertheless, the president's ability to prosecute the war was not appreciably diminished by this fact, for he did not need to tell millions of people to go fight against the Viet Cong, or the People's Republic of North Vietnam. Rather, he needed to coordinate certain of the activities that you and I performed daily and quite reliably without any notion of whether and/or how such activities contributed to the administrative output, which in that case was the war in Asia. In other words, the president's "inability" to control directly the individual's actions happens also to be the individual's inability to resist the president's policies. The bureaucracy is more like a machine that is steered, than a group of individuals doing the president's bidding. As chief executive, the president's performance of his other functions is dramatically altered by virtue of his ability to steer and coordinate the bureaucracy.

3. Chief Legislator. The president has always had the opportunity to influence legislation, and to instigate it; the Constitution of 1787 empowers the president to give information to the Congress and to "recommend to their consideration such measures as he shall judge necessary and expedient." Coupled with his role as party leader (of which more, below) the president could, in the days of the republic, be the "chief legislator"—if all conditions were right. He would have to enjoy a good popular following, his party would have to be in control of both houses of Congress, and he would have to have good working relations with the majority leadership in both houses of Congress. However, during much of the life of the republic, the president was very far from being "chief legislator." If the president lacked the will and personal qualities, or if his party did not dominate both houses, most legislation originated in Congress, and was sent to him to sign. Often, presidents in the republic would allow a bill to become law without their signature, thus expressing disapproval or noninvolvement while recognizing the likelihood that Congress would override a presidential veto.

It is not like that in the American nation-state. To be sure, the same conditions will affect the *degree of success* of the modern president in his role as chief legislator. If he cannot work effectively with congressional leadership, or if his party is not in control of Congress, then his legislative program—the package of major bills that he wants passed— may face very rough going. However, there is a very important difference between this situation and the one that faced a president in the republic. In the nation-state, almost all of the laws necessary for the day-to-day, continued operation of the country—what we might call the "nuts-and-bolts" laws of the nation—originate and are written in the executive branch. In this respect, the presidency, if not a particular president, is the chief source of legislation in the nation-state. Congress, with its constitutional authority (and responsibility) to authorize and appropriate government expenditures, has in fact become increasingly dependent upon the presidency since 1921, when the Budget and Accounting Act created the Bureau of the Budget and assigned responsibility for preparation of the budget to the president. Today, the president's responsibility and administrative capacity for preparing the budget virtually assures the fact that most legislation will originate in the presidency. Moreover, laws that do originate in Congress and are the special projects of congressmen, if passed and accepted by the president, typically and of necessity will set only broad policies, leaving to the executive branch the task of formulating explicit rules and administrative procedures required to make the policy workable. Thus the president is the chief legislator "coming and going." Because he alone coordinates the complex bureaucratic machinery, which is the day-to-day, rational-legal government, he is relied upon to request the laws and money needed for its continued operation; and where the Congress wishes to achieve a goal of its own, it must rely upon the president to transform this goal into a bureaucratic output.

On the face of things, it might seem that while the presidency controls the "nuts and bolts" of government, the Congress still has the power and wherewithal to produce—or at least have an equal say in—the broad policies and goals that are to be the outputs of the bureaucracy. This soothing notion is unrealistic, for the most part. The problem is that bureaucratization results in an increasing *interdependence* of all phases of social action—a point we will return to again and again, especially in Chapter 8—such that the *formula-*

tion of policies cannot realistically be separated from the *execution* of policies. For example: the budget is not merely a means of financial management for the government. Since it is made up by a process of reviewing and revising a vast number of subsystem budgets submitted by various governmental agencies, the budget is a means (really the only effective means) of evaluating various governmental programs and finding out just what the objectives (particular goals) of these programs are, and how they fit in with all the other programs. Even more importantly, the budget has become the chief means of managing the economy of the nation. Thus everyone in the nation (including, of course, the congressmen) is dependent upon the successful manipulation of economic tendencies by means of budget manipulation. Not unless Congress were coordinating the budget, which it is not, would it be in a position to determine or play a major part in the determination of broad policy.

A final point: we have said that the president and his staff, in order to be very successful in the implementation of his program, must succeed in pressuring and persuading Congress to cooperate. As we shall see, Congress can play a role. However, an important leadership role is virtually impossible for the Congress.

4. Party Leader. The role of party leader has changed very much from what it was in the republic. Indeed, the realities of party organization, democratic participation, and party leadership have been transformed into a curious, almost nightmarish hodge-podge of traditional party mechanisms and bureaucratic organization. What is important here is that the shift of effective power to the executive branch has produced what has been called a "four-party" system. There are two major parties, still, at least in name. But it is quite realistic to describe the party system in terms of competing "presidential parties" (Democratic and Republican), and competing "congressional parties" (Democratic and Republican). The congressional parties—of considerable but diminishing significance—remain state-based, and still operate on the model developed during the republic. Its decreasing significance for national policy is due to the shift of policymaking powers away from Congress and to the loss of a national focus in the presidency. Now, the presidential parties organize and contend for the presidency; increasingly, attention and money is funneled toward the presidential parties.[9]

As was pointed out in the previous chapter, the practice since Franklin Roosevelt's presidency has been to separate the policy-making organization from the traditional vote-getting political organization, the congressional party. Since Roosevelt's time, presidents no longer inherit with their victory the "platform" resulting from compromises and agreements between influential party bosses, Congressmen, and so on. Before long, the vote-getting organization of the presidency also began to separate from the congressional organizations—partly because the traditional patronage schemes were less and less functional, and partly because the centralized organization, the nation-state, demanded a centralized organization to run a centralized campaign.

The campaigns of Dwight Eisenhower achieved some notoriety because of the extensive use of a "Madison Avenue" advertising agency to direct and produce the campaign. John Kennedy's campaign gained notoriety because of the extensive use of modern public opinion polling techniques and tight, centralized campaign organization. And the Watergate hearings revealed the extent to which President Nixon's 1972 campaign was run from a centralized, heavily funded organization that was quite independent of the old fashioned, decentralized organization (the Republican Party) that supposedly was running the show. The president is not the "leader" of his party in the nation-state, he is the sole authority at the head of a centralized, heavily funded organization, the sole purpose of which is to elect the president. The man out of office, seeking the presidency, is also the sole leader of such an organization, except that his is not usually so well-funded, and never so powerfully augmented by the bureaucracy.

5. Commander in Chief. The Constitution makes the president "Commander in Chief of the army and navy of the United States, and of the militia of the several States, when called into the actual service of the United States . . . . " In effect, the president is commander in chief of the armed forces, when he has any. The Constitution's language (see also relevant provisions under Article I, Section 8) clearly

9. For development of this distinction, see James MacGregor Burns, *The Deadlock of Democracy* (Prentice-Hall, 1963).

anticipated that the states would maintain and supply troops when required by the national government, and that armies raised by Congress would be for emergencies, and for short duration. By and large, this is the way things worked in the American republic. The president had a (small) navy at his disposal to employ where diplomacy required, but he neither made war, nor did he command a standing army. But with the transformation of America into a nation-state, the situation has been different, to say the least. America's participation in World War I had laid the basis for nation-state military policies (including the ongoing capability of military output), and World War II sealed the pattern.

Bureaucracy is a permanent, continuous institution. Thus a policy of preparedness now is a permanent institutional fact. The United States maintains millions of men in arms; airplanes and submarines armed with nuclear weapons are deployed on a continuous basis; missile detection and launching systems are also continuously maintained in readiness. Moreover, every male in the nation-state is registered and classified according to his military potential and readiness. The power to coordinate and activate this vast, practically unlimited military potential is exclusively the president's. Harry Truman, long-time United States senator and then Franklin Roosevelt's vice president, did not learn about the existence of the atomic bomb project until he was sworn in after Roosevelt's death.

It is probably easier to see the effects of bureaucratization upon the "balance of power" arrangement in the case of the commander in chief than in any other role of the president, although the effects are similar in the other roles as well. In the republic, the role of commander in chief was limited, contingent upon the decisions of Congress; in the nation-state, the power of the commander in chief is practically unlimited, while Congress (and everyone else) must defer to his decisions.

6. Chief Diplomat. The role of chief diplomat is, basically, the role of external representation. This has always been the important function of the presidency, and it very early on in the years of the republic established the relative independence of the executive branch from the legislative branch. The president sends ambassadors as his agents, and he receives the agents of other governments, thereby establishing formal communications with other political societies (or, should he so choose, refusing such communication). He and his agents negotiate treaties (which must be ratified by the Senate), and he also negotiates executive agreements (often just as important and binding as treaties) that require no such ratification.

Today, of course, the president's role as chief diplomat is much, much stronger than it was during the republic. No longer is he much limited by Congress or the people. As commander in chief, he has at his disposal immense military means that he can readily deploy—the instance of the war in Indochina is a clear example. His powers of diplomacy, once limited by the necessity of gaining the consent and cooperation of a Congress and a people historically reluctant to engage in "foreign wars," are now augmented by his ability to apply almost unlimited military pressure to achieve his diplomatic ends. Similarly, he can manipulate the economic activities of the nation-state substantially on his own, with important implications for diplomacy. For example, even a Congress that had made a cause of eliminating foreign aid expenditure could not prevent President Kennedy from disbursing billions of dollars held "in the pipeline" from previous appropriations. Neither could a Congress appropriating billions prevent President Nixon from "impounding" those funds. Because the bureaucracy is continuous, monies are budgeted and held in complex formulas permitting great leeway over time to the office coordinating the entire apparatus.

Thus far we have emphasized strongly the centralized character of the nation-state, and the commensurate power that has been added to the presidency. The key to the president's power is his ability, by virtue of his position in the hierarchy of bureaucracy, to coordinate or "steer" the system of "assembly lines" of thoughts and actions that make up the nation-state. But we have emphasized this characteristic of the nation-state at the cost of ignoring important limitations and problems in its operation. These problems constitute fundamental dilemmas and pose fundamental challenges. We shall outline some of the main ones.

The Ghost of the Republic in the Machine

We have already mentioned that the executive branch is

not an ideal bureaucracy. Of course, nobody and nothing is "perfect," but the main reason that the bureaucracy is not a better, more workable one than it is, is the history of resistance from the legislative branch of the government. Unfortunately, there is no really satisfactory middle ground between bureaucratic performance and some other system of administration. When Congress tries to "limit" the president's power, or when it tries to retain power for itself, the result is inefficiency and mismanagement more than anything else. And not infrequently, appalling corruption breeds in these administrative no man's lands created by Congressional interference with the bureaucracy. As we shall see presently, the problem of "democratic" control over the bureaucracy is one of the dilemmas of the American nation-state.

There are a number of so-called "independent agencies" in the bureaucracy, but most of them are not independent of presidential control. Like any other agency, they are formally and practically responsible to the president, and contained in the communications net, or hierarchy; they are "independent" of the executive departments—they do not report to department secretaries—usually for good administrative reasons. However, the independent regulatory commissions *are* substantially independent of the president.

The problem is that the independent regulatory commissions are patterned on a model developed in the American republic, and do not fit the realities of the nation-state. The first one established was the Interstate Commerce Commission (ICC), created during Cleveland's presidency in 1887. This was the republic's first attempt to solve one of the worst problems of the new industrial age, the problem of railroad rates. So dependent was the nation's economy (in those pre-truck days) upon the railroads that a few powerful railroad owners could mercilessly exploit their crucial advantage. When the Supreme Court declared that states could not regulate rates on trains that delivered goods outside the states' borders (as seventy-five percent did), the problem fell, of necessity, to the Congress. The ICC was established to review rates and, when unfair practices were discovered, to prosecute the railroads in the federal courts. This did not work very well, for the Supreme Court usually found in favor of the railroads. During the early 1900s, under Theodore Roosevelt and then under Taft, the ICC's authority was extended, allowing that body to lower rates found to be unfair (subject to Supreme Court review). Then in 1914, as part of Wilson's "triple assault on privilege," the Federal Trade Commission was established and empowered to order businesses in interstate commerce to cease "unfair methods of competition" such as monopolization.

The independent, continuous status of these quasi-judicial agencies made perfectly good sense in the republic. Experience and foresight commended the national technique as the best hope of governmental regulation where state regulation was unconstitutional or impractical. It was a means of filling in that "no man's land" between federal and state law where unfair, injurious practices flourished in industrial America. But in the centralized, bureaucratized nation-state, where (theoretically) no such "no man's land" between federal and state exists, the independent regulatory agencies are anachronisms that actually perpetuate the very situation they originally were to eliminate. For now, they become sanctuaries beyond the effective reach of the regular bureaucracy, where special interests flourish. Because of the president's extensive control of the major bureaucracy, the independent regulatory agencies are not exactly utterly free; but still, the situation is a discontinuity that occasionally raises serious problems.

Table 1. The Independent Regulatory Commissions

      Civil Aeronautics Board
      Federal Communications Commission
      Federal Maritime Commission
      Federal Power Commission
      Federal Reserve Board
      Federal Trade Commission
      Interstate Commerce Commission
      National Labor Relations Board
      Securities and Exchange Commission

The independent regulatory commissions are headed by boards (commissions) of five or seven members (except ICC), appointed by the president for set, staggered terms (with Senate approval), usually five or seven years. The commissions head large, bureaucratically structured organizations within the executive. The Interstate Commerce Commission serves as an example, see page 157.

To a lesser degree, the same sort of situation may develop on an informal basis when an older governmental bureau is exempted from the general reorganizing power of the executive branch by special acts of Congress. Usually these arrangements involve a committee or subcommittee of one of the houses of Congress, a bureau that is closely tied to the committee's area, and special-interest lobbyists. These special-interest arrangements are decidedly unbureaucratic insofar as they bypass normal hierarchy, and they can be disruptive of bureaucratic functioning. However, as we shall see in Chapter 8 (where the occurrence and operation of such so-called "sub-governments" are discussed), it is still the presidency that coordinates these extra-normal arrangements, insofar as they are coordinated at all.

These "ghosts of the Republic"—carry-overs from a different kind of "machine," the spoils machine of the old party bosses—are not usually particularly edifying in their own right. But the problems they create go beyond the question whether it is "fair" or good for special interests to have special nooks and crannies in the bureaucracy wherein to pursue their own goals. The problem is that the national government *is* a bureaucracy, and it *does* function by virtue of bureaucratic procedures, especially including the existence of a reliable communications hierarchy. The emergence of the president's personal staff, the White House staff, is partly in line with standard bureaucratic practice (as a means of diminishing the span of control of the president), but in large part the president's staff will consist of persuaders, go-betweens, and "lobbyist-types" who will help, it is hoped, to narrow the gap between the normal bureaucracy and the various discontinuities we have described. What with cabinet members who do not "really" head their departments (actually, some do, some do not), independent commissions, and maverick bureaus, a good deal of informal communication is required to coordinate a coherent program. The trouble is, with so much informal communication going on as a matter of course, that communications "leaks" have become quite common, and bureaucratic reliability is considerably reduced. Moreover, something like the appalling Watergate scandal occurs largely in the interstices of these informal communications nets and the bureaucracy proper.

Bureaucracy in a Democracy

This brings us to a crucial dilemma for the American

nation-state. Most of us are accustomed to identifying with the United States—that is, we consider ourselves citizens of the most powerful country in the world, the richest, and so on. Many of us do not like the *priorities* set by some of our political leaders—we would rather have more hospitals, poverty programs, and the like, instead of more missiles, more moon shots, and so on. (Others, of course, *do* like our priorities.) Still we identify with the *power,* with the capability for output, which is the American nation-state. The problem is, how can we maintain and improve this capacity for output—military, economic, scientific, or whatever—without *decreasing* our own power to control and influence the government's actions? We shall consider this problem at the level of Congressional control in Chapter 8 and at the level of citizen participation in Chapter 9. Here, we must note that limitations on the control capabilities of the presidency serve mainly to undermine or inhibit the efficiency of the government—they do not return effective power to Congress, or to the people. Again, this is because of the assembly-line effect of bureaucracy: either it is all working together, or it is not working at all.

Does this then mean that the presidency is a threat to our democracy? Once the awesome power of the presidency became apparent with Franklin Roosevelt's administration, people began to worry. They worried about the way one man could so dominate Congress; they worried about the way one man could so consolidate his power (he was elected four times to the presidency!); and they worried at the implacable efficiency with which an income tax could be converted quite suddenly (during World War II) from a "rich man's tax" to one that reached the majority of workers. Such worries are not irresponsible, but they do not add up to dictatorship. The concerns are not silly or irresponsible because—especially for anyone whose life experience was shaped prior to the world wars—bureaucratization must seem to erode individual autonomy substantially. Things that had once been nobody's business but your own were now monitored and regulated by a centrally controlled government. However—and this is the crucial point—the power of the central government is not *personal* in a bureaucratized society. Indeed, much of the personal power of the president is an illusion of sorts. We *project* a personality upon a situation, which is, in fact, quite impersonal (that is, we "see" fully human, rational motives behind what happens to us "at the hands"

Figure 3. Interstate Commerce Commission Organization Chart

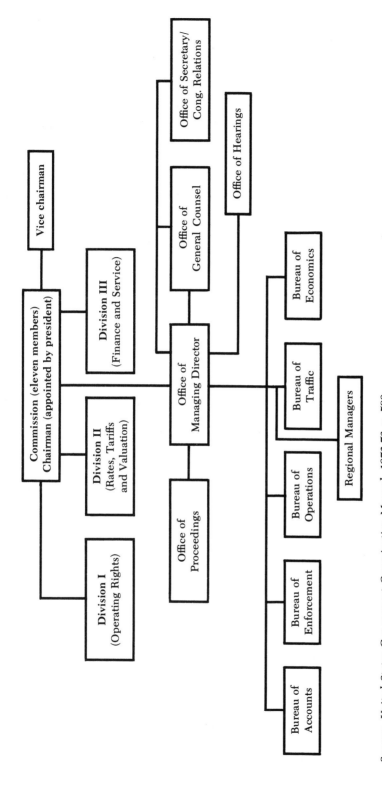

Source: *United States Government Organization Manual, 1972-73*, p. 590

of the government), because we are human and tend naturally to find human motives in others. Of course, others, including the president, *do* have human motives; but the output
of bureaucracy is not so straightforward. Remember, we
would never think of a man on the assembly line of an automobile factory as personally building an automobile;
depending upon his particular task, he may not even know
what model of car he is "building," or helping to build.
Even more to the point, the output of his personal labor may
be coordinated and recoordinated down the line so that he
is participating in the building of several different models
of automobiles. It is like that for the bureaucrat: what he
is doing has to do with governmental output, but he may
have no idea of just how. Such a situation is possible where
people obey impersonal rules, and are obedient to offices,
not men. In this sense, bureaucracy limits the ambitions of
a man who would enjoy the personal power of the dictator
as much as it limits the personal autonomy of the individual
citizen.

The second level of concern about dictatorship is much
more complicated, subtle, and ominous. Because our historical emphasis on World War II is generally (and naturally)
upon our victory over the Axis powers, and consequently
about how "evil" they were and how, thanks to the Allied
victory, that evil has at least temporarily been overcome, we
do not often reflect on the fact that it is the American nation-
state, after all, which has inherited the role of "superstate"—
and that we may have inherited the very problems we were
combating. The problem with arguing that bureaucracy
tends to limit personal, dictatorial power (and therefore, by
implication, that is not a pressing worry for us), is that the
most highly bureaucratized political society in the world at
the turn of this century, Germany, produced first an expan-
sive, imperial power dominated by "bureaucratic absolutism," and then, with Hitler, a highly personalized, dictatorial regime. We are not trying to assert a simplistic version
of the idea that "history repeats itself," but only to point out
that, apparently, circumstances can occur in a highly bureaucratized society that permit the emergence of a dictatorial regime based not on the rule of law, but on charisma, the personal appeal of the leader. Unfortunately, this fact has not
been explained adequately by anybody; and yet, for students
of American government (given its extensive bureaucratization) and for citizens of nation-states, it is a fact that needs

to be understood. It is significant that for Max Weber, the greatest student of bureaucracy, the possibility of the emergence of a charismatic leader was associated with advanced bureaucratization. Weber did not live to see the rise of Hitler, but he had already speculated that a highly bureaucratized society would produce strains upon the individual, who would still, being human, yearn for the personal meaning in his role that increasingly is absent in bureaucracy. Under such circumstances, the highly personalized claim to authority may have overwhelming appeal. The tendency to respond to a charismatic leader in a bureaucratized society may be activated if the system becomes uncoordinated, if *disintegration* occurs as the result of any one of several different causes. People in a bureaucratized society, after all, have an enormous stake in the coordination of the system, without which they are bereft of order. If disintegration threatens, people in such a society may turn to the charismatic leader who offers an alternative source of order. That is the grave danger.

Suggested Further Reading

In this chapter we have emphasized the structural characteristics of the presidency which, we believe, go farthest toward explaining American government. But—for reasons to which we have alluded—there is a very strong tendency among citizens and professional students of the presidency to emphasize the personal attributes of the presidency. Among the most representative examples are the following.

James David Barber. *The Presidential Character: Predicting Performance in the White House.* Prentice-Hall, 1972.

Edward S. Corwin. *The President: Office and Powers, 1787–1957.* New York University Press, 1957.

Richard E. Neustadt. *Presidential Power: The Politics of Leadership.* Wiley, 1960.

Clinton Rossiter. *The American Presidency.* Harcourt Brace, Jovanovich, 1960.

A good anthology on the presidency, which brings together various approaches and relevant considerations is:

Aaron Wildavsky, ed. *The Presidency.* Little, Brown, 1969.

A specialized study on one aspect of the presidency is contained in:

Richard F. Fenno. *The President's Cabinet.* Vintage Books, 1959.

For further understanding of the truly impersonal nature of large-scale, bureaucratic administration, as well as a discussion of the management technique currently most favored in the presidency and federal bureaucracy, see:

Fremont J. Lyden and Ernest G. Miller. *Planning, Programming, Budgeting: A Systems Approach to Management.* Markham, 1968.

A preliminary account of the possibly beneficial effects of Watergate on the presidency and the federal bureaucracy will be found in:

Arthur M. Schlesinger, Jr. "The Runaway Presidency," *Atlantic Monthly.* September 1973.

Since voting is so closely associated in many people's minds with voting in national elections, it might be useful in this connection to consult:

Nelson W. Polsby and Aaron Wildavsky. *Presidential Elections: Strategies of American Electoral Politics.* Scribner's, 1968.

For a discussion of the problems associated with the "imperfect" presidential bureaucracy, see:

Morton H. Halperin, "The Role of the Military in the Formation and Execution of National Security Policy." General Learning Press, 1973.

A survey and discussion of governmental promotion of and participation in "the private sector"—business activities—that goes beyond the extensive regulatory activities of the government is:

James W. McKie, "Government Policies to Control and Assist Private Business." General Learning Press, 1972.

An explicit and informative discussion of the nature of modern administrative control systems—and how they differ from age-old systems of direct command, is:

Judith A. Merkle, "Command and Control: The Social Implication of Nuclear Defense." General Learning Press, 1971.

And, finally, a goldmine of factual information on all the presidents from Washington to Nixon is:

Tim Taylor. *The Book of Presidents.* Arno, 1972.

Chapter 7
The Struggle for Legal Domination

The United States always has been a political society under the rule of law. However, just as the problem of democracy has changed with the shift from the necessarily limited power of checks-and-balances government to potentially unlimited, centralized governmental power, so has the character and meaning of "the rule of law" changed.

During the formative period of the republic before the Civil War, the federal courts were often the instruments of national ruling power, as well as the object of disputes between those who objected to national ruling power and the proponents of such power. But, in the fully articulated republic, the courts were very much a part of the checks-and-balances system that *limited,* as well as constituted, the exercise of national ruling power.

With the advent of the mechanisms of the modern nation-state in America (full, central taxing powers; large, centrally directed military forces; centrally directed, rational administrative organization), the courts inexorably were drawn back into a unified sphere of ruling power, becoming once again primarily the instruments of national ruling power.

The change is surprising because the separation of powers in the republic was well established and extremely stable, and one imagines that a public accustomed to the rule of law would not lightly have assented to a fundamental alteration of the system. The explanation for its occurrence emerges from factors we have already considered in our discussion of the transformation of America.

As we have seen, the confluence of developments peculiar to the republic and developments in the European nation-states produced the transformation of America. In the case of the courts and the American system of law, the consequences of certain of these developments generally were unanticipated. Indeed, the key issue was the question of the separation of governmental powers. When this issue was sharply in focus, the question more specifically was that of the *delegation* by Congress of *legislative* ruling powers—rule-making powers—to the president, or the executive branch of government. However, the issue was not always sharply in focus. Like two minds battling to occupy the same body, the politics of the republic and the politics of the nation-state swirled at once over the vast continent. Even with the benefit of hindsight, it is not easy for us to penetrate the disputes over claims to authority that arose in these times. Still, we now are able to separate these issues in a way that the principal participants in the transformation could not.

The "What" and the "How" of Ruling Power In the Nation-State

World War I brought America into full, nationalized conflict with some European nation-states. Inevitably, this contact with other forms of political representation, and the adaptation that followed, had consequences for America's internal disputes. In the 1890s, the cause of "radicalism" was, if feared by conservatives, nevertheless regarded as thoroughly American. In Kansas, the Populist Mary E. Lease shouted to huge audiences, "Our laws are the output of a system which clothes rascals in robes and honesty in rags." And in the East the conservative New York *Evening Post* replied, "We don't want any more states until we can civilize Kansas."[1] But after World War I, such talk as Mary Lease's immediately gave rise to the charge of "foreign doctrines." Foreigners were actually deported to newly Communist Russia; immigrants were executed on flimsy evidence as "anarchist reds," socialists were expelled from the New York legislature, and, in general, thoroughly American causes of radical economic politics were associated with the new Soviet threat to America's external security. Thus the question of

1. Arthur Meier Schlesinger, *Political and Social Growth of the American People, 1865–1940* (Macmillan, 1941), p. 228.

how America had participated successfully in the battle of nation-states that was World War I was altered to become the question of *what* America "stood for." Using war powers still technically in effect (though the war was over), Attorney General Mitchell Palmer secured court injunctions to stop United Mine Workers' strikes, and to reestablish "normalcy." Congress passed laws restoring railroads to private ownership under new, centralized organizing principles learned during government operation in wartime. As long as "private industry" was being benefited, the moves were deemed commensurate with the necessity to resist the dark forces of socialism and communism that seemed to threaten from without. The fact that the government was participating in the organization of the economy in unprecedented ways was not the center of the controversies. *What* the government did seemed important, not *how*.

The Depression and Roosevelt's New Deal reactivated these controversies, and once again the "what" tended to outweigh the "how." If Roosevelt had the backing of the near-desperate masses, he certainly was not popular with the business world. During the 1936 campaign the Hearst press ran this grim ditty, which reflected the fears of many:

> *The Red New Deal with a Soviet seal*
>
> *Endorsed by a Moscow hand,*
>
> *The strange result of an alien cult*
>
> *In a liberty-loving land.*[2]

Everywhere, the great controversy seemed to be whether the government could and should regulate the economic life of the nation. Roosevelt, of course, was in the process of doing just that, much to the dismay of many businessmen and conservatives, whose ace-in-the-hole was the Supreme Court, that lingering symbol of the republic and the system of checks and balances. Ironically, the Supreme Court did identify the key issue concerning the transformation of the United States, but the people and even the justices themselves managed to lose track of it in the hotter dispute over government control of the economy.

The real issue—which is very difficult to separate from the issue of government control of the economy—is that of separation of powers, particularly the delegation of law-mak-

---

2. Ibid., p. 565.

ing power to the executive. The reason it is difficult to separate this latter issue from the question of governmental control of the economy is that such *control (probably) could not be achieved by any means other than bureaucratic administration.* Certainly the kind of complete, positive control of the economy we know today could only be achieved through bureaucratic administration. And efficient bureaucratic administration inevitably involves centralization of effective control, which means the *de facto* delegation of law-making power to the executive.

A fine example of how the issue of delegation of power was identified but later lost is afforded by the Supreme Court decision in the case of *Schechter Poultry Corporation* v. *United States* (1935). In this decision, the Court found unconstitutional practically all of Roosevelt's "New Deal"—his National Industrial Recovery Act designed to deal with the Depression and put the nation's economy under positive governmental control. (Indeed, the Schechter decision set the stage for the famous battle between Roosevelt and the Supreme Court, which we shall discuss presently.)

In finding the National Industrial Recovery Act (NIRA) unconstitutional, the Court actually based its ruling on two separate considerations: [1] the constitutionality of the delegation of legislative power to the president; and [2] the constitutionality of the regulation of commerce by Congress. Given the recurring "Red scares" of the times, it is not surprising that the latter question was foremost in people's minds; but while the ruling on the constitutionality of economic regulation was just another in a long series of opinions hostile toward an expansion of the meaning of the interstate commerce clause in the Constitution, the ruling on delegation of powers was one of two 1935 cases (*Schechter* and *Panama,* below) in which laws were first declared unconstitutional on such grounds. Finding that the discretion of the president was, under the NRA, "vitually unfettered," the Court declared that this "delegation run riot" was an unconstitutional delegation of legislative power to the president.

The National Industrial Recovery Act
Signed in 1933, during the "Hundred Days"

A national emergency productive of widespread unemployment and disorganization of industry . . . is hereby declared to exist. It is hereby declared to be the policy of Congress to remove obstructions to the free flow of interstate and foreign commerce which tend to diminish the amount thereof; and to provide for the general welfare by promoting the organization of industry for the purpose of cooperative action among trade groups, to induce and maintain united action of labor and management under adequate governmental sanctions and supervision, to eliminate unfair competitive practices, to promote the fullest possible utilization of the present productive capacity of industries, to avoid undue restriction of production . . . , to increase the consumption of industrial and agricultural products by increasing purchasing power, to reduce and relieve unemployment, to improve standards of labor, and otherwise to rehabilitate industry and to conserve natural resources.

[The Act then established the National Recovery Administration and empowered the President to promote industry-wide agreements in about five hundred industrial fields, affecting about twenty-two million workers. These agreements were to occur in the form of "codes of fair competition" to be proposed by trade associations and approved by the President by executive order. The President was given broad discretionary powers "to effectuate the policy" of the Act.]

Schechter Poultry Corporation v. United States — 1935

[A New York poultry dealer challenged his conviction for violating the "Live Poultry Code" effectuated by Roosevelt's executive order. The Circuit Court of Appeals sustained the conviction for one of the provisions of the code, and reversed the conviction for the other violated provisions. Accordingly both Schechter and the government sought review by the Supreme Court.]

Mr. Chief Justice Hughes delivered the opinion of the Court . . . .

First . . . . Extraordinary conditions do not create or enlarge constitutional power . . . . assertions of extra-constitutional authority were anticipated and precluded by the explicit terms of the Tenth Amendment . . . .

. . . the statutory plan . . . involves the coercive exercise of the law-making power. The codes of fair competition, which the statute attempts to authorize, are codes of laws. If valid, they place all persons within their reach under the obligation of positive law . . . .

Second. The question of the delegation of legislative power. . . .

The Congress is not permitted to abdicate or to transfer to others the essential legislative functions with which it is thus vested. We have repeatedly recognized the necessity of adapting legislation to complex conditions involving a host of details with which the national legislature cannot deal directly . . . . the Constitution has never been regarded as denying to Congress the . . . flexibility . . . which will enable it to perform its function in laying down policies and establishing standards, while leaving to selected instrumentalities the making of subordinate rules within prescribed limits . . . . But . . . the constant recognition of the necessity and validity of such provisions, and the wide range of administrative authority which has been developed by means of them, cannot be allowed to obscure the limitations of the authority to delegate, if our constitutional system is to be maintained . . . .

. . . Section 3 of the Recovery Act is without precedent. It supplies no standards for any trade, industry or activity. It does not undertake to prescribe rules of conduct . . . . Instead . . . , it authorizes the making of codes to prescribe them. For that legislative undertaking, section 3 sets up no standards, aside from the statement of the general aims of rehabilitation, correction and expansion described in section one. In view of the scope of that broad declaration, and of the nature of the few restrictions that are imposed, the discretion of the President in approving or prescribing codes, and thus enacting laws . . . , is virtually unfettered. We think that the code-making authority thus conferred is an unconstitutional delegation of legislative power.

Third. The question of the application of the provisions of the Live Poultry Code to intrastate transactions.

[Here the Court delivers a long opinion denying the constitutionality of a broad application of the interstate commerce clause. We include a few lines, to indicate why so much attention was focused on this part of the decision.]

It is not the province of the Court to consider the economic advantages or disadvantages of such a centralized system. It is sufficient to say that the Federal Constitution does not provide for it. . . . Stress is laid upon the great importance of maintaining wage distributions . . . (for expanding commercial activity). Without in any way disparaging this motive, it is enough to say that the recuperative efforts of the federal government must be made in a manner consistent with the authority granted by the Constitution . . . .

Mr. Justice Cardozo, concurring . . . .

The delegated power of legislation which has found expression in this code is not canalized within banks that keep it from overflowing. It is unconfined and vagrant . . . .

. . . here in effect is a roving commission to inquire into evils and upon discovery of them correct them.

. . . If codes of fair competition are codes eliminating "unfair" methods of competition . . . , there is no unlawful delegation of legislative functions when the President is directed to inquire into such practices . . . . For many years a like power has been committed to the Federal Trade Commission with the approval of this court . . . .

But there is another conception of codes of fair competition . . . that is struggling now for recognition and acceptance. By this other conception a code is not to be restricted to the elimination of business practices that would be characterized by general acceptation as oppressive or unfair. It is to include whatever ordinances may be desirable or helpful for the wellbeing or prosperity of the industry affected. In that view, the function of its adoption is not merely negative, but positive; the planning of improvements as well as the extirpation of abuses . . . . If that conception shall prevail, anything that Congress may do . . . for the betterment of business may be done by the President upon the recommendation of a trade association by calling it a code. This is delegation running riot.

[Again, Cardozo goes on to argue that even if Congress itself had adopted this code, it would still be unconstitutional as a violation of the limits of the commerce clause.]

Since all of the justices agreed that the government was regulating commerce beyond the scope of authority permitted by the Constitution, the question of unlawful delegation of powers to the president seemed of secondary importance. But, for our analysis, delegation is the question of prime importance.

The most helpful analysis in this connection is to be found in the concurring opinion[3] of Justice Cardozo (see above). Justice Cardozo argued that there is a difference between the delegation of a "negative" power and that of a "positive" one. It is one thing, he suggests, to empower the executive branch to police specified, "unfair" competition practices. In effect, the president is empowered to seek out instances of, say, price-fixing, and when he finds them, he may take (prescribed) steps to eliminate them. But it is a different thing to empower the executive branch to do whatever would enhance or promote competitive pricing because the options for rule-making thus opened up are practically un-

---

3. A concurring opinion is one that agrees with the final decision of the majority, but is sufficiently different from those expressed in the majority opinion to justify a separate statement of reasons.

limited. By simple analogy, it is one thing for the policeman on the corner to have the power to stop you from doing certain specified things; if he sees someone doing X, Y, or Z, he may apprehend that person. But it is quite another thing to empower that policeman to make certain that everyone is engaged in productive activities; for then the policeman could—indeed, he would have to—decide what you should be doing, instead of just letting you do whatever you like as long as it is not X, Y, or Z.

Cardozo also made a related and quite important point in his opinion. Admitting that under complex and shifting conditions it may be necessary to let the executive decide when the provisions of an act of Congress should actually be applied, Cardozo employed the metaphor of delegated powers running through a canal. It is permissible to delegate powers to the executive if such powers are "canalized," that is, the source of the power is clearly the Congress, and the object of the power is picked by Congress. Thus the delegated authority flows from Congress through the executive, in the "canal" constructed by Congress and to the object of regulation specified by Congress. Cardozo had dissented from another Court decision *Panama Refining Company* v. *Ryan* (see below), which had declared a law unconstitutional for reasons of unlawful delegation of power. In that case, Cardozo thought, the act *had* "canalized" the power to be exercised by the president.

National Industrial Recovery Act, Title I, Section 9 (c)

The President is authorized to prohibit the transportation in interstate and foreign commerce of petroleum and the products thereof produced or withdrawn from storage in excess of the amount permitted to be produced or withdrawn from storage by any State law or valid regulation or order prescribed thereunder, by any board, commission, officer, or other duly authorized agency of a State. Any violation of any order of the President issued under the provisions of this sub-section shall be punishable by fine . . . or imprisonment . . . or both.

Panama Refining Company v. Ryan—1935

[*The Panama Co. appealed a conviction for violating the president's executive order prohibiting the transportation of "hot oil"—*

oil exceeding state allowances—pursuant to Section 9(c) of Title I of the NRA.]

[Chief Justice Hughes delivered the opinion of the Court.]

. . . Section 9(c) is assailed upon the ground that it is an unconstitutional delegation of legislative power. . . . Assuming . . . the Congress has power to interdict the transportation of that excess . . . , the question whether that transportation shall be prohibited by law is obviously one of legislative policy. Accordingly, we look to the statute to see whether the Congress has declared a policy with respect to that subject; whether the Congress has set up a standard for the President's action; whether the Congress has required any finding by the President in the exercise of the authority to enact the prohibition.

. . . Section 9(c) does not state whether or in what circumstances or under what conditions the President is to prohibit the transportation of the amount of petroleum . . . in excess of the state's permission. . . . So far as this section is concerned, it gives to the President an unlimited authority to determine the policy and to lay down the prohibition, or not to lay it down, as he may see fit. And disobedience to his order is made a crime . . . .

[Neither does the larger context afford adequate guidance for the President's actions, according to the majority opinion.]

. . . The Congress left the matter to the President without standard or rule, to be dealt with as he pleased. The effort by ingenious and diligent construction to supply a criterion still permits such a breadth of authorized action as essentially to commit to the President the functions of a Legislature rather than those of an executive or administrative officer executing a declared legislative policy.

. . . The point is not one of motives, but of constitutional authority, for which the best of motives is not a substitute . . . .

We are not dealing with action which, appropriately belonging to the executive province, is not the subject of judicial review . . . . To repeat, we are concerned with the question of the delegation of legislative power. . . .

We see no escape from the conclusion that the Executive Orders . . . and the Regulations issued by the Secretary of the Interior thereunder, are without constitutional authority.

Circuit Court reversed.

Mr. Justice Cardozo, dissenting . . . .

I am unable to assent to the conclusion that Section 9(c) . . . delegating to the President a very different power from any that is involved in the regulation of production or in the promulgation of a code, is to be nullified upon the ground that his discretion is too broad . . . . My point of difference with the majority of the court is narrow. I concede that to uphold the delegation there is need to discover in the terms of the act a standard reasonably clear whereby discretion must be governed. I deny that such a standard is lacking . . . when the act with all its reasonable implications is considered as a whole. What the standard is becomes the pivotal inquiry.

. . . In the laying of his interdict he is to confine himself to a particular commodity, and to that commodity when produced or withdrawn in contravention of the policy and statutes of the state. He has choice, though within limits, as to the occasion, but none whatever as to the means. The means have been prescribed by Congress.

. . . . I am persuaded that a reference . . . to the policy of Congress as declared in Section 1 is a sufficient definition of a standard to make the statute valid. Discretion is not unconfined and vagrant. It is canalized within banks that keep it from over-flowing. . . .

There is no fear that the nation will drift from its ancient moorings as the result of the narrow delegation of power permitted in this section. . . .

Almost forty years after these decisions, we can look back and separate the question of delegation of legislative power from the then hotter dispute about governmental control of the economy. But at the time, no such separation was possible, and within two years of the decisions just discussed, the Supreme Court was overwhelmed.

The transformation of the American judiciary occurred at about the time of, and in direct connection with, Franklin Roosevelt's "Court-packing" scheme, to which we have already referred. In fact, students of Constitutional law usually refer to the "pre-1937" and "post-1937" Courts, so thoroughgoing was the shift in the Constitutional doctrines of the Supreme Court after Roosevelt's attack. The courts—certainly including the Supreme Court—had been under attack before, and the Court had yielded to pressure before. Why, then, do we count this time as a fundamental change?

Roosevelt's Court-packing plan was in reality a relatively moderate scheme, and clearly constitutional. For years, the Supreme Court had been a conservative force in American politics, a veritable bastion against the solution of industrial problems proposed by state legislatures, then by Congress and the president. The range of its decisions made it plain that the Court would oppose and nullify laws regulating the national economy. The states could not regulate outside their borders and the national government lacked Constitutional authority to act. Then, as we have seen, in 1935 the Supreme Court declared the entire National Industrial Recovery Act—the heart of the original "New Deal"—unconstitutional in *Schechter*. Although the usefulness of the NRA was by then almost outlived (it had been an emergency measure), the ruling foretold the fate of upcoming, permanent New Deal legislation. After Roosevelt's sweeping victory in 1936, therefore, he moved to eliminate the Court's staunch opposition. What was "moderate" about Roosevelt's plan was that he shunned the possibility of a constitutional amendment or a statute limiting the reviewing powers of the Court (the former, of course, would have been uncertain, while the latter might itself have been struck down as unconstitutional).[4] Roosevelt's plan provided for the retirement of all justices over the age of seventy; if a justice elected not to retire, the president could appoint an additional member to the Court. At that time, six of the nine justices were over seventy; thus Roosevelt could have placed a liberal majority on the Court, one way or the other.

If Congress went along with Roosevelt's plan or not, there was no doubt as to its constitutionality. Although the Court had been a nine-member one since 1869, its size had varied up to that year. Previous changes in its size usually had been instigated on similar grounds—that is, in order to affect the output of the Court. We should not be surprised, then, to learn that some of the justices were concerned enough to reconsider their previous stances. Thus, while Roosevelt's proposal sat in a Congress neither disposed to go along with the perhaps too powerful president's latest bold move, nor happy with the obstructionist efforts of the Court, the justices made what someone called "the shift in time that saves nine." The Court began to find New Deal legislation constitutional after all, and Congress was off the hook. Roosevelt's court proposal was rejected, but its intended effect was already achieved. Virtually all of the pre-1937 decisions that had blocked the New Deal were overturned. Although the Supreme Court was not "liberal," it affirmed the constitutionality of the New Deal.

---

4. See Robert S. Hirschfield, *The Constitution and the Court* (Random House, 1962), p. 45.

The "Unshatterable" System

It is important to remember that although Roosevelt's scheme had historic precedents, its net and more important effect was in setting a precedent. When Weber referred to the "unshatterable" system of authority produced by full bureaucratization, he pointed to the fact that when each individual is but a *part* of a system that is coordinated from above, then each individual acquires a perfectly vital stake in the viability of the system itself. In this connection, two considerations are relevant to the Court crisis of 1937. First, the Court (along with the Congress and most of the population) had not yet grasped the extent to which it was *already* participating in a system that was coordinated by the presidency. Second, since 1937 the Court has exercised its role as constitutional adjudicator more as an instrument of ruling power than as an *independent* constitutional authority.

There were two main problems with the Court's pre-1937 position on delegation of powers to the president. First, the Court's ruling presumed, incorrectly, that legislative initiative lay with the Congress, and that Congress had erred when it delegated power to the president without "canalizing" that power. Indeed, many students of the Constitution have since noted that the NRA was rather hastily and loosely written, so that delegations of power to the president were, in fact, vague and unconfined. However, the critical point is this: it was the presidency that was hasty and even sloppy in writing the bill, *not* Congress. Most of Roosevelt's legislative proposals were written in full by his crew of experts in the executive branch, and presented to Congress for "rubber-stamping," in a kind of inversion of the traditional process of law-making (where Congress wrote the law and presented it to the executive for approval). As we have seen, the presidency—chiefly by means of the Office of Management and Budget—now typically produces legislative proposals, revisions, or vetoes in considerable detail and then guides these complexly interrelated proposals through Congress. The point is that, even if an act of Congress specified quite clearly what powers were to be exercised by the president, and under what conditions, the fact would remain that the real authorship of the act was the executive's, not Congress's. Now, the reason that the Court could not get behind the *appearance* of delegation of authority, to the issue of where the power to coordinate the nation's ruling power really lay, can be seen by turning to the second main problem with the Court's pre-1937 position.

In 1936, in the case of *United States* v. *Curtiss-Wright,* the Court was asked to decide whether Congress had unconstitutionally delegated legislative powers to the president when it authorized the president to prohibit the sale of arms to Bolivia and Paraguay whenever he found that such action would "contribute to the reestablishment of peace" between those countries (see below). In this case, the Court saw fit to distinguish between delegations of authority concerning *internal* matters, and delegations of authority concerning *external* matters. The distinction is so important that we have employed a similar one in this book. However, the Court in making its distinction failed to note and deal with two factors: first, the *interconnection* between internal and external representation; and second, the *new form* of external representation that had appeared around the turn of this century. The Court pointed out, correctly, that the president had always enjoyed special powers with respect to foreign affairs. However, not since the very first days of the republic— when the establishment of external and internal representation were practically the same things—had the president's role as external representative impinged so immediately upon the internal affairs of the nation. Even though the Court pointed to "a steady stream [of legislative practice] for a century and a half of time," it is curious, then, that it was not until 1937 that this landmark ruling occurred. In fact, what had happened was that *the form of external representation had changed;* now the president represented a bureaucratized society, capable of acting as a coordinated whole in response to other similarly organized nation-states. What the Court did not recognize is that the compartmentalization of presidential functions no longer reflected the reality of political representation in America. The United States had become a "system," an assembly line of thoughts coordinated from a center, the presidency.

Joint Resolution of Congress, August, 1935

Resolved by the Senate and House of Representatives . . . , That if the President finds that the prohibition of the sale of arms and munitions of war in the United States to those countries now engaged in armed conflict in the Chaco may contribute to the re-establishment of peace between those countries, and if after consultation with the governments of other American Republics . . . , he makes proclamation to that effect, it shall be unlawful to sell, except under such limitations and exceptions as the President prescribes, any arms or munitions of war in any place in the United States to the countries now engaged in that armed conflict . . . until otherwise ordered by the President or by Congress.

Sec. 2. Whoever sells any arms or munitions of war in violation of section 1 shall, on conviction, be punished by a fine . . . or by imprisonment . . . or both.

The President's Proclamation—September, 1935

Now, therefore, I, Franklin D. Roosevelt, President of the United States of America, acting under and by virtue of the authority conferred in me by the said joint resolution . . . do hereby admonish all citizens of the United States and every person to abstain from every violation of the provisions of the joint resolution above set forth, hereby made applicable to Bolivia and Paraguay, and I do hereby warn them that all violations of such provisions will be rigorously prosecuted . . . .

United States v. Curtiss-Wright—1936

[The defendent corporation was charged with conspiring to sell fifteen machine guns to Bolivia; the corporation demurred to the indictment on the ground that the delegation of power to the President was invalid. The district court sustained the demurrer, and the U.S. appealed.]

Mr. Justice Sutherland delivered the opinion of the Court.

First. It is contended that [the effect and operation of the Joint Resolution] was conditioned (a) upon the President's judgment as to its beneficial effect . . . ; (b) upon the making of a proclamation, which was left to his unfettered discretion . . . ; (c) upon the making of a proclamation putting an end to the operation of the resolution, which again was left to the President's unfettered discretion; and (d) . . . the extent of its operation . . . was subject to limitation and exception by the President, controlled by no standard. In each of these particulars, appellees urge that Congress abdicated its essential functions and delegated them to the Executive.

. . . assuming (but not deciding) that the challenged delegation, if it were confined to internal affairs, would be invalid, may it nevertheless be sustained on the ground that its exclusive aim is to afford a remedy for a hurtful condition within foreign territory?

. . . The broad statement that the federal government can exercise no powers except those specifically enumerated in the Constitution . . . is categorically true only in respect of our internal affairs. . . .

. . . .

. . . the investment of the federal government with the powers of external sovereignty did not depend upon the affirmative grants of the Constitution. The powers to declare and wage war, to conclude peace, to make treaties, to maintain diplomatic relations . . . , if they had never been mentioned in the Constitution, would have vested in the federal government as necessary concommitants of nationality.

. . . In this vast external realm, with its important, complicated, delicate and manifold problems, the President alone has the power to speak or listen as a representative of the nation.

. . . When the President is to be authorized by legislation to act in respect to a matter intended to affect a situation in foreign territory, the legislator properly bears in mind the important consideration that the form of the President's action . . . may well depend . . . upon the nature of the confidential information which he has or may thereafter receive . . . .

. . . A legislative practice such as we have here, evidenced not by only occasional instances, but marked by the movement of a steady stream for a century and a half of time, goes a long way in the direction of proving the presence of unassailable ground for the constitutionality of the practice . . . .

. . . we conclude there is sufficient warrant for the broad discretion vested in the President to determine whether the enforcement of the statute will have a beneficial effect . . . .

Lower court reversed.

Once the dam broke in 1937, the Supreme Court (and the lower courts) was drawn inside the centralized system of the nation-state—"having by its own decisions," as Robert Hirschfield has written, "been relegated largely to its original role as an instrument for strengthening the central government. . . ."[5] Since 1937, the Court has only rarely invoked the Constitution as a barrier against Congressional action. Instead, *statutory* interpretation rather than *constitutional* interpretation is invoked.[6] In other words, when the Court has

---

5. Ibid., p. 191.
6. Alpheus T. Mason & William M. Beaney, *American Constitutional Law* (Prentice-Hall, 1959), p. 698.

seen fit to limit governmental action against Communist Party members, for example, it has tended to find inconsistencies or procedural errors in the statutes, rather than finding the congressional act invalid on constitutional grounds. By this kind of device, the Court can continue to play an adjudicative role in the nation's government without asserting independent authority in relation to the system of which it is a part.

The Individual in the System: "Individual Rights" and Bureaucratic Depersonalization

The background provided by the previous sections may help us to understand the curious, almost ironic role of the courts in the administration of the rule of law in the nation-state. Since World War II several Supreme Court decisions have had a dramatic impact on individual rights. During the 1950s, for example, the Court abandoned the doctrine that "separate but equal" facilities in education satisfied the Fourteenth Amendment requirement for equal protection under the laws; in *Brown* v. *Board of Education of Topeka* (1954) the Court proclaimed that "separate cannot be equal" under any circumstances. Thereafter, segregation by race in public schools (and shortly thereafter, in any public facilities) was unconstitutional. Then in 1966, in *Miranda* v. *Arizona,* the Court ruled that an individual held for interrogation by police has a right to have a lawyer present at his initial interrogation (one must be appointed if the individual cannot afford it). Along with this requirement came several procedural rules binding on police agencies—procedures similar to FBI practices. As the Court noted, "The practice of the FBI can readily be emulated by state and local enforcement agencies." In yet another area affecting individual rights, the Court had ruled in a series of decisions—especially *Baker* v. *Carr* (1962)—that any legislative apportionment scheme that diluted the effect of certain individual voters was a violation of the Fourteenth Amendment. Later, the "one man, one vote" principle was extended to all levels of government legislatures, including Congress.

The importance and the effects of these and other individual rights cases are manifold, but an interesting and ironic coincidence is usually overlooked. Viewed from one perspective, these decisions are in the interests of the individual; but viewed from a systemic perspective, these decisions are all in line with the requirements of a bureaucratized society. After all, it is conducive to good bureaucratic practice and procedures to eliminate particularistic criteria (such as race or ethnic background) from the universal application of rules. And, as the Court's reference to the FBI reveals, bureaucratic implementation of rules should be rational, predictable, and impersonal.

Legislative districting rulings are consistent with the basis of legitimacy of bureaucratic, positive law. Positive law (as opposed to natural law) is legitimate if it is enacted according to *specified procedures* by the sole normal creator of laws, the state.

In other words, recent Court decisions have been consistent with and have contributed to the most pervasive—although largely unnoticed—change in the administration of law that has occurred with the transformation of the republic into the nation-state. At the same time that the rights of individuals have been affirmed by the Supreme Court, the individual has become a depersonalized element in the vast bureaucratic machinery of the nation-state.

Both within the vast bureaucracy, and at its margins, where it acts on clients and citizens, rules and laws are being adjudicated bureaucratically as a matter of course. That is, officials of the bureaucracy are deciding whether a rule or law has been violated, how a rule or law should be applied to a particular case, and what should be the sanction or punishment in the case of rule violation. Generally, this process of rule adjudication is strictly in the positive law category; that is, rather than deciding what is "just," or appealing to higher norms of justice, the bureaucrat simply applies the general rules to the particular case. Sanctions are applied according to well-defined rules specifying the course of action to be taken.

A very great range of day-to-day activities are regulated and adjudicated by the bureaucracy. Social Security, Medicare, and many other welfare functions performed by the government involve constant adjudication, as on the question of whether person X is indeed entitled to certain welfare checks if a member of the family is employed, and so on.

Whether a person is eligible for exemption from the military draft or whether a person has violated the income tax laws by failing to report certain income, or whether a television station has violated broadcasting rules, or whether a politician can demand equal air time, or whether a person can cross a union picket line, or whether a university must hire more women, or whether a certain drug may be manufactured and sold—all such questions, and an astonishing variety of others, are decided routinely not by the courts, but by some agency or special component of an agency of the bureaucracy. Most of these decisions are subject to appeal to the courts (which legitimizes the bureaucracy's judicial role), but most decisions do not get appealed, because the courts have already recognized the validity of the procedures used. Moreover, especially since the New Deal conversion of the Supreme Court, several important doctrines of judicial restraint concerning review of the administrative process have held sway. Of greatest practical importance is the "primary jurisdiction doctrine," which requires that no one is entitled to judicial relief for a supposed or threatened injury *until the prescribed administrative remedy has been exhausted* (*Myers* v. *Bethlehem Shipbuilding Corp.,* 1938). The exhaustion of administrative remedies rule "does not require merely the *initiation* of prescribed administrative procedures. It is one of *exhausting* them, that is, of pursuing them to their appropriate conclusion and, correlatively, of awaiting their final outcome before seeking judicial intervention."[7] As Rinehart Swenson points out, the "primary jurisdiction doctrine recognizes *de facto* the judicial character of administrative adjudication, and for its purposes incorporates administrative tribunals into the judicial hierarchy."[8]

Closely related to the exhaustion of administrative remedies rule is the rule that only *final* administrative action is reviewable. Reinforcing the significance of these rules is the now well-established rule that *administrative rules are presumed regular and valid* by the courts. That is, just as an act of Congress is presumed valid, and can only be declared void where its validity is overcome "beyond rational doubt," so are administrative rules of the executive branch now afforded such positive presumptions. (See especially, *Cities Service Gas Co.* v. *Federal Power Commission,* 1946.)

---

7. *Aircraft & Diesel Equipment Corp.* v. *Hirsch,* 1947.
8. Rinehart John Swenson, *Federal Administrative Law* (Ronald Press, 1952), p. 277.

The effectively legal, court-sanctioned adjudicative status of federal bureaucratic actions must be considered in light of the superior *efficiency* of bureaucracy—its capability for much greater administrative output. Compared to the courts, an incalculably greater number of day-to-day matters are adjudicated by the bureaucracy. The Supreme Court, and most of the many other courts throughout the judicial system of the nation, continue to operate as they did in the days of the republic. The administrative output of the courts—the number of cases tried and decided in a given period—is not and cannot be nearly as large as the administrative output of bureaucracy, although the total number of judges throughout the judicial system is quite large. But just as 1,000 partially skilled workers and a few special machines organized in an assembly line can produce hundreds or even thousands of adequate automobiles for every (perhaps excellent) one produced by 1,000 highly skilled craftsmen, so can 1,000 specialists and semi-specialists and a few computers handle thousands of cases for every one handled by 1,000 judges. The number of decisions in a year that are, technically, adjudicative ones, which are produced more or less automatically by the various levels and agencies of bureaucracy, is literally uncountable.

The point here—and it can easily elude us—is that a great number of issues and problems that technically could be a matter for legal adjudication have been absorbed in bureaucratic routine. For example, all manner of deviance from established social norms that once might have found their way into a court of law are now diagnosed and dealt with in the school bureaucracies. A great number of rules and regulations governing performance and deportment are codified in school rules, and sanctions of various sorts are prescribed and administered. Much serious deviance is "treated" as a kind of illness by counselors, clinical psychologists, and so on. Sociologists call this the "medicalization" of deviance —redefining a deviant pattern as a medical problem rather than a legal one—and the adjudication process is thus absorbed into bureaucratic procedure. Moreover, the sheer efficiency of bureaucracy makes possible the promulgation of rules, and the adjudication of cases under such rules, to an extent that was just not possible before bureaucracy, and with which no other system of administration (such as judicially administered law) can compete.

It has been suggested that an important step toward

Figure 4. The Federal Courts and Routes of Appeals.

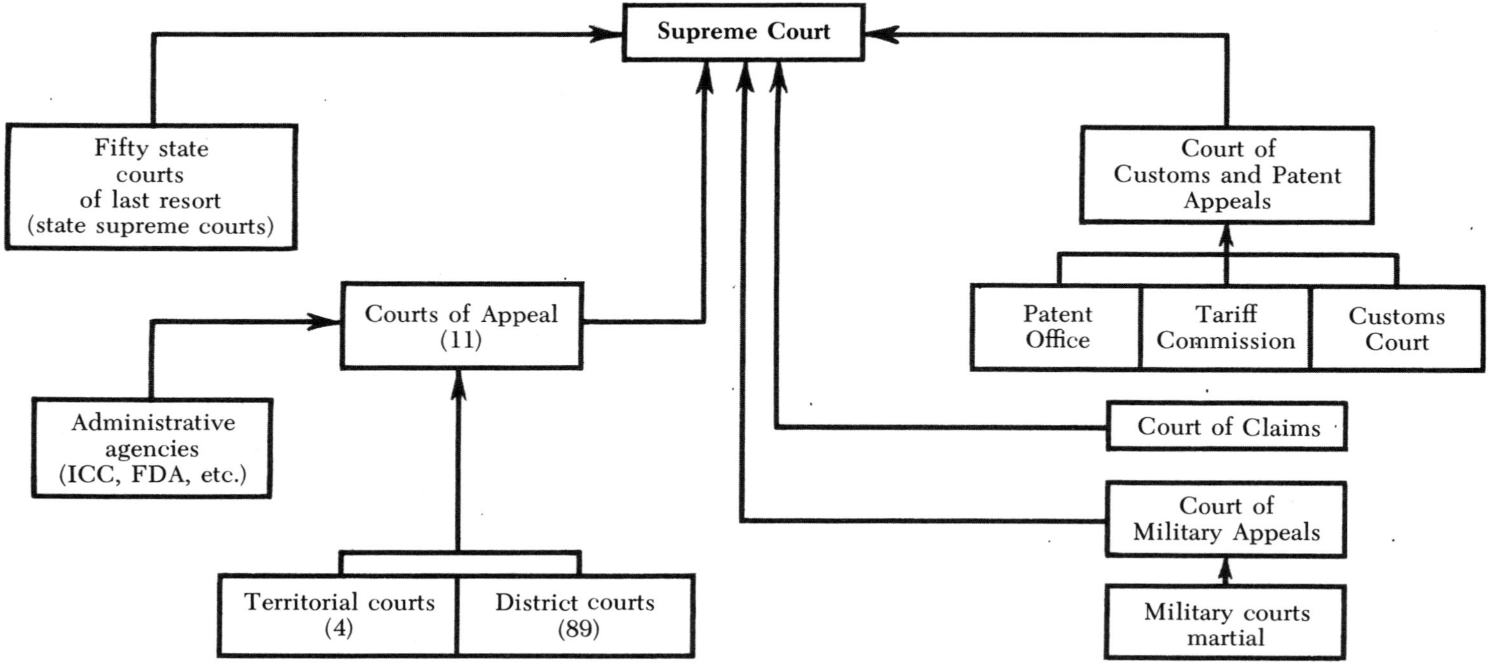

Described in *United States Government Organization Manual, 1972-1973*, pp. 55-63.

curing the malady of centralized, unresponsive government would be the restoration of the Schechter rule: "Under present conditions, when Congress delegates without a shred of guidance, the courts usually end up rewriting many of the statutes in the course of 'construction.' Since the Court's present procedure is always to try to find an acceptable meaning of a statute in order to avoid invalidating it the Court is legislating constantly. A blanket invalidation under the Schechter rule is a Court order for Congress to do its own work."[9] However, there is good reason to doubt whether the nation-state could survive such an edict. The question is not whether Congress *should* write its own laws, but whether Congress *could.* We turn now to a closer examination of that once powerful institution, to see what its fate has been in the nation-state.

Suggested Further Reading

The associated unit on the courts by Mary Walker presents a more balanced treatment of Constitutional law developments. For another balanced, brief introduction to major doctrines and decisions of the Supreme Court, see:

Carl Brent Swisher. *Historic Decisions of the Supreme Court.* Anvil Books, 1958.

Robert S. Hirschfield. *The Constitution and the Court.* Random House, 1962.

For a good, general constitutional law case book with introductory essays, see:

Alpheus Thomas Mason and William M. Beaney. *American Constitutional Law: Introductory Essays & Selected Cases.* Prentice-Hall, 1966.

For a collection of materials on a case involving the constitutionality of a presidential exercise of power, see:

Alan F. Westin, *The Anatomy of a Constitutional Law Case: Youngstown Sheet and Tube Co.* v. *Sawyer, The Steel Seizure Decision.* Macmillan, 1958.

In our opinion, one finds out only part of the story of the realities of legal domination in America by studying the courts and constitutional law; for brief considerations of administrative law, see:

---

9. Theodore J. Lowi, *The End of Liberalism: Ideology, Policy, and the Crisis of Public Authority* (Norton, 1969), p. 298.

Rinehart John Swenson. *Federal Administrative Law: A Study of the Growth, Nature, and Control of Administrative Action.* Ronald Press, 1952.

John Pfiffner and Robert V. Presthus. *"Administrative Law and Regulation." Public Administration,* Part IV. Ronald Press, 1960.

Given the crucial factor of legal authority in bureaucracy, the Supreme Court remains an institution that, arguably, could counterbalance the power of the presidency (though we think it does not and will not). For different interpretations of the Court which, in varying ways, presume a greater power in the Supreme Court than we do, see:

Theodore J. Lowi. *The End of Liberalism: Ideology, Policy, and the Crisis of Public Authority.* W.W. Norton, 1969.

Samuel Krislov, *The Supreme Court and Political Freedom.* The Free Press, 1968.

Robert G. McCloskey. *The American Supreme Court.* University of Chicago Press, 1960.

Chapter 8
The Co-Optation of Congress

Most writings on Congress, whether journalistic or academic, focus upon two topics. The first is the bewildering variety of rules and special procedures that govern a congressman's activities. The second is the surprisingly deep division of opinion about the extent and efficacy of congressional power. The two topics are related. For those who contend that the Congress is powerless, the labyrinthine structure of Congress is frequently held up as the cause of its inefficiency and haplessness. But those who contend, on the contrary, that Congress is the most—even the only—powerful legislative body among modern states often point to the limitations upon presidential power effected by powerful committee chairmen, the seniority system, filibustering, and other peculiarities of congressional structure and procedures.

Controversy about a major institution is not so surprising. But it is curious that such a basic disagreement—namely, whether Congress exercises significant power at all—should persist over the very institution which, historically, has been at the heart of American government. However, that probably is the key to the curiosity. The history of America reveals the emergence in the republic of a unique form of political representation, occurring, as it were, in the crack of history, between the crumbling of the old European order and the emergence of the bureaucratic nation-state. Unlike the parliaments of Europe, Congress did not spawn the modern executive; rather, the legislature and executive developed separately (but interdependently) in the republic.

With the transformation of America into a modern nation-state, the Congress did not come into being as a new matrix for executive preeminence. Instead, of course, it was already there, and it possessed a long history of power and independence. This power was not taken away by the executive; it was *co-opted.*

Co-Optation:
"Back Door" Presidential Control

By now a term with wide usage, "co-optation" was originally coined by Peter Selznick to describe a process that he had identified in the development or articulation of the Tennessee Valley Authority (TVA).[1] The TVA is a very large, regionally based, multifunctional public bureaucracy (it produces electricity, fertilizer, and so on), which was authorized by Congress during Roosevelt's "Hundred Days." The problems facing the TVA during its articulation, and the techniques employed to overcome these problems, are particularly instructive for us, because the situation is in some ways analogous to that of the bureaucratization of the presidency. The TVA had to establish itself in the face of considerable hostility (emerging from the still viable tradition of "free enterprise") toward governmental ownership and management of productive enterprises. Moreover, because it was *regionally* based (that is, its jurisdiction extended over several states or parts of states), the TVA also encountered the hostility of groups and individuals identified or associated with traditional governmental units (especially states) that did not correspond to the TVA's area of jurisdiction. How, then, was the TVA to overcome the hostility of and solicit the cooperation of the groups, organizations, and individuals whose cooperation was essential (such as the land-grant universities) or whose opposition was dangerous (such as that of state or local officials)? As we have indicated, Selznick identified a process he called co-optation—*the absorption of local interests into the policy-making structure of the organization.* Instead of trying to take over or preempt the power of locally based officials and interests, the TVA would offer them positions of authority in the bureaucracy. Sometimes, perhaps,

1. Peter Selznick, *TVA and the Grass Roots* (University of California Press, 1949).

a person would end up with more power by virtue of his position in the TVA than he had had before. However, as we have already seen, the nature of a bureaucrat's power is special since he may exercise great power through his *office;* yet his discretion is quite *limited* as well, again by virtue of his office. That office has a certain authority (under specified conditions) to be exercised according to certain rules of procedure. The person who occupies that office "has" its power; and, in a sense, the organization as a *part* of which the office occurs "has" the person who occupies the office. For a bureaucrat does not "decide" what the *organization* will do; instead, his (very real) decisions are part of an assembly line of thoughts and decisions which, when coordinated from above, produces the administrative output of the bureaucracy.

The situation faced by the presidency in relation to the Congress during America's transformation was somewhat analogous. The presidency, like the TVA, was undertaking to perform functions in the face of considerable hostility (deriving from the still viable tradition of "limited government") toward centralized government. Moreover, because it was *centrally* administered, the presidency also encountered the hostility of interests and individuals identified or associated with traditional governmental divisions that did not correspond to the president's new "areas of jurisdiction." In a sense, the president had a problem similar to the TVA's: how to overcome the opposition and solicit cooperation from the (preexisting) Congress. And in a sense, the same kind of process—co-optation—was put into operation. Not only local but congressional interests were absorbed into the policy-making structure of the presidential organization.

This process was by no means a conscious conspiracy engineered by a particular president. Rather, it was an instance of the tendency of bureaucratic organization to absorb preexisting interests into its policy-making structure, with the result that the preexisting interest at once loses and acquires power. The individual may still exercise power— perhaps more than he once did—but now he functions as a part of a larger system, and the center of coordination has shifted to a new location. It is this shift in the center of coordination that is all important. This concept of co-optation makes possible a more revealing description and analysis of that great institution that at once possesses so much power, and yet has no power, the Congress of the United States.

Committees and Seniority

All important studies of Congress identify the House and Senate standing committees and their subcommittees as the crucial or "real" locations of Congressional action. Not all of the committees and subcommittees (see below) are of equal importance and influence. But the decisions made in the more important committees and subsequently recommended for floor action in the appropriate chamber are, in the vast majority of cases, the final effective decisions. That is (in the case of important committees), the committees actually decide *for* the House and Senate what the form and fate of most legislation will be. And in this sense, as these committees interpret and represent reality to the membership, they preclude real politics—they avert the disputes over who will have the authority to decide.

In fact, the committee system of Congress is a queer arrangement that requires considerable analysis. Each house of Congress, confronted with a wide variety of legislative tasks, not surprisingly divides itself up into committees of "specialists" in order to deal efficiently with its work. But the method of selecting the chairmen of these committees is peculiar, and the power wielded by the chairmen is remarkable.

Since about the time of Woodrow Wilson's presidency—perhaps a bit earlier in the case of the Senate—the rule of seniority has been the single, automatic criterion for selecting the chairmen of congressional committees. Under the rule of seniority, the majority party determines the memberships and chairmanships of the committees. Within the majority party, however, preference for selection is always given to the person with the longest continuous service on that committee—the duration of which is determined by the election outcomes of the member's state or congressional district. Thus the "power" of Congress—its power to pass the laws of this nation—is in an important sense not its own power at all. For the committees make the effective decisions (most of the time), and yet the committees seem not to be the creatures of Congress itself, beholden to the larger membership of Congress. On the contrary, factors quite beyond the control of Congress as a body or institution determine who shall exercise power for Congress.

One all-important result of this situation is that the decisions and activities of the working components of the

Congress, the standing committees, cannot effectively be co-ordinated by the houses of Congress. And this surprising situation is very much aggravated by the practices of the few most powerful, broadly influential congressional committees —especially the House and Senate appropriations committees.

In the House Appropriations Committee—which exercises for the House its constitutionally granted power to initiate and control all money bills—the committee's approximately fifty members are assigned to numerous subcommittees, each of which has jurisdiction over specified parts of the total budget. And it turns out that the subcommittee chairmen are themselves "kings" of their provinces, for the recommendations of each subcommittee are virtually never overridden by the whole committee. This means, then, that even the decisions of the House Appropriations Committee are not coordinated by the committee itself, for the norm of reciprocity (that is, each subcommittee accepts the recommendations of every other subcommittee) operates as an effective rule on the committee's membership. Looked at from the perspective of Congress, such a decentralized system of power, rigidly reinforced by the seniority system, is difficult to explain. To be sure, one hears often enough the explanation that the "necessity" for specialization dictates such an arrangement. Yet, specialization and division of labor must be *coordinated* if it is to be effective at all. To put hundreds of Congressmen to specialized tasks with no means to coordinate those tasks so that they function as part of an integrated program of action is to produce chaos, not rational action. And it is well enough to defend the seniority rule as a means of avoiding divisive intracongressional battles over the question of who will exercise power for Congress, but does this explain how anything gets coordinated under the seniority rule?

We are close, at this point, to the paradox of Congress, and we are also close to a plausible explanation of the curious disagreement about the power of Congress. The paradox of Congress is that there are extremely powerful members in it who can act *for* Congress (since Congress will usually respect their decisions), and yet they are not *controlled* by Congress (they are not elected by Congress and, for most practical purposes, they are not beholden to Congress's elected leadership). Critics of Congress, focusing upon the lack of control or coordination by Congress of these men, conclude that Congress has no power, or that it has only obstructive negative power. Defenders of Congress note the fact of the great power of some of its members, and conclude that, withal, the system *works.* Strange as its methods may be, Congress does by virtue of the great power of some of its members exercise more influence over national policy-making than does any other legislative body in the world today.

This helps us to understand why the same observers see different things when they look at Congress, but it does not really explain the paradox itself. What is going on in Congress? Part of the answer, we shall venture, is that Congress itself is a kind of optical illusion. To be sure, people are elected to Congress; and when they assume office most of them are socialized into the time-honored norms of the institution during periods of "apprenticeship" on committees. Eventually a few of them, those who survive year after year in "safe" electoral districts, assume positions of great power in certain committees. But the power they exercise is not, strictly speaking, the power of Congress—it is *the power of the presidency.* To be a bit more precise, it is the power of a fairly high, policy-determining position in the federal bureaucracy, which is coordinated by the presidency. In other words, the co-optation of key members of Congress has occurred; that is, members of Congress have been absorbed into the policy-determining structure of the presidential bureaucracy.

This assertion will be qualified somewhat presently. Now, let us look at Congress in the light of this assertion in order to make sense of some of the peculiarities we have been discussing. First, there is the rule of seniority. This rule did not, and could not, become the exclusive criterion for selection to committee chairmanships as long as Congress controlled the committees. With the transformation of America, however, key committees were formed or transformed to correspond to key executive agencies or bureaus, with the committee chairmen functioning in the policy-determining processes of these executive organizations. Since the power of these chairmen was not really separable from the "office," or quasi-office, which they occupied (their "expertise" and influence was in large part the expertise of the bureaucracy within which they functioned), their power could not be taken away from their positions. Members of Congress had to "line up," as it were, for these positions, and the modern practice of exclusive application of the seniority rule was established.

The strange decentralization of Congress is also put into perspective in this light. The reason that Congress is not coordinating the activities of its own most powerful members is that the presidency is coordinating these activities. The numerous subcommittees of the House Appropriations Committee, for example, correspond to administrative offices and personnel. While each subcommittee encounters the vast expertise of relevant bureaucratic agencies, and while each subcommittee must rely on the bureaucracy with its practical monopoly on relevant information (and expertise), the whole pattern is exclusively controlled by the Office of Management and Budget, which, of course, reports to the president. This does not mean that the president can somehow "order" committee chairmen to make certain recommendations; the last thing that a committee chairman would concede is that he was beholden to the president for his position. Again, however, the president's power is not primarily the power to order, but to coordinate. We shall consider committee action to see how this works.

A bill is formally referred to the appropriate committee by order of the presiding officer (in the House, the Speaker; in the Senate, the president), but the referral of almost all bills is in fact automatic, being governed by jurisdictional rules. It is widely agreed that the bill's chances of passage most likely are determined right here, at the beginning of committee action. The bill is placed on the committee's calendar, so that the question of whether the bill ever gets considered is decided then—and most bills die at this point because they are "pigeon-holed." If the committee does not act on the bill, it is probably dead, since it is only by a discharge petition in the House (requiring a majority), or by adoption of a special resolution in the Senate, that a bill can be forced out of committee.

In general, the first thing the committee is interested in, and the information most vital to the committee, is comment or testimony from interested agencies of the government. This is true whether the question is to act on the bill, or to kill it. If the bill is acted upon, hearings (usually public, if the bill is controversial, combined with "executive" or secret sessions) are held. Government agencies may report extensively, representatives from interested parties may be called to testify or may volunteer, and interested citizens also may do so. These activities may be done by subcommittee or by the committee as a whole. Public hearings may be used to test public opinion about a proposed bill, and all testimony may be invited; or they may be used to influence public opinion, if the committee desires passage. In the latter case, the chairman's ability to call witnesses is an important power.

The committee may amend a bill, slightly or substantially, before recommending action ("ordering a bill reported") by the House. First the chamber must approve, alter, or reject the committee's amendments before voting on the bill itself. We will discuss subsequent action presently; here it will suffice to reiterate that the great majority of committee recommendations are accepted by the chamber because of the "expertise" of the committee and the norm of reciprocity (mutual respect for committee jurisdiction).

The committees, and sometimes subcommittees within them, will have practically exclusive access to all of the relevant bureaucratic information and requirements. That is, only certain members of the House Appropriations Committee will be conversant with all of the technical knowledge and planning that is part of the budgeting process. All of the congressmen are "specialists" in the sense that they carve out through committee memberships areas in which they are knowledgeable in comparison to the rest of the congressmen. However, having the "inside story" is not necessarily the same as being "expert" in a technical sense. That is, committee members may have access to reports from the bureaucracy, but they do not have the means or the expertise to produce such reports on their own, without the bureaucracy's aid. They *can* probe various governmental agencies, and check into operations here and there, so they are by no means completely helpless at the hands of the bureaucracy; in a sense, they are participants. And, for the chamber as a whole, they are certainly expert, because they spend most of their time working on bills in a certain area, and because they have access to information and advice from the relevant bureaucratic agencies.

The typical pattern of committee and subcommittee activities often leads to the formation of what have been called "subgovernments."[2] Many political scientists have noted this effect, that is, the interlocking, stable relationships among

2. See Douglass Cater, *Power in Washington* (Random House, 1964). See also Barbara Hinckley, *Stability and Change in Congress* (Harper and Row, 1971), p. 84.

three elements—the congressional committee or subcommittee, an executive agency, and a clientele group ("interest group"). Barbara Hinckley cites the example given by Douglass Cater:

Sugar legislation [was] worked out between Chairman Harold Cooley of the House Agriculture Committee, the director of the Sugar Division in the Agriculture Department, and the Washington representatives of domestic beet and cane sugar growers, refineries, and foreign producers. According to Cater, that tripartite subgovernment set price levels, indirectly influenced United States foreign policy with Latin America, and divided the sugar market to the last 'spoonful'.[3]

There are many examples of this pattern in the federal government. In it, many political scientists have seen a serious *limitation* upon presidential power, and upon his ability to determine and control national policy. Since such "subgovernments" can be quite durable, it is not difficult to see why their existence has seemed to some to limit the authority of the president. However, from our perspective, we can see such a pattern as typical of co-optation. Yes, the price of sugar is regulated (by the subgovernment), and yes, such regulation indirectly affects the United States foreign policy with Latin America. Such regulation also indirectly affects the economy, and so on. But—given such interconnections—who is really in a position to control overall policy? Who is in a position to know what the price of sugar will be *and* what United States policies toward Latin America will be, *and* what the value of the dollar on money markets will be, *and* what the taxing policies of the United States (and other) governments will be, and a host of other relevant facts and future developments which, *taken together,* spell out the economic future of individuals and collectivities? The more we look to the (unavoidable) interconnections of all the activities and sectors of the nation-state, the more we see that only the presidency could be the overall coordinator. When we look at a *part* of the process, we find a few men in apparent control—and this group does not include the president. But when we consider how many factors are beyond the control of these groups, and how much relevant information they could never acquire, then we realize the need to look for the person (or office) that does have access to that relevant information. The president is in a key position. From the perspective of the Congress, the committee

3. Hinckley, *Stability and Change in Congress,* p. 84.

chairman is independent, "uncoordinatable"; from the perspective of the marketplace, the "sugar lobby" is one of many, uncontrollables; but from the perspective of the presidency, the Sugar Division is part of the Department of Agriculture, which is part of the federal bureaucracy, monitored and coordinated by the Office of Management and Budget, which in turn reports to the president. The fact that these "subgovernments" can and do act independently or autonomously is not a *limitation* on the president's power, but the *source* of the president's power. The president would not head a very effective government if its (more or less) five million persons awaited a direct order from the president. What could anyone tell five million persons to do? "Charge!"? In fact, such a large number of persons must be organized bureaucratically, with each one performing specialized functions, *reliably*. Then, and only then, can they be controlled in a rational fashion.

Congressional Leadership: "Front Door" Presidential Control

The president does not, and could not, exercise complete coordination of and control over congressional activities by means of his capability of coordinating the bureaucracy, for several reasons. First, not all of the committees and subcommittees are susceptible of coordination, because some committees are not well-integrated, reliable "subgovernments." Some are simply unpredictable. Second, not all proposed legislation is automatically assigned to certain committees by fixed rules; in some cases, legislation could go to different committees depending on interpretation of the bill's subject matter; thus, the decision to send the bill to one or another committee can affect its eventual fate. Third, some legislation—especially new, innovative programs—cannot readily be controlled through bureaucratic manipulation because the appropriate agencies do not yet exist. (For years, federal aid to education fell in such a category.) Finally, some proposals are so controversial that a committee's decision is not taken as the final word. Some issues *will* be fought out on the chamber floors, and are too "visible" to be hidden in the secret works of some committee. There are other considerations as well, but these are sufficient to return our attention

Table 2. Standing Committees of the Congress

Senate	House
Foreign Relations	*Exclusive Committees*
Appropriations	Appropriations
Finance	Rules
Agriculture and Forestry	Ways and Means
Armed Services	*Semi-exclusive Committees*
Judiciary	Agriculture
Commerce	Armed Services
Banking, Housing and Urban	Banking and Currency
Affairs	Education and Labor
Rules and Administration	Foreign Affairs
Interior and Insular Affairs	Interstate and Foreign Commerce
Post Office and Civil Service	Judiciary
Public Works	Post Office and Civil Service
Government Operations	Public Works
District of Columbia	Science and Astronautics
Labor and Public Welfare	
Aeronautical and Space Science	*Nonexclusive Committees*
Veterans' Affairs	District of Columbia
	Government Operations
	House Administration
	Interior and Insular Affairs
	Merchant Marine and Fisheries
	Internal Security
	Standards of Conduct
	Veterans' Affairs

Note: Senate committees (except the last two) are listed in order of member preference. House committees are listed alphabetically within categories. Source: Joseph H. Harris, Congress and the Legislative Process *(McGraw-Hill, 1972, p. 91)*

to the "front side" of Congress. How is the organization managed as a body, and where does presidential influence figure here, if at all?

Coordination of congressional activities with presidential policies is more noticeable, atthough not necessarily much more effective, through the activities of the elected leaders of the House and Senate. In the House, there are five major elected leaders. First it should be clearly understood that, while the whole membership of the House elects its leaders, the deciding elections take place in party caucuses, where the majority party elects its own leaders; while elections might be contested within the caucus, everyone votes his party's choice in the formal election. The Speaker of the House is thus both the presiding officer of the House and the leader of the majority party in the House. The majority floor leader is elected in caucus, as is the majority whip. The Speaker presides over House sessions, and can—if he is skilled—use his somewhat limited powers of recognition, and the like. In addition, he does have considerable influence as the person responsible for assigning bills to committee, whenever (as occasionally happens) the rules do not require a bill to be sent to a certain committee. And he does appoint special and select committees, such as investigative committees. The majority floor leader cooperates with the Speaker and the Rules Committee (see below) to set the schedule for debate, while the whip assists the floor leader by checking the voting intentions of congressmen, lining up vote trading, and so on. For their part, the minority party also elects a floor leader who, since they cannot elect the Speaker, also serves as party leader and general strategist. The minority floor leader is assisted by the elected minority whip, plus numerous assistants. To the extent that floor action—debate and compromise on the floor, and voting on amendments and final bills—is not completely determined by committee recommendations (and it is not, partly because committees sometimes are split on their recommendations), control, persuasion, and manipulation by elected floor leaders can be quite important. Moreover, the elected leadership can exercise extensive control over House proceedings in cooperation with the Rules Committee, as we shall see.

In the Senate, the presiding officer's power is limited because of the constitutional provision that the vice president of the United States shall preside over the Senate (and exercise a tie-breaking vote). Since in practice the vice president's power over Senate activities is almost nil, the president pro tempore, who is elected and who presides in the (quite frequent) absence of the vice president, is likewise without much formal power. Again, party caucuses elect majority and minority floor leaders, both of whom function as party leaders and as schedulers of Senate business. In the much smaller body which is the Senate, these arrangements are made in consultation with minority leaders and influential individuals in the chamber. Senators also elect whips, who serve as liaison men between leaders and chamber members as in the House.

The elected leaders, obviously, reflect the party structure of Congress, and they are usually the administration's team in the Congress. When the president and the majority leaders are of the same party, then they are likely to share enough broad political stakes to cooperate effectively; if the president is of the minority party, he will have to work through the minority leaders and in whatever working relationship he can with majority leaders to coordinate his program with congressional action.

As Barbara Hinckley has written, " . . . the contemporary expectation seems to be that party leaders will support and will even actively work for presidential programs. In this way, parties, through the mediation of congressional leaders, serve to coordinate Presidential and legislative support for programs."[4]

This is the "contemporary expectation," but it has not always been so. Toward the end of the nineteenth century, congressional leadership positions (especially the Speaker of the House) became almost dictatorially strong, and included the power to determine committee chairmanships. Under these circumstances the legislative power of Congress was very great, and the president had to bargain with such leaders in order to have any influence at all upon the policies of the nation. (Of course, as chief executive the president did have considerable bargaining power.) But, as we have seen, the struggle for party realignment precipitated by the Progressive movement eventuated in an intracongressional revolt (1910–11) during which the Speaker was stripped of his powers, including the power over chairmanships and committee assignments. Thus we note in yet another way the fateful confluence of internal and external developments that transformed America.

Before the congressional power could be marshalled once again, the presidency had emerged in a new role, the role of coordinator of national policy (as a result of World War I). The committees, which had now become indispensable for Congress because of their access to information otherwise monopolized by the president's bureaucracy, never again fell under the control of congressional leadership. And as congressional leadership reemerged, the new leaders had to rely upon a cooperative, privileged access to the president in order

---

4. Ibid., p. 110.

to acquire power independent of the committee chairman. Richard Fenno describes the present-day situation: "Most of the time the two kinds of leaders cooperate—sometimes on the basis of a policy agreement, but always on the basis of a mutual need. The party leaders need the support of the committee leaders if they want any bill at all to get to the floor. The committee leaders need the support of the party leaders if they want procedural assistance and sufficient supporting votes on the floor."[5]

Thus each kind of leader depends upon and cooperates with the other in order to achieve anything at all. But both kinds of leaders also depend upon the presidency for their influence. Indirectly, the source of the committee leader's power is the presidency, for it is the committee's privileged access to (part of) the bureaucracy that is his claim to "expertise." More directly, the source of the party leader's power is the presidency, in cooperation with which the party leader can wield the power of coordination.

The Fossilization of Congress, and the Reformers

The literature on American national government devoted to the topic of congressional reform is voluminous. As David Truman has written, criticisms of Congress can be traced to three sets of circumstances. First, there is what Truman calls the "parliamentary crisis" that characterizes all twentieth-century democratic legislatures. The modern requirement for expertise and coordinated decision-making cannot be provided by legislatures, and these functions therefore fall to the executive. Second, the "separation of powers" feature of the United States Constitution has produced, in this century, a situation where the Congress is in a position to obstruct the executive in ways not possible in other systems. Finally, the power of committee chairmen, the seniority system, and other obstructive features of Congressional structure and procedure draw extensive—indeed, the most—criticism from reformers.[6]

---

5. Richard Fenno, "The Internal Distribution of Influence: The House." In David Truman, ed., *The Congress and America's Future* (Prentice-Hall, 1965), p. 74.
6. Ibid., pp. 1–4.

Figure 5. Typical Process by Which a Bill Becomes Law.

The text of this chapter has argued that only the presidency is in a position to coordinate legislative action. But the actual, formal steps by which a bill is passed into law occur in the chambers of Congress, and are coordinated by House and Senate leadership. A bill (except money bills) may originate in either house. Upon passage or approval by one house, the bill is sent to the other. Final versions from both houses are then rectified in conference, and passed again by each house in an identical form, and sent to the president for approval.

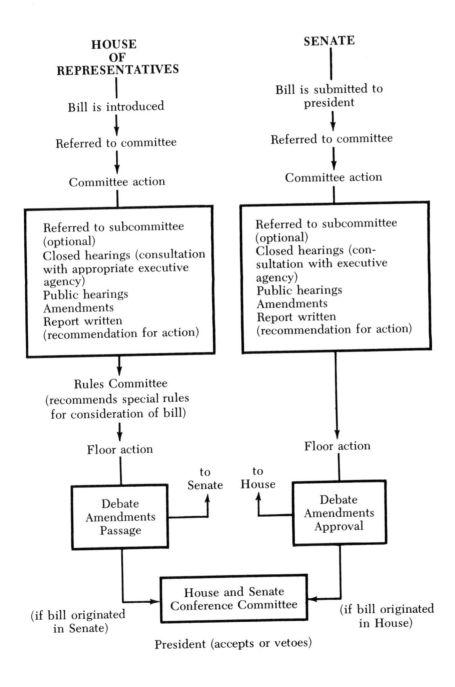

Overall, what is criticized is a "fossilized" Congress—one that has ceased to function in the ways it once did, but which endures in a form carried over from the days of the republic. Indeed, the rate of member turnover, as well as turnover in committee chairmanships and leadership positions, has decreased dramatically in this century.[7] By way of reform, two sorts of strategies are suggested. One is to "modernize" Congress, to enable it to compete, as it were, with the executive branch. Consider the following plaintive description of Congress' plight by a disillusioned congressman:

> The Committee [a House subcommittee dealing with military appropriations] and the House are dealing with this huge and difficult task, without adequate tools. Seven men almost with their bare hands are standing up to a huge organization with thousands of officials, both civilian and military, devoting their full time to the presentation of self-serving statements and documents, and inundating the committee with a plethora of testimony and charts and statistics which the committee is unable to digest, to say nothing of challenging. The Congress is at the mercy of the executive.... What if they had asked for eighty billion instead of fifty-six billion? Would the committee have been able to challenge and resist the request?[8]

In response to such situations it is suggested that Congress modernize itself. "If Congress wanted to, it could put the entire budget through a computer . . . and quickly see where the money goes . . . . The whole budget could by analyzed coldly and accurately . . . . But Congress does not own a computer."[9] Unfortunately, this kind of reasoning misunderstands the nature of computers (in particular) and technological expertise (in general). Congressional committees are already heavily dependent upon their (sometimes large) professional staffs, whose expertise is linked to key bureaucratic functions. Computers cannot do much by themselves; to be used effectively, a large one must be put in the context of bureaucratic organization, so that human and technological components are coordinated, as on an assembly line. The only thing that could compete in terms of efficiency

---

7. Nelson Polsby, "The Institutionalization of the U.S. House of Representatives," *American Political Science Review,* 1968, 62:144–168.
8. Quoted in John M. Pfiffner & Robert V. Presthus, *Public Administration* (Ronald Press, 1960), p. 525.
9. From the forward by David Brinkley to Philip Donham & Robert Fahey, *Congress Needs Help* (Random House, 1966), p. xi.

and reliable information with the bureaucracy would be another bureaucracy, similar in size and scope. This would be very expensive. And, even if it could be accomplished, Congress would no longer be a legislative body; it would be a bureaucracy.

The other kind of strategy is to break down the separation of powers by fusing the legislative and executive branches. For example, if all congressmen were elected for four-year terms along with the president, then he could lead a majority party subject to stricter party discipline in the fulfillment of centrally directed, coherent party platforms. Such proposals (which range from key changes such as the above-mentioned to complete constitutional revision) take as given the centrality of the executive, and aim to streamline the process and, hopefully, thereby enable the electorate to make more rational choices in terms of national policy.

There can be no doubt that the peculiar arrangement of power in the national government has resulted in a slower adoption of some policies (social welfare policies, governmental regulation policies, and the like) than would otherwise have occurred. But many critics have failed to notice the extent to which the executive *does* control the legislative branch, through co-optation. And in any case, the most serious problems facing the American nation-state are not "technical." The real problems reside in the very nature of modern political representation, which makes of the individual a functioning element in a vast, impersonal machine. Once he is a part of such a system, it is practically impossible for the individual even to realize his situation, let alone to do anything about it. To see this, we shall need to discuss the role of the individual in the nation-state. How does he participate in the mighty system?

Suggested Further Reading

The following is a definitive statement on co-optation and therefore is relevant in light of our analysis, even though it is not a book on Congress:

Peter Selznick. *TVA and the Grass Roots.* University of California Press, 1949.

A good general work on the Congress is:
Roland Young. *The American Congress.* Harper & Row, 1958.

For a more recent work that considers aspects of Congress in terms of a systems framework consult:

Leroy Rieselbach. *Congressional Politics.* McGraw-Hill, 1973.

The following is frequently cited and informative:

Donald Matthews. *United States Senators and Their World.* University of North Carolina Press, 1960.

Young, Rieselbach, and Matthews might be compared with this classic:

Woodrow Wilson. *Congressional Government.* 1885; Meridian Books, 1956.

A good, short work on the Congress is:

Barbara Hinckley. *Stability and Change in Congress.* Harper & Row, 1971.

A useful collection of readings on Congress will be found in the following:

David Truman, ed. *The Congress and America's Future.* Prentice-Hall, 1965.

The structure and characteristics of the traditional parties have a lot to do with the behavior of Congress. For a helpful work in which the distinction between Congressional and presidential parties is drawn, see:

James M. Burns. *The Deadlock of Democracy.* Prentice-Hall, 1963.

Another way to understand congressional behavior is from the point of view of "coalition behavior"; for examples of such studies, see:

Sven Groennings, E. W. Kelley, Michael Leiserson, eds. *The Study of Coalition Behavior: Theoretical Perspectives and Cases From Four Continents.* Holt, Rinehart & Winston, 1970.

For an analysis of the problem of bureaucracy that sees congressional control of the bureaucracy as a feasible alternative:

Charles Hyneman. *Bureaucracy in a Democracy.* Harper & Row, 1950.

Granting that legislative initiation by Congress is "abnormal" in modern times, this study considers the occasional circumstances under which policy innovation *does* occur in Congress:

John R. Johannes. *"Policy Innovation in Congress."* General Learning Press, 1972.

An informative case study of the problems facing a president who would initiate a large package of legislation in an unenthusiastic Congress, is:

Randall P. Ripley. *"Kennedy and Congress."* General Learning Press, 1972.

Chapter 9
The Problem of Participation

The transformation of America occurred over a considerable period of time. The two main stages of the transformation coincided with the great world wars of this century, wars that were at once a cause and a justification for the transformation. It is often said that the "necessities" of modern times (especially complexity and the need for speed) require that the president have immense power. But an adequate explanation of the government of the nation-state must, as we have attempted, analyze the nature of bureaucratic administration and its tendency to preempt other modes of administration. The argument from "necessity" does not explain the bureaucratization of a society, but it does help us to understand why there was not more resistance from the American people to such a fundamental, even radical, change in the structure of government. Once the successes of the Progressive movement had produced the *possibility* of bureaucratization, the great national identification with the war effort provided a *justification* for radical measures. And, once the Great Depression and the New Deal had produced the possibility of even more thorough bureaucratization, the even greater national identification with the struggle that was World War II again *justified*—made sense of—the curious dislocations of personal autonomy and traditional values that bureaucratization entails.

In other words, what is important about the apparent necessity of bureaucratic organization is that the individual is able to balance his experience of loss of personal autonomy against his personal experience of a "larger-than-life" problem. The world wars were just that—the whole world was (or so it seemed) threatened down to the last individual by powerful nations capable of raining destruction anywhere on the globe. Small wonder, then, that millions of individuals were willing—even glad—to put aside their personal autonomy for a role in the giant, coordinated task of national victory. Each individual "doing his bit," however small and apparently unrelated to killing the enemy, did not under such circumstances feel alienated or powerless. On the contrary, the omnipresent terror and exhilaration of global war lent significance to these specialized tasks, charging each one with a common meaning.[1]

And yet, how misleading, how ironically misleading, was this sense of purpose that seemed to explain the individual's role. To millions, it must have seemed rather like an old fashioned house-raising, where everyone chips in, each one performing a role in a common task to get the job done. Indeed, the aftermath of World War I suggests that many thought along just such lines, as the nation dismantled its armies, "sent the boys home," and enjoyed its peace. But as we have shown, the demobilized America of the 1920s was structurally dissimilar from the America of the 1910s; and without a doubt, America after World War II bore even less resemblance to the republic. After 1945, war and/or war-readiness had become a continuous, permanent fact of life (as the Korean war, or "police action," soon demonstrated). World War II had been no giant house-raising, where all the people pitched in, got the job done, and then went back to their "real" jobs. Rather, it was as if everyone had, almost inadvertently, signed on as permanent employees of a large construction company, one that just kept building houses forever. In addition, the final days of World War II had ushered in a strange, unanticipated dimension to the life of the individual. Nuclear weapons were first used by the United States against Japan in 1945, and suddenly two facts were plain: first, the destructive capability (and, perhaps, other capabilities as well) of the nation-state was practically unlimited; second, such capability resulted *independently* of the intentions of individuals in the system. The development and

---

1. For an interesting analysis of this phenomenon in the contemporary world, and its impact on people's consciousness, see Anton Zijderveld, *The Abstract Society* (Anchor Books, 1970).

use of nuclear weapons gave the lie to the simplistic, *physical* assembly-line model of the nation-state to which most Americans had succumbed. That is, when the *goal* of the system (the nation-state) had seemed straightforward, comprehensible and, largely, shared—to make very large-scale war on the Axis powers—then individuals could think of themselves as participating in a gigantic assembly line that produced a physical output, not unlike an automobile factory in principle. But such a model is simplistic because it implies that the individual *as individual*—that is, his mind, personality, and being—is left intact and free to comprehend his role as a (physical) part of the "gigantic assembly line." To some, the development of nuclear weapons, however, revealed a new and strange dimension. Now the output of the nation-state was found to be unforeseeable, and even incomprehensible to most of the people, who nevertheless indirectly produced that output.

In the nineteenth century, Karl Marx urged the industrial workers of the world to be conscious of the system of material production within which they toiled. It was essential (and sufficient), Marx believed, that the worker see that *he* was actually producing the output of the factory, even though the worker might not know how to build the final product himself. And yet, as Max Weber was to argue, this analysis did not speak to the problem of bureaucracy, where the individual's *mind,* not merely his body or physical activity, was but a part of a consciously coordinated whole. Nevertheless, the appealing idea that the mind, or consciousness, could comprehend (and therefore control) the (physical) conditions of its own existence enjoyed a widespread renaissance during the late 1960s. A spate of radical analyses and movements, known generally as the New Left, purported to explain and respond to the powerlessness of the individual in modern society. Ironically, as we shall show, the effect was not actually radical change, but rather conservation of the American nation-state.

Democracy in the Nation-State

The indictment of modern American democracy had begun years before the unrest of the 1960s. The seriousness of the earlier indictments often had to be inferred rather than read directly, but it was there.

During the 1950s, two kinds of criticisms of American democracy became general, and, taken together, they sounded an ominous note. On the one hand, there was a structural criticism, set forth not by "radicals" but by a relatively conservative group, the American Political Science Association. The object of the association's critique was the American political party system. The burden of the critique was that a non-responsible party organization made effective, mass democracy virtually impossible. The thrust of the association's recommendations was toward establishment of a "responsible" party system.[2] The major national parties would have to be centralized and disciplined, so that the voter could choose his representatives to Congress with the confidence that they would (have to) support their party's stated platform. If those policies proved, upon enactment into law (and the majority's policies *would* be enacted, if the party membership were effectively disciplined in the Congress), to be undesirable to the majority, then the voters could oust the responsible party in favor of its (also disciplined) opposition. Just how to effect such a structure under the existing Constitution was not obvious, but the arguments against the existing situation were telling. It was not at all clear that any kind of effective majority control of governmental policies was *possible at all* under the present arrangements.

The 1950s also saw the emergence of another sort of criticism of American democracy, at first implicit and then explicit in the fruits of behavioral science—the major voting studies. As sociologists, social psychologists, and political scientists perfected the techniques of reliable public-opinion polling, and as the results of large, heavily funded voting research projects began to be published, a disturbing picture of the American voter emerged:

We have, then, the portrait of an electorate almost wholly without detailed information about decision making in government. A substantial proportion of the public is able to respond in a discrete manner to issues that *might* be the subject of legislative or administrative action. Yet it knows little about what the government had done on these issues or what the parties propose to do. It is almost completely unable to judge the rationality of government actions; . . . the mass electorate is not able to appraise either

2. Committee on Political Parties of the American Political Science Association, *Toward a More Responsible Two-Party System* (Holt, Rinehart & Winston, 1950).

its goals or the appropriateness of the means chosen to serve these goals.[3]

The Campbell study showed that the average voter did not know enough about the issues and practical possibilities of American government to make a rational decision; and the APSA's study showed that even if he did, the party structure made an effective vote practically impossible. To be sure, such a summary statement would have seemed too harsh and simplistic during the late 1950s; but by the late 1960s, such an indictment would have seemed comparatively insipid. An awareness that *some*thing was amiss in American democracy was growing widespread, even in the 1950s when college students were dubbed "the silent generation."

The difficulty for political scientists was temporarily relieved by the emergence of a sort of "revisionist" democratic theory. This revisionist theory, known as "pluralist" democratic theory or, sometimes, "elitist" democratic theory, argues as follows: the United States is a *pluralistic,* not a polarized, society. It is made up, not of a "majority" and a "minority," but of *many minorities,* a complex field of multiple groups, in which many individuals have multiple, overlapping memberships. In such a situation, the "majority" does not rule, nor does a "minority" rule: "Minori*ties* rule."[4] Thus, the "elitist" definition of democracy by E. E. Schattschneider: "Democracy is a competitive political system in which competing leaders and organizations define the alternatives of public policy in such a way that the public can participate in the decision making process."[5] This kind of democracy is possible where pluralistic, competitive "elite strata" vie with one another, appealing for support from a broader public and compromising with each other.

Increasingly, other political scientists also began to object to this model of democracy, which, in some interpretations, found the apathy of the masses actually "functional" for the stability of the "system." "By revising [democratic] theory to bring it into closer correspondence with reality, the elitist theorists have transformed democracy from a radical into a conservative political doctrine, stripping away its dis-

3. Angus Campbell, Philip Converse, Warren Miller, & Donald Stokes, *The American Voter* (Wiley, 1960), p. 543.
4. Robert Dahl, *A Preface to Democratic Theory* (University of Chicago Press, 1956).
5. E. E. Schattschneider, *The Semi-Sovereign People: A Realist's View of Democracy in America* (Holt, Rinehart & Winston, 1960), p. 141.

tinctive emphasis on popular political activity so that it no longer serves as a set of ideals toward which society ought to be striving."[6]

However, political scientists were not to be afforded the luxury of extended, academic debate over the relative merits of their theories of democracy in America. For hardly had the debate over "elitist" democratic theory started than the very context within which such debate could occur was itself politicized. Almost everywhere—and especially in the great universities of America—disputes over claims to authority to interpret the nature of reality for the people erupted with special vigor, and even occasionally with violence.

Apparently, the nation-state was polarized after all. Yet, it was a very puzzling period, and the pattern of the events was not so clear. Somehow it seemed that everyone found himself in a polarized position, even though the concrete conditions for polarization were absent. All of the earmarks of polarization were there, including violent clashes, and even occasional deaths; yet an organized, ongoing group was hard to find.

There *were* sustained, disruptive outbursts of violence in the late 1960s. There were costly riots in Watts and Detroit, where mostly black "ghetto" dwellers poured into the streets, looting, burning, and destroying buildings and automobiles. There were all sorts of incidents on college and university campuses, ranging from passive resistance-style demonstrations through take-overs of administration buildings and classrooms to full-scale riots involving students, police, clubs, tear gas, and guns. At the same time the often populist and sometimes racist following of George Wallace was showing growing strength in huge, cheering audiences and impressive showings at the polls. Some issues were relatively durable, some rather short-lived. The issue of the Vietnam War was fairly durable, as was the theme of "participatory democracy", and the slogan of "power to the people." Other issues, such as (very) free speech, lasted only a season.

What precipitated this broad assortment of outbursts, at once so different and so similar? When we examine each movement or event separately, we are hard-pressed to find what they have in common. But, in retrospect, it seems clear

---

6. Jack L. Walker, "A Critique of the Elitist Theory of Democracy." *The American Political Science Review,* 1966, 60:288. See also Schattschneider, *The Semi-Sovereign People,* chap. 6.

that all of the movements and incidents were responses to a general feeling of *powerlessness:* George Wallace mobilized cheering crowds with the charge that "there's not a dime's worth of difference" between the major parties and called on the citizens to "send a message to Washington"; leaders exhorted throngs of students to distrust "anyone over 30," and to "take control over your own life"; while radical leaders, black and white, promised "power to the people." But what conditions produced this widespread feeling? And what has become of it?

Modern "Participation" Amendments to the Constitution

Just as the Supreme Court has been stressing egalitarian principles in its modern decisions, so recent amendments to the Constitution have been aimed at expanding and assuring the legal right of all citizens to participate in national elections. But, as we have been arguing, the context of political participation is now strangely altered by bureaucratization.

AMENDMENT XXIII
Ratified 1961

Section 1. The District constituting the seat of Government of the United States shall appoint in such manner as the Congress may direct:

A number of electors of President and Vice President equal to the whole number of Senators and Representatives in Congress to which the District would be entitled if it were a State, but in no event more than the least populous State; they shall be in addition to those appointed by the States, but they shall be considered, for the purposes of the election of President and Vice President, to be electors appointed by a State; and they shall meet in the District and perform such duties as provided by the twelfth article of amendment.

Section 2. The Congress shall have power to enforce this article by appropriate legislation.

AMENDMENT XXIV
Ratified 1964

Section 1. The right of citizens of the United States to vote in any primary or other election for President or Vice President, for electors for President or Vice President, or for Senator or Representative in Congress, shall not be denied or abridged by the United States or any State by reason of failure to pay any poll tax or other tax.

Section 2. The Congress shall have power to enforce this article by appropriate legislation.

AMENDMENT XXVI
Ratified 1971

Section 1. The right of citizens of the United States, who are eighteen years of age or older, to vote shall not be denied or abridged by the United States or by any State on account of age.

Section 2. The Congress shall have power to enforce this article by appropriate legislation.

Order and Complexity

The favorite explanation for the troubles of the 1960s, which witnessed the introduction of the foregoing amendments, has been the Vietnam War. At one time or another, practically every politician, not to mention students, college presidents, professors, labor leaders, and business leaders, called for an end to that "divisive, demoralizing" war. And it is certainly true that the war in Asia did precipitate much of this unrest. Yet such an "explanation" raises more questions than it answers if it is left at that. Why did the Vietnam War produce so much dissatisfaction? True, it was very costly, and to many observers it did indeed smack of imperialistic muscle-flexing on the part of the United States. But throughout their history Americans have frequently been willing, even eager, to resort to war in order to expand or protect holdings, or for any number of other reasons. And the fact that the Vietnamese were a poorer, less developed people does not explain America's reaction, either. Millions of American Indians, were they alive to tell the tale, would assure us that Americans are perfectly ready to do combat with nonindustrialized peoples; and millions of South Americans can attest to the readiness of America to extend its hegemony beyond the North American continent. We could go further in this vein, but the point here is not to launch a moral indictment of Americans; it is rather only to bring home the point that most of the criticisms of the American role in Vietnam, while cogent or moral enough, seem to beg a question that is particularly important for political scientists: why did the same country that jumped with such alacrity and enthusiasm into the Mexican-American War or the Spanish-American War, develop such great moral qualms about the Vietnam War?

Of course, the United States that fought the Spanish-American War was in an important sense, not the same country that fought the Vietnam War. The people of the United States today, were they still citizens of the republic instead of the nation-state, might well have taken up the cause of the Vietnam War with good spirit. At the turn of this century the majority of Americans had little trouble, apparently, supporting McKinley's concept of America's "destiny" to become an imperial power, or Theodore Roosevelt's "splendid little war" in Cuba.

What the Vietnam War really demonstrated to Americans is that war is an administrative output of the state, and that in a bureaucratic nation-state *the individual's intentions have no direct bearing on the administrative output of the state.* We have discussed, and even labored the point, that in bureaucratic organization, the individual's mind is but a segment on an assembly-line of thoughts and actions. What that means concretely is that you can be experiencing yourself as not in a war (indeed, as being *opposed to a war*), *and yet be making war* (on North Vietnam), just as surely as the man putting bolts on a wheel is indeed "making an automobile" —even though he does not experience himself making an automobile. The difference is that the assembly-line worker's mind is free to comprehend the fact that his body is but a part of the car-producing system; whereas the bureaucrat's mind is not free to observe itself as a part of a system. He knows *that* he is part of a system, but he does not always know *what* the system is "producing."

At one level it might be objected that life itself is like that, and has always been so. Man participates in a mysterious process, and the significance and meaning of his actions are partially hidden from him in an unknown and unknowable future. But the point here is different. We are not talking about the intervention of fate, or about how one's best-laid plans can go awry. We are talking about the *systematic* disparity between the individual's purposes and goals and the planned, purposeful outputs ("goals") of the nation-state. The Vietnam War was a curious frustration for Americans because year after year they received news—news from the "outside," because only from the outside could the war be experienced as such—that they were engaged in a sustained war of surprising magnitude. Small wonder, then, that they began to make that strangely anachronistic and inappropriate demand upon the nation-state; the demand for participatory democracy.

It was indeed a strange and anachronistic demand, for the emergence of the nation-state created the first situation in which the adaptation of the form of political representation to democratic participation was *technically* impossible. This is not to say that participatory democracy is itself inappropriate, but rather that participatory democracy *in a nation-state,* in a highly bureaucratized society, is a contradiction in terms.

Second in frequency to the war in Asia, as an explanation for the troubles of the 1960s, was "depersonalization" or, sometimes, bureaucracy itself. As we have seen, impersonal, rule-bound authority is characteristic of bureaucracy; and we all know that people want or need personal recognition and communication. The questions, then, are two: why did depersonalization become more or less unbearable for millions in the late 1960s (why not the 1950s?), and how did the political society get so extensively bureaucratized?

The very fact that this is a highly bureaucratized, specialized society makes generalization about it difficult to accomplish, because research and relevant analyses are scattered and, for our purposes, either incomplete or too specialized. The central importance of the world wars for the bureaucratization of America should by now be clear. But there are in addition three other important factors: the rapid growth and expansion of universal, compulsory education; the "post-industrial" economic expansion; and the heavy, accelerating use of federal grants-in-aid to state and local governmental units. These factors (which certainly do not exhaust the list of relevant developments) help account for the extension of bureaucracy into the day-to-day experiences of most Americans by the late 1960s. For it is important to remember that bureaucracy was not—and could not have been—a day-to-day, normal experience for most people in 1925, or even in 1950 (except during wars, when it "made sense"). To be sure, the nation-state was essentially a bureaucratized political representative capable of the characteristically massive outputs of bureaucracy; but millions of people who had been born in the American republic continued to experience life in its terms.

Indeed, we may wonder how such a large population could be transformed so quickly into a people accustomed to the expectations of a bureaucratic society. One factor, of course, was the spread of bureaucratic administration in the rapidly expanding economy of the American nation-state. The late nineteenth century had seen the industrialization of America's economy, and the super-production made possible and necessary by the great twentieth-century wars also made possible and necessary the adoption of bureaucratic administrative techniques in twentieth-century American corporations. The postwar economic combinations of the 1920s extended the "scientific management" practices of Frederick W. Taylor and other administrative theorists into the life-experiences of America's middle classes. By the 1950s millions of college students prepared for the "gray flannel suit" life of the bureaucrat-businessman in America's rapidly automating economy.

But the life-experience of a bureaucratized society actually extended far beyond the relatively small business-management class. Free public education, a crucial staple of the American republic, underwent stunning changes with the rise of the Progressive movement at the turn of this century and with the transformation of America. The Progressives, who had been fighting child labor practices late in the nineteenth century, saw in public education the dual opportunity to train children for a positive, responsible citizenship *and* a means of ending child labor practices. Thus as the Progressive movement crested, so did the movement in most states to make attendance in public schools compulsory. Obviously, if a child had by law to be in school, he could not very well be at work in a factory. Then, as part of that confluence of internal and external developments discussed earlier, the outbreak of World War I and the adoption of universal military conscription, revealed (from the point of view of the new nation-state) the disturbing unevenness of American public education. While compulsory education had become a (recent) fact of life for most American children, Selective Service tests revealed that the schooling was by no means standard throughout the nation. However, once national comparisons became possible, public and private efforts to standardize curricula and testing on a national basis received substantial impetus. By the time of World War II, a number of standardized, nationalized tests had been developed and put in to use across the nation. Inexorably, public (and private) education became competitive in terms of a more and more standardized, nationalized set of criteria. Furthermore—and this may be the more important point—the very enterprise of public education, now everywhere supported and supervised on a local and statewide basis, became a public bureaucracy. Only bureaucratic organization could administer the enormous task of providing a standard education to every child in a state. By the 1950s, consolidation of schools had rendered the one-room schoolhouse and other nonbureaucratic modes of public education practically obsolete. Thus, by the late 1960s, virtually every young adult in the nation, as well as a majority of their parents, had been educated by a public bureaucracy, reared in the common experience of public authority as bureaucracy.

Finally, the growth of federal grants-in-aid played an important role. Given the great day-to-day authority and responsibility of state governments in the American republic, we might wonder why these (nonbureaucratic) governments have not exerted a counterinfluence upon the tendency to bureaucratization in the nation-state. In fact, the state governments *have* exerted a counterinfluence, but this influence has been eroded by the bureaucratization of the states themselves. This bureaucratization of the states occurred because, in order to compete with the federal bureaucracy's efficiency, the states had to adopt bureaucratic organization (as best exemplified in the school systems). Secondly, the states have been bureaucratized as a direct result of federal grants-in-aid, a technique that has grown exactly in proportion with the growth of the nation-state. The grant-in-aid technique, of course, merely offers federal money to state or local government or public agencies on a voluntary basis; the state puts up a portion of the money (10 to 50 percent), and administers the program (highway building, urban renewal, "model cities," mass transit, public parks, hospitals, schools, and so on) itself. But the grant is conditional, and the conditions almost always specify the adoption of bureaucratic administrative techniques (merit personnel procedures, appropriate budgeting techniques, and the like). Thus, by the

1960s, a bureaucratized world had become the day-to-day experience for almost all Americans.

This set of conditions has generated a depersonalized, bureaucratic society. On the one hand, these conditions produced the most powerful nation-state on earth, one capable of conducting a devastating war while placing men on the moon—and all the while most of its citizens watched their televisions (sometimes in awe, sometimes in outrage) to find out what they were actually doing. On the other hand, these conditions produced a variety of public convulsions, dazzling in their diversity but always indicative of deep dissatisfaction over the powerlessness of the individual. So deep was this dissatisfaction that in 1968, President Lyndon Johnson decided not to try for reelection, after a dark-horse, antiwar candidate, Senator Eugene McCarthy, made an astonishingly strong showing in a primary election. But in 1972, the very symbol of "middle America," President Richard Nixon,[7] dealt Senator George McGovern one of the soundest electoral defeats ever recorded in the United States. What had become of the deep dissatisfaction? If bureaucratization had produced it, how then could it suddenly subside?

Experience and "Pseudo-Experience"

Political scientists have not produced anything resembling a consensus about the late 1960s—indeed, political science was (like other social science disciplines) itself polarized during the 1960s, and an "anti-establishment" wing of the profession formed under the name "Caucus for a New Political Science." Unfortunately, most of the rhetoric and writing—even that of the radicals—is *symptomatic* of the 1960s since it often exemplifies or constitutes that polarization, rather than explaining it. And, it has failed utterly to explain the sudden "disappearance" of the polarization. Our reorganization of conventionally treated American governmental materials leads us squarely to the problem: what are the experiential consequences of modern, bureaucratized nation-states? Moreover, as we suggested, the experiences of other modern nation-states should warn us that a certain dy-

7. For an interesting development of this argument, see Garry Wills, *Nixon Agonistes* (Signet, 1972).

namic, possibly peculiar to bureaucratized societies, may pose a real danger to America.

At this point, it may be helpful to remember that in the era of the American republic, the Civil War was an example of polarization par excellence. In Part II, we stressed the fact that the Civil War was, in a tragic sense, an *achievement* of the republic. That is, not until the articulation of two state-based or popularly based political parties was it possible to join the issue over ruling power at the popular level. The *organizational basis* for Civil War was lacking a mere ten years earlier, but with the emergence of the Republicans, the individual citizen could participate at a level that permitted the mobilization of his involvement in terms of *organized,* armed hostilities between the two sides. Set against the model of the Civil War, the "polarization" of the 1960s was superficial and chaotic. On the one "side" was "The Movement"—ad hoc meetings, thousands of uncoordinated pamphlets, sporadic "take-overs" of buildings, and so forth. On the other side was "The Establishment"—picture-snapping plainclothesmen, dubious "political" firings, government surveillance of "security risks," use of military forces for crisis policing of civilians, and other similar devices. In other words, the polarization consisted of a lot of intense *feeling,* a plethora of essentially *uncoordinated* action from both "sides," with occasional consequences (incarceration, property destruction, even deaths), which nevertheless only amounted to someone's bad luck, for the coordination was not there. We must speak of "sides" with quotation marks, to distinguish this phenomenon from the organized sides in the Civil War.

What was going on in the 1960s, then? Why would so many people from all over the country stampede from one "meeting" or protest to another, while equally determined policemen frantically snapped photographs of them or, occasionally, sprayed them with mace? Whence such notable zeal and concern on both "sides," without any coordinating mechanisms, without any organization, to make of them real sides, capable of doing sustained battle?

The answer, we suggest, is that the *experience,* the "feeling" of polarization was itself the *reason,* or "goal" of these movements. Bureaucratization puts the individual's mind on an "assembly line," so that he cannot experience the *goal* of the system, much as the factory worker cannot experience himself building an automobile. The feeling of polarization lent meaning to the individual's existence, albeit a dangerous and hard meaning. But if it is difficult to face the grim possibility of revolution, of civil war, perhaps this is a more satisfying experience than the soul-shrivelling experience of *anomie*—the disappearance of community, of any common meaning at all. And so, in the very nerve centers of the nation-state, in its great cities and universities, people would gather to experience—some with a shudder of dread, others with a fierce exultation—these dramas of polarization. But when they were over, where did everyone go? Back to their places—their classes, their jobs, their dwellings—in a vastly complicated system, a system coordinated from outside of their personal experiences.

Probably it is both the calming aftereffect of the catharsis and the disillusionment of seeing that nothing, after all, really changes that accounts for the "calm after the storm." At any rate, the pseudopolarization of the 1960s appears actually to have stabilized the system, rather than making it unstable. Both "sides" comprised millions of individuals who experienced a meaning in their lives, though the meaning was more illusory than real. (We do mean *both* "sides." One thing revealed by the Watergate affair is that "the establishment" was frantically—and ineffectually—"participating" in the pseudopolarization just as much as the New Left.) But we are not gainsaying the significance of the turmoil of the 1960s. Whether one feels relief or regret over the passing of those days, one should bear in mind that the conditions that produced that turmoil have not changed. And again, we should recall the fate of Germany, where the vast majority turned to regimentation and elected a demonic, charismatic leader, perhaps to satisfy a gnawing hunger for meaning in bureaucratized society.

Still, it is asking rather a lot of the individual that he think this way about America. As Weber pointed out, the system of authority wrought by bureaucracy is practically unshatterable. Each of us has a stake in it; it is such a vast system. What, except still another bureaucracy, could be posed as an alternative to it? The best hope, we believe, is to avoid the mistake of the European nation-states, which was to try to find salvation in bureaucracy, as though a state of unlimited power could somehow relieve the individual of the burden of existence. Instead of sugar-coating the reality of the American experience with the myths of the republic or the promise of "technology"—as though that could "free" the individual—we propose to begin the task of identifying the problems of the modern nation-state. But these are not to be problems that "we", the nation-state, must "solve." Rather, they are problems that the individual must face or, at least, be conscious of. Whether American education has been a great cultural achievement or the instrument of cultural destruction depends, as it were, upon one person.

Suggested Further Reading

Unlike the other chapters of this book, this one has departed substantially from conventionally treated materials. The associated unit on voting and participation by Charles McCall will help fill the gap, as will some of the following works.

For a good account of modern Germany that expresses the idea that the German experience was unique to their culture and history, see:

Peter Gay. *Weimar Culture: The Outsider as Insider.* Harper Torchbook, 1968.

For a broader introduction to the problems, ideas, and personalities that produced the modern world we live in, see:

William M. Johnston. *The Austrian Mind: An Intellectual and Social History, 1848–1938.* University of California Press, 1972.

On voting, the most representative of the studies remains:

Angus Campbell, Philip Converse, Warren Miller, and Donald Stokes. *The American Voter.* Wiley, 1960.

A good collection of articles representing different approaches and focuses on voting behavior will be found in:

M. Kent Jennings and L. Harmon Zeigler. *The Electoral Process.* Prentice-Hall, 1966.

For a more general discussion of political participation, see:

Lester W. Milbrath. *Political Participation: How and Why do People Get Involved in Politics?* Rand McNally, 1965.

Representative, essentially positive interpretations of the possibility for democratic participation in modern mass society will be found in the following:

Seymour Martin Lipset. *Political Man: The Social Bases of Politics.* Anchor Books, 1963.

E. E. Schattschneider. *The Semi-Sovereign People: A Realist's View of Democracy in America.* Holt, Rinehart & Winston, 1960.

Robert Dahl. *A Preface to Democratic Theory.* University of Chicago Press, 1956.

For a challenging theory holding that oligarchy is inevitable wherever large-scale organization occurs, see:

Robert Michels. *Political Parties: A Sociological Study of the Oligarchical Tendencies of Modern Democracy.* 1911; The Free Press, 1962.

A different kind of argument, which nevertheless reaches disturbing conclusions as to the possibility of large groups achieving collective goals without coercion is:

Mancur Olson, Jr. *The Logic of Collective Action: Public Goods and the Theory of Groups.* Schocken Books, 1968.

A landmark study of the effects of mass society upon the individual:

David Riesman, Nathan Glazer, and Reuel Denney. *The Lonely Crowd: A Study of the Changing American Character* (abridged). Anchor, 1953.

A collection of studies dealing with the same broad subject of the effects of mass society:

Maurice R. Stein, Artheur J. Vidich, and David Manning White. *Identity and Anxiety: Survival of the Person in Mass Society.* The Free Press of Glencoe, 1960.

For an analysis of the problem of the individual in a mass society from a Marxist perspective, see:

Herbert Marcuse. *One-Dimensional Man: Studies in the Ideology of Advanced Industrial Society.* Beacon Press, 1964.

A discussion of the potentialities for and limitations upon public access to policymaking processes *in the United States.*

Philip F. Beach. "Public Access to Policymaking in the United States." General Learning Press, 1974.

A good, general description of contemporary political party organization:

Hugh A. Bone. "Political Party Management." General Learning Press, 1973.

For more on contemporary social movements, including an argument against the utility of "engineering" consensus in mass populations, see:

Giuseppe Di Palma. "The Study of Conflict in Western Society: A Critique of the End of Ideology." General Learning Press, 1973.

A dispassionate look at the organizational requirements for effective social movement:

John D. McCarthy and Mayer N. Zaid. "The Trend of Resource Mobilization." General Learning Press, 1973.

An introduction to a sociology of knowledge perspective on

the problem of individual participation in society is afforded by:

Peter L. Berger and Thomas Luckmann. *The Social Construction of Reality: A Treatise in the Sociology of Knowledge.* Anchor Books, 1967.

Because the "drug culture" became such an apparently salient phenomenon during the 1960's, an interesting preliminary study is relevant here:

Robert B. Stauffer. *"The Role of Drugs in Political Change."* General Learning Press, 1971.

Part IV
American Government:
Questions for the Future

Chapter 10
American Politics in Flux

This book constitutes the context, we hope, within which a rich variety of associated units—some radical, some conservative, some conventional, some rather far-out, some "nuts-and-bolts," some theoretical—can be made the topics of focused, lively debate and critical evaluation. However, even as we warned in the introductory chapter, paradox and ambivalence are the price of our analysis. There is, we are the first to admit, more than a little of the "you can't get there from here" irony in our analysis. But the situation is far from hopeless. We may well believe that the human resources that have produced the mighty, overpowering edifice of the modern nation-state have not suddenly disappeared. Rather, to borrow Winston Churchill's phrase, we must recognize that these are still, indeed, "the times that try men's souls." As we have seen, World War II (the occasion for Churchill's remark) presented challenges for the human soul beyond the risk of physical annihilation. The challenge was not met in one sense because the transformation of America from a republic into a nation-state became permanent. Therefore, the challenge devolved upon each individual to preserve his uniqueness, his special spirit. The question that each of us must answer is, how can the individual live and act as an individual in a political society the very existence of which requires the depersonalization of authority and intellect.

If the individual is now able to perceive his own, present role as a more or less *immediate* experience of the

220

impersonal authority of the bureaucratized nation-state (instead of thinking of politics as "out there" somewhere), he will have taken a long step toward effective political understanding. And then, perhaps, it will not seem too irrelevant if we talk—in the context of a discussion of the changing nature of American politics—about school again.

Educational Illusions

Education has always enjoyed a special esteem in America. Men like Thomas Jefferson wrote provisions for public education into the very framework for expansion of the republic; and since the beginnings of the republic, countless American parents have sacrificed for the education of their children, believing that education was the surest, most respectable route to success, upward mobility, and even happiness. With the advent of the nation-state, these traditional American expectations of education were fulfilled and stimulated beyond all expectations. It became possible to calculate in dollars and cents the probable—almost certain— value of a high school degree, a college degree, and a graduate degree. Indeed, it was not long before a college degree became something more than a cherished goal; it became a virtual necessity for the middle classes.

This was another instance of that peculiar confluence of developments in the republic and developments in European nation-states. The bureaucratization of a society must proceed hand-in-hand with the extension of a system of formal education throughout the society because formal training is necessary for bureaucratic offices. The rapid bureaucratization of America was possible, in part, due to the very extensive system of public education already established in the republic. Bureaucratization, of course, transformed that system of education, standardizing it, reorienting it to national goals, and contributing to its differentiation and specialization. And in a curious way, bureaucratization has reinforced an especially naive American attitude toward education.

That naive attitude toward education, that American myth of education, might be expressed as the belief that *education relieves suffering.* To be sure, one does not find it expressed in just this way, but one infers it. All of those mothers who would "scrub floors so their children could get an education"; all of those sober laborers who had "missed their chance" by not getting an education; all of those earnest schoolteachers exhorting their students to "get all the education you can"; all of those students, even, striving for that magic degree—so many people, it seems, believe that an education will alleviate suffering, will somehow make it better for them. And, as we have said, bureaucracy rather reinforces this belief. It is true—the more school, the better job, the higher status, the more money. At least, it has been true until quite recently.

But perhaps if America had not become so thoroughly bureaucratized, and if the educational system had not been transformed into a bureaucratic training ground for bureaucracy, perhaps then America's attitude toward education would have matured somewhat. Perhaps America's attitude toward higher education, at least, would have become more like, say, the religious view of the holy man—such a man is to be admired, perhaps emulated; but one does not (if he is religious) think it is *easy* to be a holy man. This comparison is a bit strained, but we are trying to stress a point that must be recognized sooner or later. Education—"real" education—does *not* necessarily lead one away from suffering, confusion, torment, doubt, and maybe even poverty; any, or all, of these experiences are perfectly compatible with, and perhaps even necessary for, the state of being educated.

This rather moralistic-sounding exhortation is indicated, we believe, because education is at once crucial for and distant from changing American politics. On the one hand, the educational system of America (and our experience of education in it) is the most "political" of the institutions of the nation-state. It is the educational system that separates this huge population into industrial labor roles (assembly line, and so forth) and bureaucratic labor roles (management and so forth) by means of degree certification. It is the educational system that allocates and directs the huge labor force into the myriad of specializations that comprise a bureaucratized society, by means of competitive examinations, specialized courses, and so forth. It is the educational system—and *only* the educational system—which provides the "nerve centers" (mainly the great universities) where so much differentiated, specialized activity and knowledge are integrated, or held together in some sort of coordinatable fashion. And it is upon these "nerve centers" that the coordinating agencies of the nation-state (in the presidency) rely for expertise, and so forth. Moreover, the *authority* of formal education, of degrees, is vast for the nation-state. Top physicists (at least since Einstein), top engineers (at least since Werner von Braun), top policy scientists (like Henry Kissinger), and other experts exert enormous influence in the nation-state. The authority of formal degrees extends into every aspect of daily life as well—lawyers, physicians, and other "professional" people hold their power and legitimacy on account of their *formal training,* their *degrees,* after all.

But on the other hand, mainly *because* formal education is centrally a political phenomenon in the nation-state, the task of authentic education is almost impossible to pursue. It is strange because very many people experience this fact first-hand. The professor teaching this course, and many of the students in it, probably have experienced the conflict between the essentially bureaucratic expectation of their roles, that they pursue a *training* regime (aimed toward specialization) and the essentially educational goal of "knowing" in a reflective, holistic manner. But the fact that everyone is in the same situation actually reinforces that "unshatterable" system of authority. The *system* has to be relied upon to integrate each specialization, because the task of personally acquiring all that (specialized) knowledge, in order personally to integrate or "know" it, is patently impossible.

Nevertheless, the factor already mentioned, the recent, rather abrupt slowdown in the expansion rate of the educational system, presents not only dangers to, but hope for, the American political society. Just as those periods of expansion and "paper money" speculation in the republic were followed by economic panics where only gold (which the paper and bonds were supposed to "be as good as") was trusted and valuable, so will a bureaucratic "market place" flooded with too many degrees force a more discriminating attitude toward what is *behind* those degrees. In such an atmosphere, people may reevaluate bureaucratic higher education.

Disputes over Claims to Authority Concerning the Nature of Reality

Given, on the one hand, the centrality of the formal educational system for the articulation and maintenance of the American nation-state; and, on the other hand, our definition of politics as disputes over claims to authority concerning the nature of reality, the conclusion that this is a *political* book is unavoidable. We are disputing the (impersonal) claim of the nation-state to represent an authoritative definition of reality. And without a doubt, many readers of this book will dispute our own authority concerning the nature of reality. As is surely clear by now, we think that politics in education is today unavoidable; the question, really, is whether politics will be constructive and healing, or destructive. Central to this question is the subtle problem of authority, the basis of it and how it functions for the individual.

Students do not need anyone to tell them that the role, the office, of teacher or instructor brings with it a limited but very important authority. In simplest terms, it is the power of grading, derived from the authority of the office or role, authority concerning the nature of reality. At the university level, such authority is both limited and reinforced by the claim of the office to expertise. Of course, it very often happens that a student may regard a particular professor as unreasonable, biased, or even stupid. Nevertheless, the typical recourse of the student is to go ahead and submit to examination by the professor—for the authority is in the *office,* not the person. And the student, whatever he may think about grades, usually thinks that he "needs" them, in order to stay in school, in order to "get into law school" (a popular fantasy, these days), in order to graduate and get a job, and so forth. In other words, that system of authority that Weber found "practically unshatterable" is all around us; like everyone else, the individual has to participate in the system of authority—partly *because* everyone else does.

But the simple, hierarchical pattern of authority characteristic of bureaucracy is not the only kind of authority that can exist. The simple, hierarchical model of authority that obtains in the typical classroom is necessary for the efficient, bureaucratic administration of a vast educational system, it is true. But the coordination of complex patterns of knowledge and behavior thus made possible for the *system* is made *impossible* for the individual, who is limited (whether he be teacher or student) to a relatively simple pattern of authority relationships. If this simple pattern were repersonalized and broadened at the classroom level, so that the authority of the teacher assumed potentially life-changing proportions,[1]

---

1. "Potentially," that is, because the complexity of individuals makes certain institutionalization of such relationships all but impossible.

while the student became an autonomous person, capable of granting *or withholding* an acceptance of the teacher's authority, then the learning experience would become much more difficult, important, and rewarding for the people involved. The learning experience could then become creative, and that is precisely what is needed in the present situation. The bland assumption that there is plenty of knowledge there to consume, so that all we have to do is dispense and consume it efficiently (speed reading courses come to mind), is hardly supported by the individual's actual experience of bureaucratic education.

Such a change in attitude, or role identification, should not be attempted in the collective mode. That is, it is not a task for the nation-state (or in general, bureaucracies) to undertake; rather, it is a task for individuals. Indeed, only individuals could accomplish it, not bureaucrats. Of course, the problem and fact of bureaucracy will not then just obligingly go away. On the contrary, the instructor will still bear the responsibilities of his office—including that of providing unequivocal grades for (perhaps hundreds of) his students. And the student will still live in a world where staying in college is contingent upon a certain grade-point average. Mass movements, such as those that more or less tried to get underway in the late 1960s, really promise little for the individual (except the kind of temporary relief discussed in the previous chapter). For the problem remains that only bureaucracy can effectively administer anything (including education) on such a large scale. To be sure, there may be good grounds for preferring one bureaucratic goal over another; but the problem of *participating* in bureaucracy is, generally, the more serious, pervasive problem.

In a sense, the individual must try to transcend his "bureaucratic self." Instead of trying to find identity in *either* the total acceptance or total rejection of a bureaucratic role, the individual must find his important, enduring reason for being, in a set of relationships—including authority relationships—which relegate bureaucratic authority and bureaucratic relationships to a realm of secondary importance. It seems to us that such a state of mind, disturbing and occasionally full of suffering though it might be, is necessary before the interesting, meaningful new politics of America can come into view. It is on that assumption that we speak as autonomous persons to autonomous persons (who, nevertheless, struggle constantly with the problem of a bureaucratic identity), that we turn in conclusion to some of the basic problems in America.

The Nation-State as an Illusion

It begins to appear that one of the greatest problems facing an American government or history class—and facing the American citizen—is the difficulty of recognizing the tentativeness and instability of the nation-state as a form of political representation. To put a slightly finer point on it, the difficulty is in even *thinking* of the nation-state as tentative or unstable. (If something is impossible to imagine, it is at the very least difficult to see.) Our national defenses, when it comes down to it, are practically absolute; our technologies can be put to almost any task; the nation-state appears overwhelmingly secure. Naturally it is not easy to discuss it as though it were a tentative, potentially unstable system. But this is due to the illusion of timelessness and ubiquitousness produced by its organizational characteristics.

There is an ahistorical quality about a bureaucratized society that eclipses the dimension of time, or foreshortens the time dimension drastically. In the atemporal nation-state, the drama of human crises (turning points) is missing; the very idea of collective change is hard to grasp. The atemporal quality of bureaucracy is due to the impersonal and specialized nature of human participation in it. *Humans* live and die. They experience time and its turning points. Bureaucracies are, in this sense, not human. Like a machine the bureaucracy lasts forever; it is the office that has authority, not the man. The office continues, and the man passes away. Moreover, since the criteria for office-holding are impersonal and since any given office is but a part of a highly differentiated system, the quality of time that attaches to personhood cannot be attributed to the bureaucratic offices.

A related effect is the illusion of ubiquitousness of bureaucratic society. It is "everywhere" and encompasses "everything" for the individual. But this again is due to the fact that he is but a *functioning* part of a vastly complex system. For the individual, "everything" that is or can be meaningful or nonrandom is, indeed, mediated to him by the bureaucratized society. For the individual, the authority of the system of which he is a part is unshatterable. The idea of the system disintegrating is, in an important sense, literally unthinkable. If your identity—your very self—is contingent upon the integrity, the hanging-togetherness, of the system, then to contemplate the disintegration of the bureaucratized society is to contemplate your own nonexistence. Needless to say, the human mind resists such an idea.

One way, perhaps, to think about the situation "objectively" (that is, with some distance on the phenomenon, so that we are not literally identified with it) is to think about something almost as necessary to our identities as the nation-state itself, namely, modern science. We exist, of course, in a veritable sea of scientific applications, potentialities, and interpretations. And yet it may be that the very essence of science itself is no longer practicable—it may be that science itself is in crisis. In the 1930s, the great phenomenologist Edmund Husserl, working in Germany, came to just that conclusion. And the reason that science was in crisis, he found, was what he called "technization," which is the bureaucratization of the process of science to the point that thousands of scientific practitioners, each participating in the activity of science as specialists skilled at specified techniques, have individually lost an awareness of the holistic enterprise of which they are but functioning parts.

Are [current] science and its methods not like a machine, reliable in accomplishing obviously very useful things, a machine everyone can learn to operate correctly without in the least understanding the inner possibility and necessity of this sort of accomplishment? But was geometry, was science, capable of being designed in advance, like a machine, without an understanding which was in a similar sense, complete—scientific?[2]

Again, however, it is our very interdependence in terms of science, and our participation as *parts* of the whole process, which makes recognition of the crisis paradoxically difficult, almost impossible. To be sure, there are many who are ready enough to concede that science is in crisis, ready even to jettison the whole enterprise. As Germany lay in ferment, before the holocaust of World War II, Husserl acknowledged a similar attitude: " . . . we know that it has gradually become a feeling of hostility among the younger generation. In our vital need—so we are told—science has

2. Edmund Husserl, *The Crisis of European Sciences and Transcendental Phenomenology,* translated by David Carr. (Northwestern University Press, 1970), p. 52.

nothing to say to us."[3] But this is a readiness, as we might say, to throw out the baby with the bathwater. If science, if authority, if so many human ideals have been destroyed by bureaucratization, it is still not indicated that we should reject those goals along with the bureaucratized routines that are their institutional form: "The true struggles of our time, the only ones which are significant, are struggles between humanity which has already collapsed and humanity which still has roots but is struggling to keep them or find new ones."[4] The language is quaint, perhaps, and hortatory. But, in a way, it strikes the dominant theme of our book. For our reorganization of the facts of American government reveals a dramatic contrast. In the eighteenth and nineteenth centuries the story of America was the story of the construction and subsequent democratization of a unique, republican form of government. But shortly after the turn of this century a process of transformation was set in motion that eventuated in the thorough bureaucratization of the political society. Not only were the characteristic separation and balance of powers of the republic destroyed, along with the means of limiting governmental powers, but finally the very experience of our historical roots and diverse culture has been eroded. Probably it is unrealistic to think of "keeping" those roots, but perhaps it is not impossible to find new ones. The republic, after all, was an attempt to find new roots.

Corresponding to the crisis of science is the crisis of the nation-state, itself, which is threatened for the simple reason that the source of its univocal structure, its "one-piecedness," is threatened. The danger is not polarization, as we argued in the previous chapter; the danger is disintegration. An immediate consequence of disintegration, as we also suggested earlier, can be a sort of *collective denial* of the horror for the individual that bureaucratic disintegration would entail (cf. Chapter 9 on pseudopolarization). Generalization about the nation-state is difficult, because despite the widespread tendency to accept the form of representation as more or less permanent, nation-states (and modern bureaucracies) have not been around very long. Still, the fate of Germany is not encouraging: Even while Husserl was warning of a crisis of science, Adolf Hitler was promising something that most Germans took quite seriously—a "thousand-year

3. Ibid., p. 6.
4. Ibid., p. 15.

reich." And even as the ancient foundations of morality and science were laid waste among the originators of Western civilization in Europe, the German people participated in mass regimentation rituals and promised, in the name of order, to follow the personal whims of a charismatic leader.

The track record of the modern nation-state is not at all good; it is not clear that one is able to last very long. At the same time, however, it *is* clear that individuals, once identified with the bureaucratized nation-state, can hardly imagine alternatives to that *form* of the political society (though they may be quick enough to fantasize a completely different set of *goals*). But the key may be something other than a political "system;" the key may be the individual.

The Neglected Individual

The same organizational characteristics of bureaucratized society that produce the illusion of permanence and ubiquitousness for the nation-state also limit and circumscribe the significance of the individual. The limited significance of the individual is not characteristic of a particular ideology or economic system; in modern socialism and modern capitalism alike, the individual is required to submerge himself in a system coordinated from a center outside of the individual. It is not just a matter of size, for the republic was vast and populous; but, to take one example, in the republic a Jeffersonian concept of the self-reliant individual doubtless contributed to the huge growth of the United States—size, in other words, was not necessarily inconsistent with individualism. The limited significance of the individual in the nation-state has to do with the fact that he is a *part* of the coordinated system, but this does not say quite enough. After all, the *individual* in the American republic was part of a coordinated system, too (think of the system of checks and balances). The difference might be put this way: in bureaucracy, it is a *part* of the individual that is, in turn, *part* of the system. In a sense, individuals are not coordinated; offices are coordinated. Rules of conduct, stipulated procedures, and so forth, *sharply limit* the discretion of the individual in the performance of his role in bureaucracy; the very predictability of the office makes possible the coordination of vastly complicated systems of activity—at the cost of depersonalizing the individual's role.

Now, if it were actually possible to do away with the human self, the terms of the problem we are discussing would be strictly moral. *Ought* we to permit the submersion of individuality? However, the problem has a decidedly practical side, since it seems likely that it is not, in fact, possible to eliminate individuality. True, in modern times an extremely efficient mode of organization has insinuated itself into the structure of political societies, and the efficiency of that mode of organization requires the depersonalization of the individual's function in the system. But a corollary of this depersonalization has been a growing, collective hunger for meaning expressible in human terms; and this hunger has manifested itself in systemic paroxysms ranging from pseudopolarization to charismatic dictatorships. These paroxysms do not solve the problem of depersonalization, but they are symptomatic of the problem.

If the nature of this problem can be recognized, then the possibility of positive political resolution can follow. Instead of looking always to the nation-state to assimilate more and more of our precious (and dwindling) human resources, we should perhaps begin to see the unassimilated persons among us as a *goal,* not something to be eliminated. It is amazing, in a way, how assiduously the nation-state labors to eliminate divergent or unassimilated elements of the population. For cultural minorities, whose typical family backgrounds do not prepare them for ready assimilation into our bureaucratic educational system, we have "headstart" programs designed to substitute a standard preschool environment for the "substandard" one provided by the cultural minority. Children of all races are herded at earlier and earlier ages into compulsory, public schools—partly to "prepare" them for "productive lives" and partly to "free" women to take jobs in the bureaucratized society. And old people are severed from work as though age were a disease, and turned out to (hopefully pleasant) pastures, separated from normal society.

All of these policies are "for" the individual, in the sense of helping and encouraging the individual to adapt to and identify with roles in the bureaucratized society. But there is another way to look at the unassimilated elements of our society, which is to think of them as our best links to the secrets and promises of individuality. The old, after all, are the only people among us who have ever known life in a different kind of society: they do not need us—we need them. And perhaps some of those cultural minorities that the state labors so mightily to eliminate have still clung to their rare and unassimilated roots; if so, we should *learn* from them, not train them. And women: if there are millions still who have discovered meaningfulness in child rearing and the creation of "home" in our wastelands, should we perhaps consider begging of them their secret, instead of "liberating" them? Then there is that living, ancient symbol of divinity, the child, which modern society so arrogantly proposes to "educate" from birth—as though the secret of life belonged to the state, instead of the "child of seven days."

It will be a step in the right direction if our society can cease to exploit education and begin, instead, to nurture it. Rather than being a process to be used, to serve the training needs of the bureaucratized society, schools should be a goal in and of themselves, to be achieved by a society.

> Meaningfulness of life . . . can be experienced only by the individual and not by a State, which, on the one hand, is nothing but a convention of independent individuals and, on the other, continually threatens to paralyze and suppress the individual. . . . all our social goals commit the error of overlooking the psychology of the person for whom they are intended and—very often—of promoting only his illusions."[5]

Suggested Further Reading

For a revealing account of the struggle for individuality in timeless, ubiquitous environment of a bureaucratized society, see:

Arthur Mitzman. *The Iron Cage: An Historical Interpretation of Max Weber.* Knopf, 1970.

A brief, interesting argument that the structure of modern mass organizations tends to diminish the consciousness of the modern individual is:

Carl G. Jung, *The Undiscovered Self.* Little, Brown, 1958.

A much more optimistic account of the development of modern consciousness in present-day society:

Charles Reich, *The Greening of America: How the Youth Revolution Is Trying to Make America Liveable.* Random House, 1970.

---

5. C. G. Jung, *The Undiscovered Self* (Little, Brown and Co., 1958), p. 124.

Reich's argument is of a type criticized in:
Eric Voegelin. *Science, Politics and Gnosticism.* Henry Regnery, 1968.

A sobering and relevant discussion of the political implications of technology and the ecology:
Margaret Sprout and Harold Sprout. "Ecology and Politics in America: Some Issues and Alternatives." General Learning Press, 1971.

For a representative attempt to recover individual consciousness in a disintegrating, bureaucratized context a complex, unfinished work is:
Edmund Husserl. *The Crisis of European Sciences and Transcendental Phenomenology: An Introduction to Phenomenological Philosophy.* Translated by David Carr. Northwestern University Press, 1970.

Index